Educational Technology in the Classroom

Educational Technology in the Classroom

Patricia Ann Brock

Trenton State College

Educational Technology Publications
Englewood Cliffs, New Jersey 07632

Library of Congress Cataloging-in-Publication Data

Brock, Patricia Ann.
    Educational technology in the classroom / Patricia Ann Brock.
       p. cm.
    Includes bibliographical references (p.) and index.
    ISBN 0-87778-269-5
    1. Educational technology. I. Title.
  LB1028.3.B74 1994
  371.3'078--dc20

                                       93-23417
                                         CIP

Printed in the United States of America.

Library of Congress Catalog Card Number:
93-23417.

International Standard Book Number:
0-87778-269-5.

First Printing: January, 1994.

DEDICATION

To my teachers ...

My parents, who taught me to be respectful of yesterday's memories

My husband, Mark, who taught me to be receptive to tomorrow's promises

My T.S.C. students, who taught me to be responsive to today's realities.

Preface

If you are a novice in educational technology, this book is for you. Since the information is directed to an audience of elementary through college educators and preservice teachers, the content is written in a non-technical style for the purpose of creating more "EdTech" competent individuals in school settings. Easily used as a library reference, self-help resource book, or preservice/inservice text, *Educational Technology in the Classroom* was developed to help erase the mystique and techno-skepticism connected with the variety of teaching and learning technologies appearing in classrooms, computer labs, and media centers.

To make the book as beneficial to educators as possible, I had to determine what educators needed to know. First, I completed a review of the literature regarding educational technology and read articles apprearing in current journals and publications. Based on this study, I next designed a 12-page EdTech Survey, which I randomly distributed nationally to more than 400 educators from elementary through higher education levels. Essentially, I sought answers to the following questions to guide the development of this book:

• What educational technologies do you know and use?

• What are some advantages of these technologies?

• What are some disadvantages of these technologies?

• How do you address any technology problems or concerns?

• Which educational technologies do you know little or nothing about?

• What factors encourage you to use educational technologies?

• What factors discourage you from using educational technologies?

Based on survey replies, school site visitations, and personal interviews not only of educators, but also of representatives from educational technology companies, I developed and wrote this book.

The practical style of this publication is a direct, question-and-answer format. Part One: Computer Fundamentals provides the knowledge foundation for further computer-based technologies. Chapters One through Four present information on commonly asked questions about computer systems. Part Two: Integrated Telephony discusses the merger of telephone and computer technologies and the new role they play in distance learning. Part Three: Educational Radio and Instructional Television continues the discussion of distance learning, focusing upon two common mass communication technologies. Part Four: New Technologies for Instruction introduces the most recent developments in educational technologies, including CD and videodisc technologies, desktop computer music, and multimedia. The final chapter takes a brief look into the future of educational technologies including desktop video and virtual reality.

ACKNOWLEDGMENTS

I would like to thank all of the American educators who completed the comprehensive and time-consuming surveys; the teachers, administrators, and college students whom I interviewed in the many school systems that I visited; and the business representatives who explained their technologies and provided the materials to enhance the visual presentation of this book.

A special thank you must be offered to the students in my computer literacy classes at Trenton State College, who read through the rough drafts of this manuscript and offered suggestions for improving the document.

Acknowledgment also goes to many people who reviewed the concept or content areas of this book, including Dr. Kathryn Jaye Biacindo, California State University at Fresno; Ms. Marie Blouin, Marshall Middle School, Billerica, Massachusetts; Mrs. Nell Burgeson, former teacher at Spotswood Elementary School, New Jersey; Dr. Amy Dell, Trenton State College; Mrs. Diane Gerlach, Keyport High School, New Jersey; Dr. Fred Hurst, University of Maine at Augusta; Mr. Bill Hudzig, ham radio specialist; and Ms. Linda Huffines, Corey Elementary School, Arlington, Texas.

In addition, I would like to thank other Trenton State College authors, including Dr. Blythe Hinitz, Dr. Dorothy Rubin, and Dr. Jim Silver, for their moral support.

I must especially thank Mark S. Anderson and H. Milton Anderson, who provided typesetting and graphic design assistance with this book.

Of course, I must thank Larry Lipsitz of Educational Technology Publications for supporting my idea and research endeavors, providing permission to include illustrations from his professional journal, *Educational Technology*, and being a constructively critical and very helpful editor.

Patricia Ann Brock

Contents

DETAILED CONTENTS   PAGE

PART I

COMPUTER FUNDAMENTALS

Microcomputers in education are here to stay. A few traditionalists still claim that this technology is just another expensive bandwagon that will someday collect dust in a storage room. Not so. Unless, of course, educators don't learn to use them. That means all educators – not just computer or media specialists, but also classroom teachers. A few educators fear a threat to job security, predicting that teachers will one day be replaced by computers. Not so again. Good teachers will only become better teachers by using computers as professional tools to extend their teaching and managing skills.

Now, ask yourself the following questions: Would I like an assistant to work with students when I can't do so because I am working with a group? Would I like extra clerical help in keeping my records straight and up-to-date? Would I like an extra secretary to communicate with colleagues, administrators, students, or parents because I just don't have the time to write so many letters? If you answered ''yes,'' you should know that all of these tasks are possible with the electronic assistant called the microcomputer.

What should you know about computers? First, you need a basic introduction to computers as presented in Chapter One. Brief answers to commonly asked questions are discussed. If you need more details on certain topics, references are noted for further descriptions in succeeding chapters, or you can refer to the Glossary.

Next, Chapter Two: Microcomputer Hardware presents the electronic devices you need to understand. Then, the remaining chapters in Part I focus upon computer software. Chapter Three: Computer Software for Programming and Courseware introduces computer disks, programming, Computer Assisted and Computer Managed Instruction (CAI and CMI), and Integrated Learning Systems (ILSs). Chapter Four: Computer Software for Applications presents computer applications including word processing, desktop publishing, database software, spreadsheets, graphics, and telecommunications.

1

1

Chapter One:
Introduction to Computers

What is a computer system?

Essentially it is a modern technology that has two major components, which are electronic devices, called **hardware**, and information usually stored on disks, called **software**. Think about this as similar to the relationship between a VCR player and a videotape. In order to make the technology useful, you need both components working simultaneously.

What can a computer system do?

A computer system can do four tasks: **input, process, store**, and **output**. This simply means that as you put information into the computer (input), the computer follows your directions (process). As the computer works, the information is saved in its memory (stored) and this processed information is presented to you (output). Further details about these tasks and the required hardware needed are discussed in this chapter.

Are there different categories of computers?

There are three categories based on size, speed, and capabilities. First, the largest, most powerful, fastest, and most expensive computer is the **mainframe computer**. In many cases more than 100 users may simultaneously share the capabilities of this computer by working on terminals, basically keyboard and monitor devices, that are connected to one mainframe. You might have heard of the **supercomputer**, the most powerful computer presently available, which is used, for example, in large governmental institutions.

The second category of computers is the **minicomputer**. Less powerful, comparatively slower, and less expensive than the mainframe computer, the minicomputer can be shared simultaneously by at least 20 users.

The last category, probably the one you use, is the **microcomputer**. Also called the **micro, personal computer**, or **PC**, the microcomputer is primarily designed to meet the needs of the individual user. However, it is becoming more common in educational settings to see microcomputers connected together in configurations called **networks** so that information or peripherals (e.g., printers) can be shared. Networks are further explained later in Chapters Two and Three.

You might be familiar with the different sizes of microcomputers called **desktop**, **transportable, laptop**, and **notebook**. If you would like more information about these microcomputer varieties, read Chapter Two: Microcomputer Hardware.

Although less powerful, slower, and less expensive than the mainframe and minicomputer, the microcomputer is the most common computer in educational settings today. For this reason, microcomputer usage will be emphasized in this book.

What are the common microcomputer system components?

Certain basic hardware requirements are needed for a practical microcomputer system. To input information, many microcomputer systems in schools today use only a **keyboard**, but a device called the **mouse** is becoming more common. To process information, a **CPU** (Central Processing Unit), sometimes called a **microprocessor**, is used. The CPU is a fingernail-sized computer chip housed inside of your microcomputer. There are also other computer chips called **memory** that store information. To input data from computer disks, **disk drives** are needed. The newer microcomputers used in educational settings often include **internal hard drives** as well as **floppy disk drives**. Finally, to output information, a **monitor** is required and a **printer** is highly recommended.

But, computer hardware is not enough. You also need **software**, which is usually provided on a floppy disk, sometimes called **a diskette** or just **a floppy**. For more details on hardware, read Chapter Two. For more information about disks and software, read Chapters Three and Four.

What are the most popular microcomputers in education today?

Most educators agree that the "big three" microcomputers found most often in educational settings today are *Apple* (including *Macintosh*), *IBM*, and *Tandy* products. However, many other brands, including *Amiga* and *Commodore*, are also used in educational settings.

Which microcomputer is best in an educational setting?

Each company, of course, says its product is your best selection for education. But which one is really the best? The answer is simply the one is that best meets your specific computer needs.

First, consider what you want to do with your microcomputer. Then you need to review software. For example, do you want to type papers (word process), or do you plan to use instructional software? Next, you must consider what hardware you will need to run the software which you want to use. Remember, *look at the software before you decide on the hardware.*

To help you in deciding which software and hardware products are best suited to your needs, there are Decision-making Guidelines for specific educational technologies provided at the end of Chapters Two through Thirteen. As you decide, keep in mind the following three important basic points about microcomputers: 1) there is no microcomputer standard; 2) there are different operating systems; and 3) there are competing microcomputer environments called text-based and graphics-based. The following discussion will explain these points.

What is a standard?

A standard means that all software can run on all microcomputers and all brands of computer hardware can interconnect. This computer incompatibility problem is similar to one that existed a few years ago with VCRs. In the USA and Canada there used to be two VCR standards, VHS and Beta. Videotapes could not run on both systems. This problem is largely resolved today in North America, since VHS has become the dominant standard. However, there are more varieties of standards in other parts of the world. To resolve the incompatible standard dilemma, some VCRs in other countries (e.g., India) are designed to play multiple standards. Before you plan to take your VCR tapes to show to your friends abroad, ask if they have a compatible VCR available.

Like VCRs, computers do not have one accepted standard with international acceptance. Maybe one day there will be one international standard so that all software could run on any computer hardware and any VCR tape could run on any videoplayer, but none yet exists.

What is an operating system?

The second point is that each microcomputer brand uses a particular **operating system,** which means there is special software that manages the file and input/output operations. Each operating system is defined by the type of microprocessor or CPU that is used.

Most *IBM* PCs use PC-DOS (Disk Operating System) as an operating system. This system is compatible with MS-DOS, which is used with many *Tandy* computers and many other *IBM* **compatible** computers or **clones**. Both PC-DOS and MS-DOS were written for a family of microprocessors developed by *Intel*. Beginning with the CPU called the 8086, successive developments have lead to the improved 80286, 80386, and 80486. More commonly the newer chips are referred to as the 286, 386, and 486. The latest in this series is called the Pentium, rather than the 80586. The important fact is that each improved chip is progressively faster and more powerful.

You might be familiar with a new operating system for *IBM* computers called the OS/2. This operating system is not commonly found in educational settings today because it offers limited compatibility with MS-DOS.

Like *IBM*, *Apple* microcomputers also run two incompatible operating systems. *Apple* OS or ProDOS is the operating system used with the older *Apple II* family. The *Apple II* family consists of *Apple II*, *Apple II+*, *Apple IIe*, and the *Apple GS*. These microcomputers are common in classrooms, but have very limited power.

On the other hand, the *Apple Macintosh* family is more powerful. The Mac family of microprocessors was developed by *Motorola*. These chips are called 68000, 68010, 68020, 68030, 68040, 68050, and 68060. Again, the higher numbers indicate more speed and power. The Macs include the *Mac LC* varieties which use MAC-DOS as the operating system. Unlike the *IBM*, *IBM* clones, and *Tandy PCs* with MS-DOS operating systems, *Apple* computers are **proprietary systems**, meaning that there are virtually no clones available. *Apple* microcomputers use only *Apple*-compatible hardware and *Apple*-specific software.

One important feature to note about any CPU, whether developed by *Intel* or *Motorola*, is that it is measured according to a MHz (megahertz) internal clock speed. As with newer microprocessors, the newer microcomputers have higher MHz speeds. So, while in the late 1980s 8MHz to 10MHz were common, in the 1990s much faster speeds of 25MHz, 33MHz, and even 50MHz and 66MHz are now available for microprocessors within microcomputers.

What is a microcomputer environment?

The last point is the competition between microcomputer **text-based** (or command line) and **graphics-based** (or menu driven) **environments**. Historically, *IBM* users had text-based environments in which typed text commands and functions were used to control the computer. In comparison, *Apple Macintosh* users were guided through screen displays by images called **icons** (e.g., trash can to discard data) usually manipulated by a mouse. This graphics-based environment, sometimes called GUI (pronounced goo-ey) or Graphical User Interface, has been growing in popularity. To alleviate the text-based versus graphics-based competition in the microcomputer market, *Microsoft*, the giant software company, developed a package called *Windows*. This software allows the formerly text-based environment of the IBM and clone computers to be transformed to the more popular graphics-based environment. Now both *IBM* and *Mac* environments support icons.

So, which microcomputer is the best in education? Some advocates claim that MS-DOS PCs will be standard, while others insist Mac-OS or something else will be the standard. The important thing to realize now is that there is no standard operating system, even though competitive operating systems exist. However, it is interesting to note, that even though there is no standard microcomputer, there seem to be educational favorites. At the elementary level, the Apple IIe is still popular because of its relatively low cost and software availability. Some primary and middle schools are also using older models of Tandy. At the higher levels of education, *IBM* PCs seem to be more prevalent, but the Mac series is gaining ground.

What is the best type of software in education?

There are basically three main types of microcomputer software in education: Programming, Courseware, and Applications Software. Again, the decision is yours. Trends, though, show that Applications Software, particularly word processing, is most popular. For detailed descriptions of software types, read Chapters Three and Four.

Where do I find educational software?

There are basically two categories of software distribution: **commercial** and **non-commercial software**. Commercial software can be purchased from computer dealers and software catalogs. According to the policy of the company, you might even be able to borrow and test drive a product for 30 days before purchasing. Advertisements and software reviews, often included in educational and general technology journals, are good sources for software selection. Listings of recommended periodicals for educators are included at the end of all chapters in this book.

If you are buying a new microcomputer system, the dealer might include free commercial software. This type of software distribution is called **bundled** software and is not selected by you but, instead, by the dealer or company selling the hardware.

In comparison, non-commercial software products are not widely advertised, bundled, or distributed by large software companies. Generally, small advertisements are found at the back of computer magazines. **Shareware** and **freeware** are two kinds of non-commercial software. Shareware costs are low and freeware costs are non-existent. Usually, private individuals design and distribute these products through computer magazine mail orders or in-person distribution at computer conferences.

The last, but not the least, way to learn about computer software is to ask colleagues and friends what they use and recommend. But don't only take their word for it; the best way to learn about software is to try the software yourself. If you don't know how to use a piece of software, ask someone to help you or read through the packaged manual or documentation (commonly referred to as "The Docs") and run the software yourself. It is a very good idea to use a Software Evaluation Form as a professional assessment guide while you review the software. For more information about such a form, see Chapter Three.

Can't I just copy software rather than buy it?

It is easier and cheaper to make a copy of someone else's software rather than buying it, but copying commercial software for use on another computer is against the law. Due to budget constraints or lack of knowledge about illegal software use, illegal copying or **pirating** seems to be a commonly accepted practice among educators.

Many educators aren't aware that commercial software is protected by the copyright law. When you remove the plastic shrink-wrap covering from a sealed software product, you are permitted to make an extra copy called a **backup** (also referred to as **archival** copy) for your own use, but no others. Individuals who break the agreement can be liable for as much as $50,000 for each illegal copy of software. Don't ever claim that you didn't know copying is illegal, since all products include serious license agreements.

Summary

This chapter has listed and answered common fundamental questions asked by many new computer users in the educational setting. By understanding these introductory concepts, you can begin to build a knowledge base for educational computing. With microcomputers becoming a very prevalent educational technology, computer knowledge and skills are essential components in the teaching/learning process.

Recommended Periodicals

BYTE
Classroom Computer Learning
Computers & Education
The Computing Teacher
Education Computing News
Educational Computing
Educational Technology
Electronic Learning
Journal of Computer-Based Instruction
Journal of Computers in Math and Science Teaching
Journal of Computing in Childhood Education
Journal of Computing in Teacher Education
Journal of Educational Computing Research
Journal of Research on Computing in Education
Journal of Technology and Teacher Education
Microcomputers in the Classroom
Microcomputers in Education
PC Magazine
PC World
Perspectives in Computing
Popular Computing
Technology & Learning
T.H.E. Journal

Resources

Association for the Advancement of Computing in Education (AACE). PO Box 2966, Charlottesville, VA 22902. (804) 973-3987.

Association for the Development of Computer-based Instructional Systems (ADCIS). 229 Ramseyer Hall, 29 W. Woodruff Ave., Columbus, OH 43210. (614) 292-7900.

International Society for Technology in Education (ISTE). University of Oregon, 1787 Agate St., Eugene, OR 97403. (503) 346-4414.

EDUCOM. 1112 16th St. NW, Washington, DC 20036. (202) 872-4200.

References

Azarmsa, R. (1991). *Educational computing: Principles and applications.* Englewood Cliffs, NJ: Educational Technology Publications, Inc.

Bork, A. (1987). *Learning with personal computers.* New York: Harper & Row.

Brownell, G. (1987). *Computers and teaching.* St. Paul, MN: West Publishing Company.

Flake, J.L., McClintock, C.E., & Turner, S.V. (1985). *Fundamentals of computer education.* Belmont, CA: Wadsworth Publishing Company.

Freedman, A. (1993). *The computer glossary* (6th ed.). New York: AMACOM.

Heinich, R., Molenda, M., & Russell, J.D. (1993). *Instructional media and the new technologies of instruction* (4th edition). New York: Macmillan Publishing Company.

Hohmann, G.R. (1990). *Young children and computers.* Ypsilanti, MI: High/Scope.

Hurschbuhl, J.J. & Wilkinson, L.F. (Eds.). (1992). *Computers in education* (5th ed.). Guilford, CT: The Dushkin Publishing Group, Inc.

Kearsley, G., Hunter, B., & Furlong, M. (1992). *We teach with technology: New visions for education.* Wilsonville, OR: Franklin, Beedle & Associates, Inc.

Lauckner, K.F. & Lintner, M.D. (1993). *Computers: Inside and out.* Ann Arbor, MI: Pippen Press.

Lillie, D.L., Hannum, W.H., & Struck, G.B. (1989). *Computers and effective instruction.* New York: Longman.

Schellenberg, K. (Ed.). (1992). *Computers in society* (4th ed.). Guilford, CT: The Dushkin Publishing Group, Inc.

Simonson, M. & Thompson, A. (1990). *Educational computing foundations.* Columbus, OH: Merrill Publishing Co.

Snyder, T. & Palmer, J. (1986). *In search of the most amazing thing: Children, education & computers.* Reading, MA: Addison-Wesley Publishing Company, Inc.

Walsh, A.W. (1990, March). Technology and education: A reappraisal. In N. Estes, J. Heene, & M. Thomas (Eds.), *Proceedings of the Ninth International Conference on Technology and Education* (pp. 687-689). Brussels, Belgium: CEP Consultants, Inc..

2 Chapter Two:
Microcomputer Hardware

What is microcomputer hardware?

Microcomputer hardware is the physical components of the microcomputer system. Hardware can be part of a basic computer system or connected as an additional piece. Each additional piece of hardware is called a **peripheral**. Peripherals generally include four types of devices: **input, output, telecommunication**, and **musical sound**.

What is an input device?

An input device enables you to enter data or information into the microcomputer. Although there are many varieties, the seven most common input devices found in the educational setting are **keyboards, light pens, touch screens, joysticks, mice, graphic tablets**, and **scanners**. To provide for a better understanding of what each device is and how it works, the following question-and-answer format is presented.

What is a keyboard?

A keyboard is a set of keys arranged on a flat surface, basically like a typewriter keyboard. However, besides the regular letter, number, and symbol keys called **alphanumeric keys**, there are arrow keys and a set of special keys called **function keys** for specific computer tasks. Sometimes there is also a calculator keypad located on the keyboard.

Keyboard types include either the non-movable, **fixed keyboard**, which is attached directly to the computer, or the separate **independent keyboard**, which is connected to the computer by a curly cord similar in appearance to a telephone cord. You might prefer the independent keyboard for position flexibility, since it can be placed on your lap, or angled on a desktop or table. In addition, it is important to know that some computer systems provide at least one **upgraded keyboard**.

What is a light pen?

A light pen is another input device. You simply touch the monitor with the tip of the pen and the computer responds. It is now possible on some microcomputers to handwrite your input directly onto the screen.

What is a touch screen?

Similar to the light pen is an even easier input device called a touch screen. By touching (i.e., with your finger) a selection appearing on the screen, you may request the information you need. This device is becoming more common in settings where students have physical disabilities and cannot manage keyboarding skills.

What is a joystick?

The joystick is a small stationary input device that attaches by a cord to the microcomputer. By moving the joystick or by pressing specific buttons, images on the screen can be selected and moved. If you have played any computer games, you are probably familiar with the joystick peripheral.

What is a mouse?

A mouse is a small palm-sized pointer peripheral connected by its "tail" or cord to the computer or keyboard. Moving the mouse over a flat surface moves a pointer on the monitor. By skills called **pointing**, **clicking**, and **dragging** (specific manipulations using the mouse), screen commands are carried out.

A mouse can have from one to three buttons for clicking. Some new microcomputers have a new line of lightweight mice particularly handy for laptop and notebook models. Some computer experts predict that the mouse, as a peripheral, may become extinct since some new microcomputers have **trackballs** built directly into the keyboards to replace the cabled mouse.

What is a graphics tablet?

A graphics tablet is an input device that allows the user to write or draw on a flat square surface with a plastic tipped pen. As you write on the flat surface, your input appears on the microcomputer monitor.

If you have not seen graphic tablets for on-computer freehand drawing, you might have seen this input device used on television sports and newscasts. For example, sports broadcasters use the graphics tablets to highlight or trace football plays made on the field, displaying them on the television screen.

What is a scanner?

The scanner is an input device that can "read" text, photographs, graphics, and handwriting from paper into your computer. This process is accomplished by changing the image into digital format so that the computer "understands" the information it is receiving.

With OCR (Optical Character Recognition) software, a scanner can be used by the visually impaired to "read" the printed word. OCR readers when passed over printed words can "speak" with synthesized voices the words being scanned.

What is an output device?

An output device enables your data or information to exit the microcomputer. There are at least four categories of computer hardware output devices including **disks drives**, **monitors**, **printers**, and **LCD output devices**. The following presentation will discuss each category in detail.

What is a disk drive?

A disk drive is a small box-like component that stores output data. There are two types of disk drives: the **floppy disk drive**, which reads the inserted **diskette**, and the **hard** or **fixed disk drive**, which reads and stores programs and data. Although hard disk drives are more expensive, they have a larger storage capacity for your data and programs and operate much more quickly.

What is a monitor?

A monitor, also called a **screen**, is a hardware device for viewing your programs. Similar in appearance to TV screens, monitors vary according to size, shape, color ability, adjustment flexibility, and screen clarity. (See Figure 2.1.)

The physical size of the most common microcomputer desktop screen varies from five to 20 inches measured diagonally. Screen size is an important consideration when purchasing a computer. For the young child and the visually-impaired user, a larger

Figure 2.1. Viewing the *Compton's MultiMedia Encyclopedia. (Courtesy of Compton's)*

monitor is better. If you plan to do word processing, screen size also plays an important role in your computer decision-making. While a 25 line viewing screen (one-half of a doublespaced 8.5 by 11 inch paper) is standard for desktop microcomputers, some laptops provide as few as four lines of visibility.

Both monochrome (one-color images on a different colored background) and color screens are available. For word processing, color, although very attractive, is not necessary. Some computer users prefer amber or green monochrome monitors, rather than black and white, since they believe that these colors are more relaxing to the eye.

Adjustment flexibility is important in monitor selection. Some monitors are non-movable, while others can tilt back and forth or swivel from left to right to adjust to your needs. Rigid monitors can be uncomfortable to use, especially for long periods of time when glare from lighting is a concern.

Screen clarity or resolution measured in picture elements or **pixels** is important to consider. The more pixels, which appear as tiny dots on your monitor, the clearer and sharper are your screen images. Also, the higher number of pixels in each direction, the clearer the monitor's images.

What is a printer?

A printer, which is an electronic device, is necessary for printing information on paper. The paper output is called **hard copy** to distinguish it from the **soft copy** which appears temporarily on the screen. Printers are available in the following four general types: dot matrix, daisy wheel, ink jet, and laser.

Usually the least expensive is the dot matrix printer, where alphanumeric and graphic symbols are formed by a variety of dot patterns. (See Figure 2.2.) The more pins and dots per inch (DPI), the clearer your picture will be. Although you can adjust the older models of dot matrix printers to print near letter quality (NLQ), the letters will generally not be quite as clear as if typewritten. In addition, these printers are noisy to use especially if they are placed in adjacent locations (e.g., computer labs).

However, newer models are quicker and quieter and some products can produce near laser quality letters. Currently in education most dot matrix printers are used for making hard copies of document drafts, graphics, and pictures.

A recent development in dot matrix printers are portable printers designed to

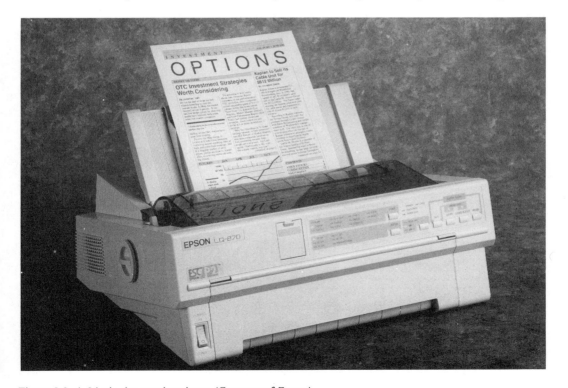

Figure 2.2. A 24-pin dot-matrix printer. *(Courtesy of Epson)*

accompany laptop computers. Weighing usually less than seven pounds, some printers are lightweight and small enough to fit into a briefcase.

The daisy wheel printer derives its name from a small part frequently shaped like a flower. From the center of this printing device radiates separate "petals," each with an alphanumeric symbol at the end. Since the daisy wheel turns and is struck to print each letter exactly like a good typewritten one, printing time is longer.

Definitely not desirable for graphics, the daisy wheel can create clear final text. This type of printer is being used less often as ink-jet and lower priced laser printers are gaining in popularity due to their speed, quiet operation, and graphics capabilities.

The ink jet printer is reasonably priced, and is becoming more common. Alphanumeric and graphic characters are formed by spraying droplets of liquid on the surface of a paper. Similar to dot matrix printers, some ink jet printers are available in portable sizes to provide a device for making hard copies from laptop computers.

One characteristic that dot matrix, daisy wheel, and ink jet printers have in common is that their speed is measured in characters per second or **CPS**. For example, a 180 characters per second would be called 180 CPS. However, the speed of the next type of printer, the laser printer, is not usually measured in CPS, but rather, pages per minute, or **PPM**.

The final and usually most expensive printer type is the laser printer. Quiet and fast, laser printers print precisely. Because laser printers produce whole pages at a time (much like photocopy machines), output is very fast. Although expensive, laser printers have decreased in price dramatically since they were first introduced a few years ago.

A major benefit of the laser printer is that it can produce both professional-looking text and graphics. Because of the printer's capabilities, commercial graphic artists and publishing houses are no longer the sole sources for typesetting and creating finished printed documents. Desktop publishing software for the microcomputer coupled with a laser printer has provided a tool for educators and students to create documents like newsletters and resumes. The pages for this book were produced on a laser printer.

What is an LCD output device?

Relatively new on the educational scene is an LCD device which looks like a picture frame mounted around a thick piece of glass. Connected by a cord to a computer, the liquid crystal display (LCD) device is placed upon the flat surface of an overhead projector, which permits the image from a computer monitor to be enlarged and projected onto a wall screen. Not only is this a convenient device in a one-computer classroom, but also it is a visual resource for presenters at conferences, seminars, and workshops who need to share computer screen images and data with an audience.

What is a telecommunications device?

A telecommunications device allows you to send and receive information from other computer and electronic devices.

Suppose that you wanted to send or receive computer information via electronic devices. In communicating with another computer, you would need a **modem** (modulator-demodulator) to connect your computer to your telephone. A modem acts as an interpreter between telephone and computer signals. Since telephones use analog signals, such as tones and voices, and do not understand the off-on (like a light switch) computer digital signals, the modem creates the necessary translation. In order to telecommunicate or send messages via telephone lines by computer, one modem is needed for the computer at each end so that signals can be changed from digital to analog and back again.

Modems vary by the speed of data being transmitted. Measured in bits per second or **BPS**, transmission rates vary from a slow speed of 300 BPS to 1200 BPS, 2400 BPS, 4800 BPS, and 9600 BPS or more. In educational settings today, the popular speeds are 1200 BPS and 2400 BPS. Since long distance telephone usage can be expensive, the faster your data goes through the telephone lines, the less you pay on your telecommunication calls.

So, how do schools use modems? **Electronic mail, bulletin board services**, and **online databases** are telecommunication uses gaining popularity in educational settings. See Part Two: Integrated Telephony for more information.

What are musical sound devices?

Musical Sound Devices provide the capability of developing and playing high-quality electronic music through the computer. You might already know that a computer can make a simple beeping sound through internal speakers. But suppose you want a more sophisticated, varied, or high-quality sound? It is possible to add these qualities to your PC by adding a Musical Instrument Digital Interface or **MIDI**. With an internal device called a sound card and external connection called a MIDI port, you can connect electronic devices such as a **keyboard synthesizer** or a home stereo. Many kinds of sounds can be made with a MIDI sound card or sound source. For example, many different sounds can be played at one time, called multi-timbral sound, or several notes can be played at once, which is called polyphonic sound. To create these sounds, special software is needed. For more information on MIDI, please see Chapter Twelve: Desktop Computer Music.

What are the types of microcomputers?

Most input and output devices commonly used in education attach to one type of microcomputer, called a **desktop**, which coincidentally fits on the top of your desk and can weigh more than 30 pounds. This weight factor plus the need to connect it to an electrical wall outlet makes the desktop stationary. (See Figure 2.3.)

Figure 2.3. Using a Desktop Computer. *(Courtesy of The Learning Channel)*

In comparison, the three other types of microcomputers, which include **transportable**, **laptop**, and **notebook**, are more lightweight and portable. How do portable microcomputers differ?

Transportable or lunchboxes are lighter than desktop computers and can be transported. However, they weigh up to 18 pounds, which is still quite heavy for carrying.

The laptop is smaller yet and, as the name implies, you can place it on your lap. One form of laptop is the notebook, which is about the size of an average yellow-lined notepad, but, of course, thicker. A notebook microcomputer can weigh as little as 4.4 pounds and fit easily into a briefcase or carry bag. (See Figure 2.4.)

If you would like an even lighter and smaller laptop, your answer is a **palmtop**, which can weigh as little as 1.3 pounds. The newest laptops, which are sometimes referred to as subnotebooks, have high-quality color monitors and touch screens which allow you to input data by touching the screen with a special device rather than using a keyboard.

Although both are classified as microcomputers, there are three important differences between desktop and laptop microcomputers. First, a laptop is presently somewhat more expensive than a desktop variety of equal power. The notebook microcomputer is usually the most expensive. Second, a laptop microcomputer is portable. Since you are not limited by the distance to the nearest wall outlet, a battery-operated microcomputer notebook can be used at the location of your choice, whether in a plane or in a park, rather than being confined to one desktop. Students and teachers are now commonly seen typing class, seminar, conference, and meeting notes into laptops. Third, desktops and laptops are very different in size. The **footprint** or space required on a table or desk for a desktop microcomputer is twice the size of a laptop. In comparison, some laptops are twice the size of the newest palmtop microcomputers.

If you are interested in purchasing a laptop microcomputer, two very important physical factors to consider are the size and clarity of the monitor and the size and spacing of the keyboard. Notebook computers sometimes have smaller than standard size keyboards, which can be very difficult and uncomfortable to use, especially for the high-speed typist.

What do the various microcomputers look like?

Since desktop computers are usually available to examine in on-site educational locations, and laptops or notebooks are less common, some photographs of laptops and notebooks are included for comparative review. Figure 2.4 shows a Compaq notebook computer, while Figure 2.5 pictures the *Tandy 102* Portable Computer. The *102*, weighing three pounds, has been on the market since the late 1980s. Notice the **QWERTY** keyboard, which is very similar to the traditional typewriter design, plus the addition of a top row of

Figure 2.4. Student Using a Notebook Computer.

special keys called function keys, including arrow keys, which accomplish tasks like moving quickly forward or backward through your document. Notice also the small-size

Figure 2.5. Tandy 102 Portable Computer. *(Courtesy of Tandy Corporation)*

screen built in to the computer and the dark circle (actually a red light) beneath the name label indicating the battery power.

It is important to remember that many other companies sell computers similar in features to those illustrated. For example, a new popular notebook from Macintosh is called *Powerbook*, while a new model from IBM is called *Think Pad*.

What is microcomputer networking?

All microcomputers are designed as **stand-alone computers**, which means that they can function individually. You should know that although microcomputers can operate independently, they can also be connected to work together, sharing peripherals, files and software. When microcomputers are connected to other microcomputers or peripherals, the configuration is called a **network**. For example, the connection of several microcomputers to one or more printers is called a printer-sharing network. (See Figure 2.6.)

What is a LAN?

A **LAN** or Local Area Network is hardware and software which permits microcomputers and peripherals to be interconnected and operate together. In a network, each microcomputer can share all of the software and data, and all of the printers and other devices, which are connected anywhere on the network.

Figure 2.6. A Printer-Sharing Network from COMWEB Technology Group. *(Courtesy of COMWEB Technology Group)*

LANs are becoming more common in educational settings because hardware and software costs can be saved through the sharing of various computer components. For example, rather than purchasing one printer or CD-ROM drive per computer, these hardware resources can be shared by several microcomputers at one time. Rather than connecting one printer to one microcomputer, users spool or queue up printing jobs on a first-come-first-served basis. In other words, you give the command to print, and since you are sharing the printer with other users, you must wait until your turn in the printing line to have your hard copy completed. Because of their rapid printing time, laser printers are more practical in a networking setting than are dot matrix printers.

LANs are usually controlled by **file servers**, which are relatively expensive computers with hard disk drives. The file servers act as librarians by storing and sending out to the user the requested software programs and data. Because programs stored on file servers can be used simultaneously on multiple microcomputers, networked system and applications software require network versions or the payment of **site licensing fees** to the publishers. These fees are generally less expensive than purchasing multiple copies of an individual program.

How does a computer work?

After learning about microcomputer hardware, you might be wondering how computers actually work. Since a computer is an electronic device, you either need to plug it into an electrical outlet or, when possible, use batteries to allow for portability.

Although a computer can store and move massive quantities of data very quickly, it only understands numbers. Since the computer is an electronic device, it relies on the same on-off concept as a light switch. When the light is on, a one is represented on the computer. When the light is off, a zero is represented. Using a series of rapid on-off electronic one and zero combinations or **binary digits** called **bits**, the computer translates the electric code of each eight-bit set, called a **byte** or character. To define which number will define which character, a standard numerical code called **ASCII** (American Standard Code for Information Interchange) has been developed. Each ASCII code symbol represents a character which can be typed on the keyboard and displayed on the screen. Characters include letters, numbers, and symbols which are composed of bytes. Standard ASCII character sets range from 0 - 127. For example, any word you type on the computer is composed of bytes. If your word has three letters, you will have used three bytes. Chart 2.1 presents the computer coding equivalent for the word "tom."

Character	=	ASCII Code	=	Byte Equivalent
t		99		01100011
o		111		01101111
m		109		01101101

Chart 2.1. Computer Coding Equivalents.

Why is it important to understand bytes?

The number of bytes a computer can store is one measure of its power and capacity and is called **memory** size. Memory comes in two types, **ROM** and **RAM**. ROM is "Read Only Memory" which stores factory-programmed instructions for the computer that cannot be changed. When the computer is turned off, ROM still remains.

Its opposite is RAM or "Random Access Memory." This type of memory allows you to read and write changeable information. But you must remember that when the computer is turned off, the information in RAM is lost unless battery power is used to maintain the memory (available on some systems), or the information has been saved on a hard or floppy disk. RAM size describes the amount of information that can be stored only while the power is on. RAM is typically listed in computer advertisements.

Which computer memory size is better: K or Mb?

Two computers used in various school settings are the Apple IIe computer, which in its standard configuration has 128K RAM, and the Apple Macintosh LC computer, which has 4MB RAM. In order to understand this RAM measurement, it is important to know that approximately 1,000 bytes (actually 2^{10} or 1,024 bytes) equals 1 kilobyte or 1K, and 1,000 kilobytes equals 1 megabyte or 1 MB. So, 4MB is 32 times greater than 128K, meaning that the power and capacity of the Mac LC RAM memory is much greater than the Apple IIe. So, Mb RAM capacity is better than K RAM capacity.

You might be interested to know that some of the more powerful computers (not readily available in educational settings) have gigabytes or G of memory. Each G is equivalent to 1,000 megabytes or 1,000,000 kilobytes. Chart 2.2 shows the byte hierarchy.

```
8 bits = 1 byte(1 character)
1,000 bytes = 1 kilobyte(1K)
1,000 kilobytes (1,000K) = 1 megabyte(1MB)
1,000,000 kilobytes = 1,000 megabytes = 1 gigabyte(1G)
```

Chart 2.2. The Byte Hierarchy.

How much RAM is enough?

The more RAM you have, the better. For example, a common word processing program for the Apple II family computers is *AppleWorks*, which requires 128K of memory, whereas a basic Logo program requires only 64K of memory. Generally speaking, many programs or software designed for classroom use require only 64K. However, more sophisticated software like *PUBLISH IT!* (which has been used to lay out this book) requires at least 640K.

What happens when the memory runs out?

The most common occurrence is a message on the screen stating something like "no more space." A remedy for the more advanced computer is a **virtual memory** system which uses a computer component called the hard disk drive as an extension of the computer's RAM memory. The program information and data not in current use are stored in temporary areas and then exchanged with other program information and data when they are needed. This swapping provides more usable space in memory.

What is the importance of the CPU and Processing?

Another measure of speed and power is the type and speed of the chip called the **microprocessor** or **CPU**. Often referred to as the brain of the computer, it directs all the activities including processing and controlling the data flow between the devices connected to the computer, like the printer and the monitor.

One point to remember when buying a computer is to consider both the CPU and the K (or better the MB) sizes. Ask also if the K or MB memory measurement is expandable, allowing you to add more power to your computer. The expandability upgrade is becoming a more common option in microcomputer purchasing.

What are the advantages of computers in an educational setting?

There are many advantages of using computers in an educational setting. The following discussion describes the primary advantages of using computers in the teaching and learning process:

Computers have special capabilities useful to educators. Computers can: 1) calculate and process data at great speeds; 2) work 24 hours each day at top efficiency; and 3) store large quantities of data in their memories for lengthy periods of time.

Assistive technologies, which assist disabled people to see better, hear more clearly, use **synthesized speech**, learn, and become more mobile have educational advantages. Such advancements assist in mainstreaming more learners. An example of assistive technology is *BrailleMate*, a pocket computer for the visually impaired, which has a braille keyboard and acknowledges input with a speech synthesizer. Then it automatically translates text for printing onto a hardcopy braille or ink printer.

Learner motivation is increased as students are provided hands-on experiences with computers. Because of our visually-oriented society, many students have spent hours watching television or playing computer games, so the microcomputer is a natural extension of these interests. Unlike traditional television, but similar to computer games, microcomputers provide interactivity, allowing the student to sense control over learning through individualized tasks.

Flexibility in teaching/learning styles is encouraged through computerization. The traditional sage-on-the-stage model can be transformed to a guide-on-the-side model in which the teacher can provide independent and cooperative learning opportunities via personalized software programs or groupware programs designed for discussion.

Location versatility can encourage the integration of computers into the classroom environments. Whether used as a stand-alone or networked into a LAN, microcomputers can be placed individually in each classroom, clustered in a media-library area, mobilized on carts for regrouping and distribution, or permanently organized in a lab setting.

What are some specific examples of computer usage in education?

There are many examples of computer uses in education. The following examples have been selected to focus on previously discussed computer advantages.

Computer speed and calculation abilities are easy to understand. For example, finding class averages on tests can be accomplished in a fraction of the time taken by manual calculations. The computer can decrease your clerical time and provide you with accurate data that can be stored on disks or paper.

Assistive technologies permit paralyzed persons to communicate with the computer and other individuals by using devices which respond to voice commands, a headwand, subtle head movements, or a blink of the eye. Eldon Nelson, manager of the IBM National Support System for Persons with Disabilities, summarized the use of electronic devices in the following manner: "For the able-bodied, technology makes work easier, but for a person with a disability, technology often makes things possible" (Fox, 1991).

An example of at-risk students being motivated by technology can be found in Orangeburg-Wilkinson High School, Orangeburg, South Carolina. Dramatic changes occurred in the at-risk student population when one computer was provided for every 20 students. The drop-out rate decreased while 30% more students met basic reading standards and 62% of the students went on to college.

Computers can provide in-class assistance to instructors. Rather than relying on the direct lecturing approach using only chalk or whiteboard as a visual aid, computers can now be utilized to provide an enhanced version of the overhead projector. Small team student workstations or independent learning centers can be designed to meet the individual needs and interests of learners, providing electronic remedial to advanced presentations. Depending on the software, students can be pre-tested, provided appropriate practice, monitored, and post-tested via computers with a minimum of teacher-directed interaction.

Computers can also be used successfully in a number of different settings. For example, one stationary computer in the classroom provides the opportunity not only for the integration of computers into whole-class instruction, but also for student cooperative learning experiences. On the other hand, a computer lab provides many opportunities for hands-on experiences by many students simultaneously and, in addition, the equipment is generally located in a more secure location. Mobile computers are used for on-the-spot demonstrations and are group-shared according to teachers' needs. Finally, the library setting for microcomputers creates an equal-access climate and students can receive assistance from knowledgeable librarians.

What are some computer hardware problems and solutions?

There are several predominant computer problems which have been reported by educators. The following discussion will describe them.

It is a difficult to choose a computer system. There are many products and brands on the market. Since operating systems are not standardized, it is important to choose one that best fits your needs. The first step in hardware selection is deciding what main function or application you will use. For example, do you want the system primarily for word processing, running instructional software programming, or graphic designing? Become familiar with products which are compatible with the system of your choice. Product name recognition might be important to you, so you might want to choose an *IBM*, *Apple*, *Mac*, or *Tandy* computer. If you are willing to buy a less-known, less-expensive brand, then you would buy a microcomputer referred to as a **clone**. Of course, you need to match the costs of the hardware and software with your projected budget.

Setting up the system can also be a problem. You might want to seek the guidance of computer-experienced colleagues, or you might want to hire computer dealers or computer-training professionals to help you. You might be comfortable enough to follow the step-by-step guidelines and diagrams presented in hardware manuals.

As a computer system is up and running, it is important to identify an individual or team to provide a support system in assisting when a hardware problem occurs. Some hardware companies provide a hotline to answer questions. Whatever your choice, it is a good idea to have some back-up support from a knowledgeable and skilled person.

Another problem concerns understanding the purchasing or leasing agreement. Read all of the fine print before signing any agreement. Be certain to know the answers to the following questions: (1) What are the warranty terms? (2) What provisions are made for service for hardware repairs? Warranties can vary from 90 days, which is common, to as many as 60 months, so shop for a reputable company with good references. Be certain that you understand exactly what parts of your computer system are covered by the warranty.

A further concern is the repair or service contract. Again, only do business with a reputable dealer. Be certain to ask whether the service contract requires you to take your computer in for repair or whether the repair person will repair your computer on-site. If your computer must be taken to the dealer for repairs, ask if there will be a substitute one during the repair process. Also, be certain that repairs are made with high-quality parts, preferably with the original brand. Ask about hourly rates. Computer repair and service costs can be very expensive and provide you with **downtime** or computer non-use time.

The last problem commonly mentioned by educators is the potential incompatibility of computer systems and additional peripherals. Since most peripherals require some kind of controller board in the computer, it is important to find out and understand whether add-ons are possible. You can check at the back of your microcomputer to see if there are **ports** or plug-in areas for connecting peripherals. Often, the symbols or numbers on the ports will provide an indication of what peripherals can be connected. Your computer manual should also help explain this process and indicate your computer's limitations.

Decision-making Guidelines: Computer Hardware

1. Objective: What types of computers would best enhance the teaching and learning environment? Will the microcomputers be stand-alones or will they be networked together?

2. Integration: How will computers be used within the educational setting? For example, will they be utilized for instruction, clerical support for teachers, or part of a multimedia system? (See Chapter Thirteen for more details.)

3. Cost: What is the budget for computers? Do you intend to purchase a total system or essential components parts? Do you plan to add peripherals? What operating system will you choose? How much initial RAM will you need? Will you purchase an upgraded keyboard? Do you need a mouse? What other input devices will you need? Will the system be purchased or leased? Are there educational discounts? Is there a service contract? What are the long-range plans for computer hardware expansion?

4. Location: Will the computer system be placed in a classroom, media center, or lab?

5. Security: What measures will be undertaken to prevent computer damage or theft?

6. Equal Access: What policy measures will be designed to ensure that all students and teachers have an equal opportunity to use the computers?

7. Updating: Who will be designated as the "computer specialist" or "computer contact" to recommend additional equipment, review service and warranty contracts, be responsible for computer repairs, suggest upgrading/replacing equipment when necessary, and organize training sessions?

8. Training: Who will be trained to use the computers? When and where will the training occur? Will there be special time or financial allotments available to the trainees?

Summary

Computer hardware is the electronic equipment needed to run software. This chapter has focused on a detailed description of computer components relevant to education. Included topics were computer tasks, and networking, followed by a basic introduction to the "inside workings" of microcomputers.

Recommended Periodicals

Byte

Compute

Computer Journal

Computer Music Journal

The Computing Teacher

Educational Technology

EDUCOM Review

Electronic Learning

Electronics

IBM Systems Journal

Instructor

Journal of Educational Technology Systems

Journal of Research on Computers in Education

Journal of Special Education Technology

Library Hi Tech

Mac World

Media & Methods

Microcomputers in the Classroom

PC Laptop

PC Today

PC World

Tech Trends

Technology & Learning

T.H.E. Journal

Resources

Alliance for Technology Access. Apple Computer, Inc. 20525 Mariani Ave., Cupertino, CA 95014. (800) 732-3131.

Apple Computer. 20525 Mariani Ave., Cupertino, CA 95014. (408) 996-1010.

Association for the Advancement of Computing in Education (AACE). PO Box 2966, Charlottesville, VA 22902. (804) 973-3987.

Association for the Development of Computer-based Instructional Systems (ADCIS). 229 Ramseyer Hall, 29 W. Woodruff Ave., Columbus, OH 43210. (614) 292-7900.

Association for Educational Communications & Technology (AECT). 1025 Vermont Ave. NW, Washington, DC 20005. (202) 347-7834.

Brother International Corp. 200 Cottontail Lane, Somerset, NJ 08875. (908) 356-8880.

Citizen America Corp. 2450 Broadway, Suite 600, PO Box 4003, Santa Monica, CA 90411. (310) 453-0614

Eastman Kodak Co., Printer Products Division. 343 State St., Rochester, NY 14653. (800) 344-0006.

EDUCOM. 1112 16th St. NW, Washington, DC 20036. (202) 872-4200.

IBM National Support Center for Persons with Disabilities. PO Box 2150, Atlanta, GA 30301 (800) 426-2133 (voice); (800) 284-9482 (TDD)

IBM Corporation. 4111 Northside Parkway, Atlanta, GA 30327. (800) 426-9402.

International Society for Technology in Education (ISTE). University of Oregon, 1787 Agate St., Eugene, OR 97403. (503) 686-4414.

Lexmark International, Inc. 740 New Circle Rd. NW, Lexington, KY 40511. (606) 232-3000.

Seikosha America, Inc. 10 Industrial Ave., Mahwah, NJ 07430. (800) 338-2609.

Star Micronics America, Inc. 420 Lexington Ave., Suite 2702, New York, NY 10170. (212) 986-6770.

Tandy Corporation. 916 One Tandy Center, Fort Worth, TX 76102. (817) 390-3477.

References

Artwick, B.A. (1989). *Microsoft Flight Simulator: Information Manual and Flight Handbook.* Redmond, WA: Microsoft Corporation.

Barron, A.E. & Orwig, G.W. (1993). *New technologies for education.* Englewood, CO: Libraries Unlimited, Inc.

Collis, B. (1988). *Computers, curriculum, and whole-class instruction.* Belmont, CA: Wadsworth Publishing Company.

Electronic Learning. (November/December 1988). Technology and the at-risk student. *Electronic Learning, 8* (3), 36-49.

Fox, J. (March 1991). Unlocking the door: PCs and people with disabilities. *PC Today, 3* (5), 43-51.

Gevirtz, G. & Kelman, P. (1990). *The Scholastic guide to educational computer networks.* New York: Scholastic Inc.

Glitman, R. (1992, January). Pen PCs: Mission-critical note takers that return to basics. *PC World, 10* (1), 89.

Heinich, R., Molenda, M., & Russell, J.D. (1993). *Instructional media and the new technologies of instruction* (4th ed.). New York: Macmillan Publishing Company.

Hogan, M. (1992, January). Compaq does a power lunch box. *PC World, 10* (1), 83.

Hogan, M. (1993, January). The whole world in his windows. *PC World, 11* (1), 43-44.

Kearsley, G., Hunter B., & Furlong, M. (1992). *We teach with technology: New visions for education.* Wilsonville, OR: Franklin, Beedle & Associates, Inc.

Kraft Systems, Inc. (1990). *Thunderstick User's Guide.* Vista, CA: Kraft Systems, Inc.

Landry, R. (1991, March). PenPoint puts it in writing. *PC World, 9* (3), 83-86.

Leyenberger, A. (1991, May). Computers for the rest of us, Part XI. *PC Laptop Computers Magazine, 3* (5), 59-63.

Mason, J. (1992). Warning: Here come the software police. In K. Schellenberg (Ed.), *Computers in Society* (4th ed.). Guilford, CT: The Dushkin Publishing Group, 91-95.

Melville, R. (1993, March). Dot matrix lives! *PC World, 11* (3), 175-179.

Miastrowski, S. (1992). Tag-along hard copy. *BYTE's Essential Guide to Portable Computing, 17* (13), 41-44.

O'Brien, D. (1990, November/ December). *Media and Methods, 27* (2), 24-25.

Schwebach, L. (1991, July). Making sense out of SCSI. *PC Today, 7* (5), 28-33.

Spector, L. (1992, January). Color and Light: The new color notebooks. *PC World, 10* (1), 73.

Smarte, G. (1992). First impression. *BYTE's Essential Guide to Portable Computing, 17* (13), 8-9.

Smarte, G. (1993, January). Two Toshiba systems to go. *BYTE, 18* (1), 46 & 48.

TeleSensory. (1992, January). Braille in a pocket computer. *PC World, 10* (1), 62.

Timeworks. (1991). *Publish It! Manual.* Version 2.0. Timeworks, Inc., Northbrook, IL.

Troutman, A.P. & White, J.W. (1988). *The micro goes to school: Instructional applications of microcomputer technology.* Pacific Grove, CA: Brooks/Cole Publishing Company.

Walkenbach, J. (1991, June). Equipping your PC for high-quality sound production. *PC Today, 6* (5), 32-38.

Yacco, W. (1991, May). Portable pointers. *PC Laptop, 3* (5), 23-29.

3

Chapter Three:
Computer Software for
Programming and Courseware

What is computer software?

Computer software is a general term applied to programs or instructions written in special computer languages which make computers function. Since microcomputers can only process one program at a time, the purpose of computer software is to store data or other programs for future use.

In educational settings, there are three categories of software: First is **programming software** used to write programs (lists of sequenced directions) in languages like Logo or BASIC; second is **courseware** used for instruction, such as on-computer tutorials. Third is **applications software** used for specific tasks like word processing. For organizational purposes, this chapter presents programming and courseware, while Chapter Four focuses on the most rapidly growing software category — applications tools.

Software, regardless of category, looks basically similar in appearance. All data are encoded on circular pieces of plastic, aluminum, or metalicized disks. To input software data into the microcomputer, you must place a diskette or disk into a disk drive. In the disk drive your data will be read and stored either permanently or temporarily. There are four types of microcomputer disks that can be used in the reading and storing task: (1) the 5.25-inch floppy disk, (2) the 3.5-inch floppy disk, (3) the hard disk, and (4) the compact disc or **CD-ROM (Compact-Disc, Read-Only Memory)**. For further information on CD-ROM, read Chapter Ten: Compact Disc Technology.

Traditionally for microcomputer uses, most software comes on two sizes of **floppy disks**. The older variety is the 5.25-inch (often pronounced five and a quarter-inch) floppy disk, which was truly floppy. Made of coated mylar material, the floppy disk is round but encased in a thin square plastic envelope for protection. For example, the Apple II family and older microcomputer series use this size disk to store and transfer data.

The newer version floppy disk is only 3.5 inches in diameter with a hard plastic casing. Besides being less fragile, the smaller diskette (still called a floppy disk) can store much more data than the larger-sized disk. The 3.5-inch disk is is more common with the newer microcomputers. Both sizes of floppy disks have holes in their plastic jackets which expose the mylar material to a device called a disk drive. The purpose of this disk drive is to read and write information from the floppy disk.

Next, the hard disk is made of metal or metal-coated platters inserted, stored, and read on hard disk drives. Although similar in size to a floppy disk (either 5.25-inch or 3.5-inch), a hard disk can store more information and retrieve the information faster. Because of its storage capacity and speed, all new microcomputers have the ability to store software data on hard disks. The hard disk is read by the hard disk drive.

The most recent form of computer disk for storing data is the CD-ROM (Compact Disc-Read Only Memory) which measures 4.72-inches in diameter. This metalicized disk coated in clear plastic can store massive amounts of text and graphic data. Compared to floppy and hard disks, a CD-ROM can store and retrieve the most data. For example, a complete encyclopedia can be stored on one CD-ROM. Because of CD-ROM capabilities, CD-ROM drives are now included with many new Mac and PC microcomputer systems. Chart 3.1 presents a comparison of approximate storage capacities on a CD-ROM.

To better understand the differences among a 5.25-inch floppy disk, a 3.5-inch floppy disk, a hard disk, and a CD-ROM, Chart 3.2 presents specific data on appearance and storage capacity.

As you can see, the capacity to store software or data depends upon the disk used. With the development of CD-technology, the storage ability of the microcomputer has increased tremendously. For example, a CD-ROM can store 250,000 pages of text, which is equivalent to 1,520 350K floppies or eight 70Mb hard disks!

```
CD-ROM = 250,000 pages of text
       = 1,520 5.25-inch floppy disks
       = 695 3.5-inch floppy disks
       = 8 70 megabyte hard disks
```

Chart 3.1. CD-ROM Comparative Storage Capacities.

No matter which disk you use, safety precautions must be taken to prevent the erasure of disk contents. Since the 5.25-inch and the 3.5-inch floppy disks are still the most common software storage mediums in educational settings and most sensitive to data erasures, it is important to understand how to care for them. Unlike the hard disk, which is generally sealed within the hard disk drive, or the CD-ROM, which uses optical rather than magnetic technology, floppy disks need special care. For more information on CD or optical disc care, see Chapter Ten. Chart 3.3 lists some important safety reminders for floppy disk users:

DISK	APPEARANCE	STORAGE CAPACITY
5.25-inch Diskette	Thin mylar plastic disk enclosed in a stiff but flexible plastic case	Double-sided, 340 to 360K; double-sided high-density, 1 to 2Mb
3.5-inch Diskette	Thin mylar plastic disk encased in a non-flexible plastic case	Double-sided, 700 to 800K; double-sided high-density, 1.4Mb
5.25- or 3.5-inch Hard Disk	Metal or metal-coated platters enclosed in a metal housing	40 to 100Mb common in educational settings
4.72-inch Compact Disc CD-ROM	Silver-colored metalized clear plastic disk	Approximately 550Mb

Chart 3.2. Comparison of Microcomputer Disks.

SAFETY PRECAUTION	REASON FOR PRECAUTION
1. Keep disks away from magnetic and electrical devices such as TVs, telephones, stereos, tops of PCs or monitors, etc.	Since disks are recorded magnetically, magnetic fields can erase data easily.
2. Protect your disks from extreme temperatures. Keep them out of direct sunlight and away from cold locations.	The plastic materials are sensitive to extreme conditions.
3. Do not bend, use paper clips on, or write directly on 5.25 disks.	A bent or creased disk will not make good contact with the disk drive.
4. Never touch the magnetic surface of the disk with a finger, or with dirt, dust, or liquids.	Any foreign material can prevent good contact with or contaminate the disk drive.

Chart 3.3. Caring for Microcomputer Floppy Disks.

You might ask, which size and type of disk should I use? Check the slot size of your disk drive. Although many microcomputers have one or two same-sized disk drives, some have two differently sized drives that run 5.25-inch and 3.5-inch disks. If you have a new model microcomputer, you might have a CD-ROM drive as well. To identify the types of drives you have on your computer, either read your microcomputer manual or ask someone who is knowledgeable about microcomputers.

Another concern is **disk version** or which disk works in which microcomputer. If you are using a blank disk, you need not worry about a correct version. However, if you are purchasing software with information already stored on it, you need to buy the correct version. What does that mean?

As mentioned in Chapter One, different computers use different operating systems. For example, if you were to buy software to use on an *Apple IIe* machine, you would need *Apple OS (Apple II)* software. If you wanted the same program for an IBM compatible or any PC, you would need to purchase an *MS-DOS* version of the software. Has anything been done to simplify this sometimes confusing situation?

Presently, long-time microcomputer competitors Apple and IBM are working on a cooperative venture which should produce a compatible standard for both systems. This simply means you won't have to worry about software versions. Their new system is still in the planning stages and may not appear in the educational setting for some time.

But, regardless of which operating system you choose, you generally cannot use the computer without putting in or **loading** the operating system from a disk into the microcomputer's memory. This process is called **booting up the system**. If your computer is networked, the booting is generally done in advance for you.

What is networking software?

If you want more than one student to simultaneously use a specific software program, you will need a disk for each microcomputer. For example, if you have a class of 25 students with 25 microcomputers, you will need 25 disks. To save money on multiple disks and to save time (no individual booting up the system), you can set up a computer network and purchase one piece of software with a site license. This single piece of software is loaded into a file server where it is shared by all users in the network.

As discussed in Chapter Two, specific hardware is required including workstations (networked computers), a file server (powerful computer with a hard-disk drive which stores, directs, and monitors information among the workstations), and a network system (user-interface between operating system and software). Examples of popular educational network operating systems include *Novell Netware* (generally compatible with *IBM PCs*) and *AppleTalk* (generally compatible with *Macintosh* and *Apple II* family microcomputers). A popular network management system software is the *Schoolmate Education Network* for Tandy PCs.

How are computer programming software and courseware used in education?

First, programming software and courseware will be defined. Next, examples will be presented of each educational use.

What is programming?

Programming is the process of learning to encode sets of instructions in computer languages. In the educational setting, the most popular languages today for non-specialist computer users are **BASIC** and **Logo**. BASIC was the first language available on a large-scale educational audience for microcomputer users in the 1970s. During that time, applications software and courseware were generally unavailable to teachers, so BASIC was the "basic" component of any computer literacy course taught. Chart 3.4 presents an example of a BASIC program.

```
10 REM THIS IS A BASIC PROGRAM
20 PRINT ``BASIC IS FUN.''
30 PRINT ``THIS IS A SAMPLE.''
40 END
```

Chart 3.4. An Example of a BASIC Program.

In comparison, Logo is not only a programming language but, also, a philosophy of education. Specifically designed by Seymour Papert at M.I.T. (Massachusetts Institute of Technology) to further develop thinking skills, Logo has been historically confined to elementary school and introductory computer literacy classes for teachers. Although a very powerful language, Logo's graphics capabilities, called Turtlegraphics, make up the most popular component. Within the computer's **microworld** the learner can discover, explore, and understand a variety of mathematical concepts. More recently, Logo has added a three-dimensional aspect to programming with **robotics**. With new Logo software, called *Lego Logo*, students can animate self-designed robots through Logo programming. Other less used capabilities of Logo are speech synthesis, music enhancements, advanced graphics, word processing, and more complex mathematical problem-solving features. A very good introductory free 25-page book on Logo is entitled *Why Use Logo? An Overview of Logo in Education* by *Terrapin Software, Inc.* So that you are familiar with the style of a simple Logo program, Chart 3.5 presents an example.

```
REPEAT 4 [FD 30 RT 90]
RT 60
REPEAT 4 [FD 50 LT 90]
```

Chart 3.5. An Example of a Logo Program.

Together with other programming languages, including **C, FORTRAN, Pascal,** and **COBOL,** the concept of programming as a focal point for computer literacy is declining among educators. Better quality courseware and applications software are assuming major roles in classrooms. If, though, you plan to design your own software, **author** (modify) existing software, or teach programming to students, knowledge of programming fundamentals is still important.

What is courseware?

Courseware includes two categories: **Computer-assisted** or **Computer-aided Instruction (CAI)** for teaching and **Computer-managed Instruction (CMI)** for managing instruction. Both are used in educational settings.

What is CAI?

CAI programs sometimes include **Computer-based Training** Programs or **CBT**. General categories include: **drill and practice, tutorial, simulation,** and **problem-solving**. These four areas will be presented in detail.

What is drill and practice software?

Drill and practice software is skills-development CAI which often emphasizes response accuracy, speed, self-pacing, and convergent question-answering abilities. Colloquially referred to pejoratively as "drill and kill," this type of CAI earned its nickname because of the dull, repetitive presentation which some of the first-marketed commercial drill and practice software contained.

Drill and practice software is often the easiest area to integrate into an existing curriculum, since it serves as an "electronic" review sheet. You need little or no previous computer experience to use it. If you teach language arts, social studies, foreign language, ESL, or science, you might already have discovered a use for this individualized and often student-paced skills-development CAI. You also may have noticed the convergent-thinking opportunities for factual content review. If you are a remedial or enrichment teacher, you certainly realize the value of immediate feedback (correct or incorrect answers) for the students on computers. As you are very aware, a teacher with a class of 25 students cannot provide immediate, individualized feedback for all learners simultaneously. Twenty-five computers can. For this reason, computers for drill and practice use are sometimes viewed as "non-human teacher aides."

How are drill and practice software packages commonly used in today's classrooms? There are three uses: (1) as learning stations, (2) as "free time" choice activities, and (3) as **groupware** (where an entire class or small group uses a software package together).

What is tutorial software?

Tutorial software is sequenced, interactive, and user-paced CAI that introduces new concepts. Better quality tutorials use a process called **branching** in their programming designs, allowing a choice of various optional responses. For example, if you need more explanation of a concept before proceeding to the next line of information, you can use **remediation loops** or programmed digressions from the main sequence of learning steps. Tutoring is electronically personalized. Figure 3.1 shows a tutorial product.

Most computer companies provide floppy disk software tutorials to teach you how to use the machines. These tutorials are step-by-step guides that instruct, often in an entertaining manner. Also, some software companies provide introductory tutorials to introduce their products. These introductory promotions are called **demo disks**. Demo disks are either distributed free of charge or at a low cost.

What is simulation software?

Simulation software programs are interactive computer analogies of real-life decision-making situations. CAI educational simulation software is not to be confused with computer games. Although similar in many ways to visual stimulus-response action adventure games, a CAI simulation presents facts and problem-solving situations, but in not always the win-lose format of computer games. For example, simulations are popular for on-computer science

Figure 3.1. Spanish Assistant. *(Courtesy of Microtac Software)*

experiments and historic you-are-there decision-making adventures. Figure 3.2 presents a scene from a very popular social studies simulation called *The Oregon Trail*.

In educational training programs, interactive simulations are used to train pilots and astronauts. For the amateur pilot or pilot hobbyist, less sophisticated and more reasonably priced software simulations are available for school or home microcomputers.

What is problem-solving software?

Problem-solving software is CAI for the purpose of further developing logical or visual-spatial relationship skills. Sometimes similar to logic problems presented on I.Q. tests, problem-solving software allows you to practice strategy development, including both inductive and deductive reasoning.

What is CMI?

The second category of courseware is **CMI** or **Computer-Managed Instruction**. It is software that allows you to monitor, to keep records, and to evaluate academic progress whether the students are taught traditionally or on computers. Another aspect of CMI is **Computer-based Testing** or **CBT**, where monitoring is focused on testing. Manually

Figure 3.2. A Scene from the Simulation, "The Oregon Trail." *(Courtesy of MECC)*

managing learning programs of individual students can be a complex task as well as time consuming. However, by using CMI, you can easily update the performance and accomplishments of every student automatically and electronically via the computer.

A beneficial function of CMI is the testing component. Most CMI software cannot only score tests, but also can access on-line (computerized databases) test items to be used plus provide a test-item analysis of teacher-created items. The test-item analysis identifies sound items, and indicates which items should be eliminated or improved.

What are the advantages of using computer programming software and courseware in education?

There are several major advantages for using programming software and courseware in the educational setting. Some advantages relate to the learner, others to the instructor. Both sets of advantages will be discussed.

Learner advantages include five major areas: (1) logic skills development, (2) problem-solving abilities development, (3) individualization of learning tasks, (4) increase of motivation, and (5) interactivity with the microcomputer. Through programming software, students learn the necessity of logical, sequential decision-making and planning to design end products. While the nature of cause and effect is further developed in programming, it is also enhanced by problem-solving and simulation experiences. Students can be provided with personalized learning plans based on their needs and interests through CAI courseware. It is important to remember that no matter which software is used, learners are interacting with their microcomputer environment and are provided individualized feedback through immediately reinforced responses.

For you, the instructor, there are several major advantages, which are: (1) programming is an instructional tool for the demonstrating and teaching of sequence logic through computer interaction; (2) CMI offers clerical assistance with administrative and recordkeeping tasks in less time than manual methods; (3) personalized monitoring of student performance is enhanced; and (4) with the combination of CAI and CMI, you can use the computer as a "classroom assistant" presenting and reviewing information on a step by step basis according to individual learner needs.

It should be made clear that you do not lose control of the curriculum. Instead, the curriculum is personalized and paced as you assume the role as the "guide on the side," supervising, coaching, monitoring, and assessing each student's progress whether in programming, CAI, or CMI uses.

What are some specific examples of computer programming software and courseware in education?

A mountain of software products is available from a growing number of companies. An entire book can be written to review specific packages so the following sampling is just the tip of the iceberg of some popular products:

First, programming software, like BASIC, is sometimes "built into" the computer. So when you turn on the computer you can easily begin programming. Many popular books and programming course textbooks have been written for teaching BASIC in educational settings and are available in many bookstores. Skim through some selections and see which one best suits your needs. On the other hand, Logo programming software has mushroomed from a two-dimensional screen "microworld environment" to three-dimensional robotics with the addition of Lego building blocks and materials. Again, many books exist. However, there is one that I highly recommend: *Mindstorms: Children, Computers, and Powerful Ideas* by the creator of Logo, Seymour Papert. This book describes the educational value and potential of this exciting, very versatile programming language, too often misunderstood by educators.

Second, courseware products, both CAI and CMI software, are becoming "teaching and clerical aides" for instructors. Again, there are many products. The following samples with descriptions represent just a few:

• A CMI example is a program called *ClassMaster* by *TECHBYTE International*. This software combines a comprehensive grading system with a filing system, student attendance data, biographical information, performance in raw point or percentage scoring, and a performance projection system.

• *Barney* by *DLM* is a CAI software product for young children (pre-school through eight years old). Based on a Public Television character, this software teaches numbers, the alphabet, and colors and shapes.

• A popular example of CAI problem-solving software is *The Factory* by *Sunburst*, where learners from grade 4 through adult levels use color graphics and animation to create geometric ''products'' on a simulated machine. Concepts stressed include visual discrimination, understanding sequence, spatial perception, and logic.

• *Flight Simulator* is CAI simulation software by *Microsoft* that provides you with the on-computer experience of piloting not only a single-engine aircraft, but also a business jet, sailplane, and a World War I bi-plane. Three-dimensional screens complete with sound effects enhance your adventure.

• There are several versions of Logo. One is *Krell Logo Language* by *Krell Software* and another is *Terrapin Logo* by *Terrapin, Inc.* Both programming language software packages offer Logo's basic components.

• *Nigel's World* by *Lawrence Publications* is a CAI simulation that combines photography and geography skills as the 7- 12-year-old travels on photo assignments around the world. There are four difficulty levels for the 40 maps so the program can be adjusted to meet individual needs. Digitized speech, music, and animation are valuable enhancements to the program.

• *PILOT* and *SUPERPILOT* by *Apple Computer, Inc.* are authoring languages that have been used by educators for many years.

• *Principles of Chemistry* by *Cliffs StudyWare*, designed for beginning or advanced chemistry students, is a serious, comprehensive study aid covering 26 chemistry topics. To enhance learning, multiple choice test for each topic, a CAI drill practice, and a tutorial are included in the software package.

• *SimLife, the Generic Playground* is the newest in a series of simulation programs (e.g., *SimCity* and *SimAnt*) by *Maxis* designed to provide decision-making opportunities for middle through high school students. SimLife focuses upon the development and evolution of a student-designed and student-controlled ecosystem challenged by mutagens and natural world disasters.

• *Stickybear's Reading Room* by *Optimum Resource, Inc.* is language arts CAI to help young students (4- 8-years-old) learn sentence structure and reading comprehension in both English and Spanish.

• *Where in America's Past Is Carmen Sandiego?* is a recent addition to the popular line of *Where in the ... World, Europe, Time, etc. ... is Carmen Sandiego?* This traditional favorite software CAI simulation package that incorporates geography skills is available from *Broderbund*.

• *Zoo Keeper* by *Davidson & Associates, Inc.* is a simulation for primary through middle school students. In this software package students assume the responsibility of the absent zoo keeper. Problems such as habitat conditions and endangered species protection caused by troublemakers must be resolved.

• *Zug's Race Through Space*, published by *Zugware*, is a "talking" software program which includes problem-solving adventures emphasizing and teaching facts about the solar system, asteroids, comets, and meteors to 5- 12-year-olds.

What are some computer programming software and courseware problems and solutions?

There are several common concerns regarding the use of programming software and courseware. These concerns will be discussed in the following presentation.

First, one of the most common problems is the search for high-quality, educationally-sound programs. It is common knowledge that teaching/learning software, especially as produced in the past, has not always represented sound educational practice. Too often software did not take full advantage of microcomputer capabilities and became expensive "ditto sheets."

To identify good products, you can read software reviews, talk to your colleagues, and, best of all, borrow or request demo disks (sometimes called trial disks) from a publishing company to evaluate. You generally need not return demos. If you are borrowing software for a review period of approximately 30 days, review the software individually or in teams prior to purchase. Many software publishers provide the potential buyer with a review period for a "trial run." Remember, though, that if the software is not returned within the specific loan period, the reviewer must purchase the package, whether satisfied or not.

A second problem with software is the clarity of the "how to" manuals or **documentation** that explains the use of the software. With a large volume of software now available, competing companies are improving the understandability of software directions. You might like to learn how to use new software either alone or in a team. Whichever setting, it is helpful to find an individual to use as a resource guide who is already familiar with the software. The "human element" in learning new technology is still a favored one by many educators.

To address both software quality and documentation concerns, you could design a customized Software Evaluation Form. There are many samples already available for you to use, but if you would like to develop your own, what are some questions that should be included? Generally, comprehensive evaluation forms include the following: (1) Introductory Information, (2) Technical Data, (3) Teaching Information, (4) Subject Content, (5) Sensitivity Issues, and (6) Recommendation/Rejection. Chart 3.6 illustrates some basic questions for each area.

INTRODUCTORY INFORMATION:
1. What is the name, publisher and date of the software?
2. What is the cost of the software?
3. If the software is on limited review time, when must it be returned to the publisher?
4. Who is/are the software reviewer(s)?
5. What is the date of the software review?

TECHNICAL DATA:
1. What type of microcomputer is needed? (e.g., Apple IIe, IBM, etc.)
2. How much RAM is needed? (e.g., 64K, 128K, 2MB)
3. Is a printer needed?
4. What version of software is needed? (e.g., Apple OS, Mac OS, DOS)
5. Is a software site license needed (e.g., to use with a LAN network)
6. Is the documentation understandable?

TEACHING INFORMATION:
1. Does the software provide helpful feedback?
2. Does the program branch, allowing each student to proceed at his/her own pace?
3. Is there recordkeeping available for students or teacher?
4. Is the presentation logical and appropriate for the intended grade/age level?

CONTENT DATA:
1. What is the type of software? (e.g., programming, CAI, CMI, applications)
2. What are the main objectives of this software?
3. What subject area/s is/are included in the product?
4. What must students need to know prior to using this software? (e.g., keyboarding, basic map skills)

SENSITIVITY ISSUES:
1. Are there both male and female positive role models?

(Chart continued on next page)

Chart 3.6. Evaluation Form Questions.

2. Is there unbiased minority representation?
3. Are software packages available with multilingual options?
4. Is the subject content multicultural in nature?

RECOMMENDATION/REJECTION:
1. Will the software motivate students? Why?
2. What are two software strengths?
3. What are two software weaknesses?
4. Do you think it's worth the cost? Why?
5. Would you recommend or reject its purchase? Why?

Chart 3.6. Evaluation Form Questions. (Continued)

Software evaluation can be a tedious and time-consuming process. That's why it's important to design a comprehensive, yet, concise format. How can this task be done? Chart 3.7 presents design tips:

1. Include as many ''Yes and No'' responses as possible. (e.g., I think we should have site license for this software.... ___Yes ___No)
2. Include ''Multiple Choice'' responses. (e.g., The printer needed is... ___Dot Matrix ___Laser)
3. Include ''Short Answer'' space. (e.g., I think we ___ should ___ should not purchase it because _____)
4. Leave lots of ''White Space'' on your form. Don't try to crowd too much on one or two pages.
5. Use various editing techniques to emphasize areas. (e.g., boldface, underlining, etc.)

Chart 3.7. Evaluation Form Designing Tips.

A third problem concerns multicultural and non-biased imagery. Sometimes, inadverently, publishing companies and software designers present insensitive image presentations on software. When reviewing software, be certain to evaluate sensitivity issues. If you find some concerns with the product, write or telephone the publishing company. (For contact information, see Resources at the end of this chapter.)

A fourth problem is the integration of software into the traditional educational setting. You will find flexible and cross-disciplinary uses for many software packages, which provide opportunities for cooperative learning, and on-computer and off-computer experiences. For example, additional "off the computer" materials such as reproducible worksheets, lesson plans, picture cards, and "extensive" or "comprehensive" teachers' guides are included with some packages. Occasionally, research study results are also added to the documentation to promote the program's success.

A fifth concern is the lack of practical knowledge for mainstreaming computers into the current curriculum. Often the "when your work is done" and the "hit and miss" approach to computer software are used.

One way of addressing the fourth and fifth problems is through the use of a new **instructional delivery system** called the **Integrated Learning System** or **ILS**. An ILS is a complete hardware, software, and curriculum "package" growing more popular in schools today. Within this framework of the educational process, the microcomputer plays a central role. Rather than using software products on a short-plan basis, a multi-year curriculum sequence is designed. Each ILS is personalized to focus upon the major basic skills instructional objectives of each individual school district. How does an ILS work?

There are several companies that are pioneers in developing the ILS, including Computer Curriculum Corporation, part of Simon and Schuster, and Wicat, which is now part of Jostens Learning Corporation. As a popular example, let's examine the components of the *Jostens ES ILS*. An interactive, networked educational software program, this ILS is available for preschool through high school students as well as basic education skill development for adult learners. Programs begin with *Tapestry Early Learner* for pre-kindergarten through grade 3. Next, the *Renaissance Elementary Learner* adds the dynamics of interactive multimedia (see Chapter Thirteen) for reading, research, writing, ESL (English as a Second Language), and math for kindergarten through grade 6. Then *Discovery Middle School Learner* emphasizes cross-curricula studies teaching independent, self-directed skills. Lastly, *Explorer Secondary Learner*, besides teaching math, reading, and writing also teaches life and employability skills needed for adolescent learners.

How can ILSs be personalized to meet school needs?

First, samples of the textbooks in use by the particular school district are sent to the company. Members of the company staff, in turn, correlate the major instructional objectives of the textbooks with computer lessons. Using a database of more than 1,800 lessons in language, math, reading, and science, *Jostens ES* plans a pre-test, three different learning activities, a learning game/reinforcement activity, and a posttest for each instructional objective. When the preliminary work is done, the *ES* system is installed on a local computer area network or LAN connected to a very powerful host computer with the curriculum stored on a CD-ROM and the management system on a hard disk drive component. Using a mouse controlled environment, IBM, Tandy, and Apple networks can support an ILS. So, when a student or teacher uses the system, this personalized match of textbook and computer merges traditional print text enhanced by the computer, thus bringing the microcomputer from a peripheral to a central role in the educational setting.

To help you assess an ILS, a workbook for educators called *Assessment and Evaluation of Integrated Learning Systems: A Kit for School Districts* is available for a fee from the Texas Center for Educational Technology or TCET. See Resources at the end of this chapter for contact information.

Although an ILS seems like the ideal computer-based instructional delivery system, you must also realize that this design has one limitation: an ILS needs a network that only runs ILS software. This defining feature is called a closed architecture. In comparison, an open architecture runs any software program written in networkable format which is also compatible with the file server.

The sixth problem is the threat of **computer viruses**, which are programs that hide inside other programs for the purpose of altering or destroying data. Viruses can range from simple mischievous messages appearing on the screen at unexpected times to more serious data losses in hard drives. Most often transmitted through "infected" floppy disks or data obtained through modems, viruses are illegal sets of instructions usually created by individuals called **hackers**. There are many viruses in existence with two of the most familiar being *Ping Pong* and *Jerusalem*. You might also remember the notorious MS-DOS virus called "Michelangelo" which was programmed to trigger on March 6, 1992 and continue every March 6th (which is Michelangelo's birthday). This virus did write "garbage" on all disk tracks, which destroyed data.

Two common questions regarding viruses are: 1) What are some symptoms of a computer virus? and 2) What can be done to prevent viruses? The following discussions will address these concerns.

If you notice your system acting strangely (e.g., longer booting time, unusual number of error messages appearing on the screen, less RAM and disk space than usual, garbled messages, or disappearing files), your computer probably has been infected by a virus. At this point, if your data is not saved on hardcopy or on backup disks, you may have a major problem on your hands. To prevent a computer loss disaster, Chart 3.8 lists recommendations.

The last problem identified by educators in the use of programming software and courseware is the illegal use of software. As you may know, most computer software can be easily copied. All you need is a formatted blank disk and a few instructions. However, this process, called **pirating**, is illegal. Publishing companies print warnings on commercial software packages limiting legal copying to one or two backup, or **archival copies**, but no more.

1. Purchase anti-viral solutions — programs that can help prevent the infection of disks and disk drives.
2. Buy software from reputable software dealers. As tempting as shareware, freeware, and illegally copied software from another colleague or friend might be, you may be a candidate for a computer virus that can ruin all of the data and programs you have on your computer.
3. In a networked computer system, always run an anti-viral program prior to using any software. This process generally takes less than 30 seconds, and might save your software and data.

Chart 3.8. Tips for Preventing Computer Viruses.

The temptation, though, is very strong to make more copies, since school budgets are limited. Pirating has become a too common practice among teachers who want to save money and share software with their friends and colleagues. Many teachers don't realize they might be committing an ''intellectual property'' crime. Remember, even if pirates don't get caught, software companies must increase the price of legal software in order to make up for lost sales, so eventually we all pay.

There are two solutions to this problem: (1) Purchase **site** or **district licenses**. This allows one piece of software to be shared by a limited number of users (sometimes up to 50 users are permitted to load software from one file server), and (2) make teachers aware of the illegal act. You might consider including a caveat at the completion of a Software Evaluation Form such as: ''I have not nor has anyone at my request attempted to illegally copy this software'' and request a signature.

Decision-making Guidelines: Computer Programming and Courseware

1. Objective: Why use programming software or courseware in your educational setting? Will an ILS meet your needs?

2. Integration: How will the selected programming software or courseware be integrated into the various curriculum and administrative areas?

3. Cost: What will be the budget limits for purchasing stand-alone microcomputer or networking system software?

4. Location: Where should the software disks be stored? For example, in the library, media center, individual classrooms, administrator's office, or teachers' room?

5. Security: What precautions will be taken so that disks don't "disappear?" What preventions will be taken to avoid computer viruses? What preventions will be taken to prevent illegal program copying?

6. Equal Access: Will all educators who wish to use the software packages have equal access or will disks be used only by specific staff members?

7. Responsibility: Who will be the individual or team "in charge" of making certain that the disks are working properly? Who will review new software on 30-day trial basis? Who makes recommendations for new software purchase? Who will decide which software will be ordered? Who keeps an inventory of software?

8. Updating: Who will decide when a new version of a software package needs to be ordered?

9. Training: Who will be trained on the use of new software? Will educators be self-taught through manuals and hands-on experiences or will they be personally or group tutored?

Summary

This chapter presented software as an integral component of a computer system which is stored on a variety of disks. Two important categories of software discussed were programming and courseware. Both are commonly used in educational settings.

Recommended Periodicals

A+: The Independent Guide for Apple Computing

AmigaWorld

Apple Education News

BYTE

Collegiate Microcomputer

Compute!

The Computing Teacher

Computer Technology Review

Computers in the Schools

Education Computing News

Education and Computing

Educational Technology

Educational Technology Research & Development

EDUCOM Review

Electronic Education

Electronic Learning

Instructor

Journal of Computing in Childhood Education
Journal of Computing in Mathematics
Journal of Educational Computing Research
Journal of Research on Computers in Education
LOGO and Educational Computing Journal
Logo Exchange
MacUser
MacWorld
Media & Methods
Microcomputers in Education
PC Today
PC World
Personal Computing
Teaching and Computers
Technology & Learning
Text Technology
T.H.E. Journal

Resources

Appletalk. Apple Computer, Inc. 20525 Mariani Ave., Cupertino, CA 95014. (408) 996-1010.

Association for the Advancement of Computing Education. PO Box 2966, Charlottesville, VA 22902. (804) 973-3987.

AntiVirus Plus. T.C.P. Inc. Rego Park, NY 11374. (800) 922-0015.

Borland International. 1800 Green Hills Rd., Scotts Valley, CA 95066. (408) 438-5300.

Broderbund Software. 500 Redwood Blvd., Novato, CA 94948. (800) 527-6263.

Cliffs StudyWare. PO Box 80728, Lincoln, NE 68501. (402) 423-5050.

Davidson & Associates, Inc. 19840 Pioneer Ave., Torrance, CA 90509. (800) 545-7677.

Diamond Computer Systems, Inc. 470 Lakeside Dr., Sunnyvale, CA 94086. (408) 736-2000.

DLM. One DLM Park, PO Box 4000, Allen, TX 75002. (800) 527-4747.

Dr. Solomon's Anti-Virus Toolkit. Ontrack Computer Systems. Eden Prairie, MN. (800) 752-1333.

EduCorp. 7434 Trade St., San Diego, CA 92121. (800) 843-9497.

Hartley Courseware. PO Box 149, Dimondale, MI 48821. (800) 247-1380.

Houghton Mifflin Educational Software Division. Dept. 39, Box 683, Hanover, NH 03755. (800) 258-9773.

HyperGlot Software Co. 505 Forest Hills Blvd., Knoxville, TN 37919. (615) 558-8270.

Intellimation. PO Box 1922, Santa Barbara, CA 93116-1922. (800) 346-8355.

Jostens Learning Corporation. 6170 Cornerstone Court East, San Diego, CA 92121-3710. (800) 521-8538.

Lawrence Productions. 1800 South 35th St., Galesburg, MI. 49053. (800) 421-4157.

The Learning Company. 6493 Kaiser Dr., Fremont, CA 94555. (800) 852-2255.

LEGO Dacta. PO Box 1600, Enfield, CT 06083. (800) 527-8339.

Logo Computer Systems, Inc. PO Box 162, Highgate Springs, VT 05460. (800) 321-1380.

McGraw-Hill. 1200 NW 63rd St., Oklahoma City, OK 73116. (405) 840-1444.

MacroMind. 410 Townsend St., Suite 408, San Francisco, CA 94107. (415) 442-0200.

Maxis. Two Theater Square, Suite 230, Orinda, CA 94563. (510) 254-9700.

MECC (Minnesota Educational Computing Corp.). 6160 Summit Dr. North, Minneapolis, MN 55430. (800) 685-MECC.

Microsoft Corp. One Microsoft Way, Redmond, WA 98052-6399. (800) 426-9400.

MicroTac Software. 4655 Cass St., Suite 214, San Diego, CA 92109. (619) 272-5700.

MindLink/Problem Solver. 44 Merimac St., Newburyport, MA 01950. (508) 462-8340.

Mindplay. 100 Conifer Hill Dr., Building 3, Suite 301, Danvers, MA 01923. (800) 221-7911.

Mindscape. 3444 Dundee Rd., Northbrook, IL 60062. (800) 221-9884.

National Geographic Society Educational Services. Dept. 88, Washington, DC 20036. (800) 368-2728.

Novell Netware. Novell Inc. 122 E. South, Provo, UT 84606. (800) 453-1267.

Scholastic Software. PO Box 7502, 2931 E. McCarty St., Jefferson City, MO 65102. (800) 541-5513.

Schoolmate Education Network. Tandy. 1700 One Tandy Center, Fort Worth, TX 76102. (800) 321-3133.

Spinnaker. One Kendall Square, Cambridge, MA 02139. (617) 494-1200.

Sunburst Communications. 39 Washington Ave., Pleasantville, NY 10570. (800) 431-1934.

TCET (Texas Center for Educational Technology). PO Box 5155, University of North Texas, Denton, TX 76203-5155. (817) 565-4433.

Teacher Support Software. 1035 NW 57th St., Gainsville, FL 32605. (904) 332-6404.

TECHBYTE International (USA) Inc. 4025 Woodland Park Blvd., Suite #380, Arlington, TX 76013-4314. (817) 261-8487.

Terrapin Software Inc. 400 Riverside St., Portland, ME 04103. (207) 987-8200.

Tom Snyder Productions. 90 Sherman St., Cambridge, MA 02140. (800) 342-0236.

Wings for Learning. 1600 Green Hills Rd., Scotts Valley, CA 95067. (800) 321-7511.

Zugware. PO Box 2961, Torrance, CA 90509. (310) 793-0610.

References

Advertisement. (1991, September). ObjectLogo. *T.H.E. Journal, 19* (2), 92.

Bailey, G.D. (Ed.). (1992, September). Integrated learning systems [Special issue]. *Educational Technology, 32* (9).

Bennett, R.E. (1987). Identifying a purpose for computer education programs. In R.E. Bennett (Ed.), *Planning and evaluating computer education programs.* Columbus, OH: Merrill.

Birch, A. (1988). *Logo Probability.* Portland, ME: Terrapin Software, Inc.

Braun, J.A. (1986). *Microcomputers and the social studies classroom.* Boulder, CO: Social Studies Education Consortium.

Brock, P.A. (1992). *The Logicreative approach to learning Logo.* Unpublished manuscript. Trenton State College, Elementary and Early Childhood Education Department, Trenton, NJ.

Bowers, C.A. (1988). *The cultural dimensions of educational computing: Understanding the non-neutrality of technology.* New York: Teachers College Press.

Cannings, T.R. & Finkel, L. (Eds.). (1993). *The technology age classroom.* Wilsonville, OR: Franklin, Beedle & Associates, Inc.

Charishak, I. (1988). *Creating dynamic stories with LogoWriter.* White Plains, NY: Dynamic Classroom Press.

Charles, R. & Silver, E. (1989). *The teaching and assessing of mathematical problem solving.* Hillsdale, NJ: Lawrence Erlbaum Associates, Publishers.

Dudley-Marling, C. & Owston, R.D. (1988). The state of educational software: A criterion-based evaluation. In J.J. Hirschbuhl (Ed.), *Computers in education* (3rd ed.) (pp. 71-76). Guilford, CT: The Dushkin Publishing Group, Inc.

Flake, J.L. (1990). *Computer-intensive middle and secondary mathematics education.* Belmont, CA: Wadsworth Publishing Company.

Flake, J.L., McClintock, C.E., & Turner, S.V. (1985). *Fundamentals of computer education.* Belmont, CA: Wadsworth Publishing Company.

Gagne, R.M. (Ed.). (1987). *Instructional technology: Foundations.* Hillsdale, NJ: Lawrence Erlbaum Associates, Publishers.

Heinich, R., Molenda, M., & Russell, J.D. (1993). *Instructional media and the new technologies of instruction* (4th ed.). New York: Macmillan Publishing Company.

Holzberg, C.S. (1993, February). Take a byte out of crime. *Electronic Learning, 12* (5), 28-30.

Kearsley, G., Hunter, B., & Furlong, B. (1992). *We teach with technology: New visions for education.* Wilsonville, OR: Franklin, Beedle, & Associates, Inc.

Lathrop, A. & Goodson, B. (1984.) *Courseware in the classroom.* Reading, MA: Addison-Wesley.

Lewis, P.H. (1992, November). Simulating life. *The New York Times: Education Life*, Section 4A, 38-40.

Lillie, D.L., Hannum, W.H., & Stuck, G.B. (1989). *Computers and effective instruction.* New York: Longman.

Lockard, J., Abrams, P.D., & Many, W.A. (1987). *Microcomputers for educators.* Boston, MA: Little, Brown and Company.

Moscardini, A.O., Curran D.A.S., & Middleton, W. (1990, March). Innovative methods of teaching the mathematically unadapted. In N. Estes, J. Heene, & D. Leclercq (Eds.), *Proceedings of the Seventh International Conference on Computers and Technology* (pp. 496-498). Brussels, Belgium: Page Bros. Ltd.

New Software Releases. (1989, November). LogoWriter Secondary. *The Computing Teacher, 17* (3), 49.

New Software Releases. (1987, October). LEGO TC Logo. *The Computing Teacher, 15* (2), 57.

Papert, S. (1980). *Mindstorms: Children, computers, and powerful ideas.* New York: Basic Books.

Papert, S. (1993). *The children's machine: Rethinking school in the age of the computer.* New York: Basic Books.

Picciotto, H. (1990). *Logo math: Tools and games.* Portand, ME: Terrapin Software, Inc.

Riedesel, C. & Clement, D. (1985). *Coping with computers in elementary and middle school.* Englewood Cliffs, NJ: Prentice-Hall.

Roblyer, M.D. *et al.* (1988). *The effectiveness of computer applications for instruction: A review and synthesis of recent research findings.* New York: Hawthorn.

Rooze, G.E. & Northup, T. (1989). *Computers, thinking, and social studies*. Englewood, CO: Libraries Unlimited.

Sheingold, K. & Hadley, M. (1990). *Accomplished teachers: Integrating computers into classroom practice*. Center for Technology in Education, Bank Street College of Education. New York: Bank Street Press.

Sheldon, K.M., Linderholm, O., & Marshall, T. (1992, February). The future of personal computing? *BYTE, 17* (2), 99-102.

Shimabukuro, G. (1987). *Thinking in Logo: A sourcebook for teachers of primary students*. Menlo Park, CA: Addison-Wesley.

Tipps, S. & Bull, G. (1987). *Beginning with Logo: Terrapin version*. Englewood Cliffs, NJ: Prentice-Hall.

Van Horn, R. (1992). Educational power tools: New instructional delivery systems. In J.J. Hirschbuhl & L.F. Wilkinson (Eds.), *Computers in Education* (5th ed.) (pp. 31-36). Guilford, CT: The Dushkin Publishing Group, Inc.

Vockell, E. & Schwartz, E. (1988). *The computer in the classroom: Enhancing academic learning time*. Santa Cruz, CA: Mitchell Publishing Co.

White, C.S. & Hubbard, G. (1992). Tips for evaluation, documentation, and preview of software. In J.J. Hirschbuhl & L.F. Wilkinson (Eds.), *Computers in education* (5th ed.) (pp. 85-87). Guilford, CT: The Dushkin Publishing Group, Inc.

Willing, K. & Girard, S. (1990). *Learning together: Computer-integrated classrooms*. Markham, Ontario, Canada: Pembroke Publishers, Ltd.

Willis, J. (1987). *Educational computing: A guide to practical applications*. Scottsdale, AZ: Gorsuch, Scarisbrick, Publishers.

Willis, J., Hovey, L., & Hovey, K. (1987). *Computer simulations: A sourcebook to learning in an electronic environment*. New York: Garland Publishing Co.

Woerner, J., Rivers, R., & Vockell, E. (1991). *The computer in the science curriculum*. New York: McGraw-Hill.

4

Chapter Four:
Computer Software for
Applications

What are computer applications programs?

Computer applications programs or **applications software** are packages designed for specific tasks, which include **word processing, database, spreadsheet, graphics**, or **telecommunications**. All of the these generic applications share a common feature: personal, customized use for the individual.

What is word processing software?

Word processing is the most popular software used in educational settings. As a tool for writing, word processing allows you to easily correct and revise characters, sentences or paragraphs in **soft copy** (screen display) prior to printing the document in **hard copy** (paper). What types of revisions are possible in word processing? Some of the most commonly used ones are **inserting, deleting, moving, formatting,** and **word wrapping.** These editing functions are detailed below in Chart 4.1.

TERM	DEFINITION AND EDITING CAPABILITY
Insert	To add letters, words, or paragraphs, or simply "open a space" within the document. The original text is automatically rearranged by the computer.
Delete	To erase letters, words, paragraphs, or blocks of text by a few simple keystrokes.
Move	To rearrange information within the document to new locations of choice; sometimes referred to as "cut and paste."
Format	To change margins, center words, provide visual emphasis, such as underlining and boldfacing, add headings, etc., with a few simple keystrokes.
Word Wrap	To automatically move a word which is too long for the current line to the next line.

Chart 4.1. Common Editing Functions Defined.

Other, more advanced editing functions include automatic indexing, hyphenation, and footnoting. Some word processing software will even allow you to change the sizing of the characters called **points,** and the actual shapes of the characters called **fonts.** These terms will be further explained in the discussion on desktop publishing.

There are two other popular enhancements to many word processing software packages, which are: (1) a **spell checker** and (2) a **text-analysis program.** First, a spell checker assists in correcting any spelling errors in your document by comparing your word with the words in its dictionary or **lexicon.** If it "questions" the spelling pattern, your word will be highlighted for correction. Although most spell checkers are used to proofread a completed document, some spell checkers can be used during the writing process. These include a **pop-up dictionary** and a **pop-up thesaurus** which are on-line (already on the computer) for easy accessibility.

Second, a text-analysis program analyzes the grammatical structure of a word-processed document. Computerized feedback, for example, can include, sentence length, readability index, repetitious word frequencies, unmatched sets of brackets or quotation marks, and sexist language.

With these automated proofreading assistants, you can make your final document more professional in appearance and more coherent in context. The traditional, three-staged writing process, which includes: (1) prewriting, (2) composing, and (3) revising, is naturally enhanced. Since the primary reason for writing is communicating ideas to an audience, the traditional three-stage process should include a fourth stage, which is publication. The best applications programs for this purpose are called **desktop publishing**.

What is Desktop Publishing or DTP?

Desktop publishing or **DTP** is a relatively new concept that allows you to create professionally typeset documents on the microcomputer. Typesetting tasks (e.g., text columns, pasteup of graphics, etc.) once limited to publication or graphics design professionals, are now possible by any individual with the following prerequisites: (1) Hardware including a microcomputer with sufficient RAM, a mouse connected to **GUI** (Graphical Users Interface), a laser printer, and if desired, a scanner; (2) desktop publishing software; and (3) a preliminary understanding of graphic design.

By using desktop publishing, you can create documents in a variety of letter styles, sizing, and column presentations. With some practice the non-professional artist can create documents that combine word processing and graphics to design resumes, newsletters, book manuscript layouts, and other text-based, graphically enhanced products without the use of professional artists, typesetters, or graphic designers.

What are some introductory terms you should know in DTP?

Learning at least four basic terms will introduce you to desktop publishing: (1) **Font** is defined as a collection of characters that combine to make a specific standardized set of **typestyle**; (2) **typestyle** refers to the general outline or shape of the character; (3) **typeface** describes the variety of the typestyle; and (4) **point sizing** or **sizing** refers to the precise measurement of the character in increments from 1 to 72 point with 72 = 1 inch, 36 = 1/2 inch, etc. Chart 4.2 illustrates a variety of sample fonts.

Another important aspect of general graphic design that you should understand is the concept of layout. Layout is the creation of an aesthetic and appealing page setup. Since the main purpose of DTP is to clearly and creatively present printed information, certain basic guidelines need to be followed. Chart 4.3 lists some of the most important criteria in developing a professional document.

This sample is 10-point Swiss.

This sample is 12-point Dutch.

This sample is 18-point Brushwood.

This sample is 36-point Drury Lane.

Chart 4.2. Sample Desktop Character Fonts.

If you have the hardware and software for DTP, don't be alarmed or dissuaded by a lack of graphic designing knowledge and experience. Again, you can enroll in a formal course or you can teach yourself. Read the DTP manual or documentation for your software application product. If you need an additional resource to help you create desktop published materials, a recommended book is *Preparing Instructional Text: Document Design Using Desktop Publishing* by Earl R. Misanchuk.

But suppose you do not use desktop publishing software and want to add graphic designs to your text documents; what do you do? Since desktop publishing is so popular, some word processing applications products are enhancing their capabilities by adding a special software for designing called graphics software. This applications use will next be briefly discussed.

What is graphics software?

Graphics applications software is basically art and visual representation which is divided into two categories: (1) freehand and clip art, and (2) charts and graphs. In freehand and clip art graphics software, you can either design artwork by drawing original or freehand designs on to the computer screen with a mouse peripheral (e.g., *Super Paint*) or by selecting, locating, and re-sizing predrawn designs from an available set which is called **clip art** (e.g., *Print Shop*). Popular graphics software for artwork is available for pre-school beginners through graphic artists. At the basic level you can easily create posters, cards, stationary letterheads, calendars, and banners which are then printed either in black and white or color on a dot matrix printer. If your artistic talents are very limited, you can choose to use a clip art rather than a freehand graphics software package.

1. Use no more than three fonts per document. Too much variety confuses the reader.
2. Select appropriate point sizing according to the visual needs of your readers. With standard 12-point as a guideline, you should increase the sizing for younger readers or visually-impaired individuals. If you want to be paper efficient decrease the point sizing for the average readers.
3. Avoid too much clutter on each page. Aim for at least 50% white space which includes spacing between your lines and margins or borders.
4. Keep graphics to a reasonable quantity. Again adjust the number according to the readers' needs. Younger or less-able readers need more stimulating graphics that enhance, not detract, from the text content. Always face any characters "looking into" the page rather than gazing uninterestedly off the page.
5. Don't over-emphasize! It is tempting and fun to use all types of special effects in your DTP document. If you use too many, however, nothing is emphasized. Remember the use of yellow highlighting in textbooks to locate important facts? Too much highlighting leads to all yellow pages with no emphasis of the important areas.
6. Research and compare other documents similar to the style that you plan to DTP. What formats or styles made some documents more interesting to read? What effects attracted and kept your attention?
7. Complete your document, put it aside for a day and then review it as a "new" reader. You can hold the final product up to a mirror to see if the reverse image looks aesthetically pleasing-which it should.
8. Find a good DTP resource book as a guide.

Chart 4.3. Tips to Good Graphic Design.

In comparison, there is graphics applications software which allows you to convert data into charts and graphs. You can easily create professional-looking pie charts and series graphs by following a set of directions. In *Microsoft Works*, for example, the charting program is called an overlay because this process is described as a program-within-a-program. You cannot create a pie chart or series graph unless you have created a spreadsheet file first. So, in other words, the text, numerical, and formula data, initially presented in grid format on a spreadsheet, are converted into visual format via the chart or graph format that you select.

Next, you will learn more about other applications software that present data that are organized and manipulated in chart or grid format. These applications software components are databases and spreadsheets.

What is database software?

Database software is an organized collection of information which can be created and easily rearranged. Similar to a file card set, this electronic database can be also be saved on hard copy (printed paper). But an electronic database can be stored on your disk or hard drive as well. In addition, unlike a typical file card collection, you can electronically rearrange and access information in extremely short amounts of time. So, how do you use a database?

Databases are useful for both teachers and students. A common use for a database by the teacher is the creation of a list of names, addresses, telephone numbers, birthdates, or classes. This database can be added to, deleted, or rearranged based on the user's needs. If, for example, you created a class database with student's birthdates, you might want to rearrange your database so that only students born in March are displayed on your screen. You can then read this new list from your microcomputer screen (**soft copy**) or print the listing to **hard copy** (paper). You might want to rearrange your database alphabetically or by age. Once you've designed your **fields** or **categories**, you can in a few seconds rearrange and view or print the data in your new format. There is no time-consuming shuffling or reshuffling through a set of file cards.

A database is also a valuable research tool for students. With the amount of information available to us doubling every five years, it is not possible, nor meaningful, to memorize facts in isolation. Developing inquiry skills, through organizing, accessing, manipulating, and evaluating electronically stored information should be encouraged. Students need to learn how to organize and sort data into meaningful categories and relationships. Through hypothesizing, students can prove or disprove their statements by researching and rearranging databases.

Suppose, for example, students were interested in studying the tropical rain forests. By researching through reference resources, they can create a database with categories or fields including country location, continent location, hemisphere location, size of rain forest, numbers of animal species, and rate of deforestation. Next they might hypothesize that "All rain forests are in the Southern Hemisphere" or "Most deforestation is occurring in Central America." By rearranging their database they could prove or disprove their statements.

Another applications software presented in chart or grid format that can also be used to hypothesize or forecast is the spreadsheet.

What is spreadsheet software?

Spreadsheet applications software allows you to calculate and make predictions or forecasts based upon numerical data. In appearance a spreadsheet looks similar to a bookkeeper's general ledger with rows and columns of information. This electronic bookkeeping process was one of the earliest and most useful types of business applications software developed for the microcomputer. Computerized spreadsheets can easily, efficiently, and accurately calculate requested data. Large numerical listings can be added, subtracted, multiplied, or divided automatically, saving many hours of time.

Unusual at first in educational settings, spreadsheets are now most commonly used for budgeting in administrative offices. Teachers are finding spreadsheet programs helpful in their own bookkeeping needs such as grading. Students can develop personal or organizational spreadsheets to help monitor income and expenses. As newer spreadsheet programs add a graphics dimension, for example, pie chart graphing, teachers and students will find spreadsheet software a more interesting and valuable tool for teaching and managing clerical tasks.

To simplify the use of applications software, different varieties are combined in special packages. Since desktop publishing focuses on professionally designed documents, word processing, spreadsheet, and graphic capabilities are automatically combined into most sophisticated software packages. In comparison, a combination of word processing, database, spreadsheet, graphics, and telecommunications, which is simply sending and receiving data via the computer (see Part II for a detailed explanation) are available in a combination called an integrated software package.

What is integrated software?

Integrated software is an applications package that allows you to interconnect word processing, database, spreadsheet, and sometimes graphics and telecommunications components into one document. Educators and students especially find that the incorporation of spreadsheet plus database enhance a communications or research report.

With the trend in this "integration" concept growing in popularity, it is important to familiarize yourself with the concept. If you cannot find a formal course or workshop, you can teach yourself. To do this you need a microcomputer, compatible software, and a manual. Usually there is an on-the-computer tutorial or tour of the product plus a step-by-step hardcopy of instructions.

If you would like an additional resource which offers more guidance and activities, here are two recommended books: For the *Apple Macintosh* computer, *An Introduction to Computing Using Microsoft Works* by Presley and Freitas is excellent. If you need better keyboarding skills, there is a "Developing Keyboarding Skills" appendix that will teach you to touch type. Another good publication that serves as a tutorial to learning *Microsoft Works* is a book entitled *Microsoft Works for Educators* by John F. Beaver. Included with the text is a 3.5 inch floppy which provides practice activities. If, however, you own or use an IBM or IBM-compatible computer, an MS-DOS version of the book is also available.

What are the advantages of applications software in education?

There are several major advantages of using applications software:

One of the most important advantages is the creation of original, professionally-designed materials for the teaching/learning process. By using editing functions, electronic spelling and grammar assistants, or graphic enhancements, word processing, database, and spreadsheet documents are technically easier to develop.

Written communication is increased. Since it is faster and easier to correspond with teachers, students, and other individuals as well as to design newsletters, the use of word processing and desktop publishing enhances and increases the frequency of written contact.

Motivation is heightened. Writing and publishing of documents become easier due to the computerization of manual tasks.

Clerical responsibilities are more efficiently accomplished through the use of spreadsheet capabilities. Tedious, mundane tasks can be completed easily through the electronic bookkeeper.

Individuals, whether students or teachers, who have special needs can communicate more easily within text-based communications. For example, both very young children and physically disabled individuals of any age who lack the manual dexterity to form letters accurately can type and easily edit the documents via word processing. Students or teachers with learning difficulties such as dyslexia can improve their written legibility through the use of spell checkers and text-analysis programs.

Telecommunications applications software connects you with other teachers and students in far corners of the world. (See Part II for more specific advantages.)

What are some specific educational uses for applications software?

There are many uses for applications software in the educational setting. Specific product examples presented alphabetically provide some packages available to you:

• Since the 1980s, versions of *AppleWorks* by Apple Computer, Inc. have been popular integrated application packages in elementary schools using Apple II series microcomputers. The newer versions include spell checkers.

• *Bank Street Writer* and *Bank Street Speller* by Bank Street Publications are word processing packages suitable for young learners. The on-screen guidance and simple structure of the programs provide an easy introduction to word processing.

• Versions of *Microsoft Excel* by Microsoft Corporation are sophisticated programs for spreadsheet development and database manipulation. This software enhances visual presentations and written reports with, for example, three-dimensional data graphing of numerical representations.

• Versions of *Microsoft Word* by Microsoft Corporation and *WordPerfect* by WordPerfect Corporation are more complex word integrated packages which include spell checkers better suited to older students.

• Another popular integrated application package for both Mac and IBM plus clones is *Microsoft Works*. This sophisticated software includes a fine drawing program as well as word processing, database, spreadsheet, and telecommunications. A mouse is needed in this GUI environment.

• The newest version of *Professional Write 2.2* by Software Publishing Corporation is a popular sophisticated word processing package that has added a grammar checker to its thesaurus and dictionary components.

• Several versions of *Publish It!* by TimeWorks are fine examples of desktop publishing software. Through the integration of graphic designing and typesetting, professional-looking documents can be created by educators.

• *RightWriter* by Macmillan Computer Publications is a grammar checker which provides information in such areas as Readability Index (suitable reading grade level), Strength Index (directness of phrasing), and Jargon Index (use of colloquialisms). After the grammatical analysis, Sentence Structure Recommendations are offered to the user.

What are some applications software problems and solutions?

As with programming and courseware, applications software users have the following similar concerns:

Because there are many software packages available for applications, it is important to determine what best suits your needs. An important concept that makes word processing easier is called **WYSIWYG** or What-You-See-Is-What-You-Get. This term describes that your screen soft copy will look exactly like your printed hard copy. Not all programs, however, provide this feature.

Another technical feature that concerns educators is the size of the text display. Left to right spacing on the screen is divided into columns. Each column contains one character. There is an inverse correlation between the text size and number of letters displayed horizontally on the screen. Common sizes vary from 20-, 40-, to 80-column displays. The 20-column version uses large primary type most suitable for young children and the visually impaired. The 40-column is appropriate for intermediate school learners whereas the 80-column version is best suited for high school and college students or teachers. Since the printed page of text presents 65 columns, the 80-column version is most popular.

Because applications software packages are user-centered, the documentation (descriptions of how the program works) must be clear. Although improving in format, many manuals still seem to be written with the assumption that all users are computer literate. This is one reason to check to see if there is an on-computer tutorial or introductory tour that accompanies the explanation in the manual.

Curriculum integration of applications software is less of a problem than programming or courseware. Since students are constantly being encouraged to increase their writing skills, microcomputers are natural technical assistants. However, two problems exist concerning word processing: (1) Educators frown upon the use of grammar and spell checkers in creating completed documents. The attitude has been expressed by some educators that students should correct errors manually (and traditionally) without the assistance of a machine; and (2) a controversy still exists regarding the appropriate age or grade for introducing keyboarding skills. As educators become more confident with word processing themselves, they will better understand the benefits of electronic assistants and the early introduction to keyboarding skills. Word processing and desktop publishing will create a more interactive, student-centered language arts environment.

The last two problems in applications software concern computer viruses and the illegal use of software. Similar to programming software and courseware, applications software can be exposed to viruses, and disks can be illegally copied. Again, the best remedy to viruses is to install an anti-viral program in your computer system (particularly if it's on a network) and purchase software from reliable sources. (See Chapter Three for more information on computer viruses.) To resolve the problem of unauthorized software copying, it is important that educators and students are made aware that this process is illegal — although very tempting. (See Chapters One and Three for more information on illegal copying.)

Decision-making Guidelines: Applications Software

1. Objective: Which applications programs will be integrated into the present curriculum? Will an integrated applications package be used? Will desktop publishing software be necessary?

2. Integration: What are specific plans to integrate applications software into the curriculum?

3. Cost: What is the budget cap for software expenditures? Which applications would be of greatest use in the curriculum?

4. Location: Where should a pilot study be done to assess the quality of the applications software? Will integrated packages be available in the teachers' room, teachers' offices, or in individual classrooms? Will the software be placed on a LAN? What is the cost for a software site license?

5. Security: Where should the original applications disks be stored? Where will the backup copies be placed? What will be done to discourage illegal software copying?

6. Equal Access: Who should have access to software applications? All teachers, and students, or just a selected initial pilot study sample?

7. Updating: Who will be responsible to make certain that the applications packages are current? Who will make recommendations for future selections and purchases?

8. Training: Who will be taught to use the software? How, when, and where will they be instructed?

Summary

This chapter has presented information on applications software, which is currently the most popular software usage in education. A variety of applications, including word processing, desktop publishing, databases, spreadsheets, graphics, and telecommunications, were discussed.

Recommended Periodicals

BYTE
The Computing Teacher
Education Computing News
Educational Technology
Educational Technology Research & Development
EDUCOM Review
Electronic Education
Electronic Learning

Instructor
Journal of Computer-Based Instruction
Journal of Computers in Mathematics and Science Teaching
Journal of Computing in Childhood Education
Journal of Research on Computing in Education
MacUser
MacWorld
Media & Methods
Microcomputers in Education
Online Access
PC Today
PC World
Teaching and Computers
Tech Trends
Technology & Learning
Telecommunications
T.H.E. Journal

Resources

Apple Computer, Inc. 20525 Mariani Ave., Cupertino, CA 95014. (408) 996-1010.

Bank Street Story Starters. Mindscape. 3444 Dundee Rd., Northbrook, IL 60062. (800) 221-9884.

Bank Street Writer. Scholastic Software. PO Box 7502, 2931 East McCarty St., Jefferson City, MO 65102. (800) 541-5513.

Children's Writing and Publishing Center. The Learning Company. 6493 Kaiser Dr., Fremont, CA 94555. (800) 852-2255.

Computer Literacy through Applications. Houghton Mifflin. Educational Software Division. Dept. 39, PO Box 638, Hanover, NH 03755. (800) 258-9773.

Cotton Tales. Mindplay. 100 Conifer Hill Dr., Building 3, Suite 301, Danvers, MA 01923. (800) 221-9884.

Create with Garfield. DLM. One DLM Park, PO Box 4000, Allen, TX 75002. (800) 527-4747.

Designasaurus. Britannica Software. 345 Fourth St., San Francisco, CA 94107. (800) 572-2272.

Explore-a-Story. D.C. Heath. 125 Spring St., Lexington, MA 02173. (800) 334-3284.

Ibis Software. 90 Montgomery St., Suite 820, San Francisco, CA 94105. (415) 546-1917.

Microsoft Corporation. One Microsoft Way, Redmond, WA 98052-6399. (800) 426-9400.

Minnesota Educational Computing Corporation (MECC). 6160 Summit Drive North, Minneapolis, MN 55430. (800) 685-MECC.

Newsmaster. Unison World. 1320 Harbor Bay Parkway, Alameda, CA 94501. (510) 748-5680.

Newsroom. Springboard. 7808 Creekridge Circle, Minneapolis, MN 55435. (800) 654-6301.

Print Shop. Broderbund. 17 Paul Dr., San Rafael, CA 94913. (800) 527-6263.

Que Corporation. PO Box 90, Carmel, IN 46032. (317) 573-2500.

Super Print. Scholastic, Inc. PO Box 7502, 2931 E. McCarty St., Jefferson City, MS 65102. (800) 541-5531.

Teacher Support Software. 1035 57th St. NW, Gainsville, FL 32605. (904) 332-6404.

TimeWorks. 625 Academy Dr., Northbrook, IL 60062. (708) 559-1300.

Tom Snyder Productions. 90 Sherman St., Cambridge, MA 02140. (800) 342-0236.

References

Apple Computer. (1990). *Writing curriculum guide.* Available from LIST Services, 10810 Harney St., Suite 202, Omaha, NE.

Alessi, S.M. (1991). *Computer-based instruction: Methods and development* (2nd ed.). Englewood Cliffs, NJ: Prentice-Hall.

Beaver, J.F. (1992). *Microsoft Works for educators.* Pacific Grove, CA: Brooks/Cole Publishing Company.

Black, R. (1991). *Roger Black's desktop design power.* New York: Bantam.

Bluhm, H. (1987). *Administrative uses of computers in the schools.* Englewood Cliffs, NJ: Prentice-Hall.

Bolter, J. (1990). *The writing space: The computer and the history of writing.* Hillsdale, NJ: Lawrence Erlbaum Associates, Publishers.

Brock, P.A. (1991, May). Networking by electronic newsletter. In G. McKye & D. Trueman (Eds.), *Proceedings of the Twelfth Educational Computing Organization of Ontario Conference and the Eighth International Conference on Technology and Education* (p. 103). Toronto, Ontario, Canada.

Burns, D., Venit, S., & Hansen, R. (1988). *The electronic publisher.* New York: Brady.

Cannings, T. & Finkel, L. (1992). *The technology age classroom: Using technology as a tool.* Wilsonville, OR: Franklin, Beedle & Associates.

Collis, B. (1988). *Computers, curriculum, and whole class instruction.* Belmont, CA: Wadsworth Publishing Company.

Costanzo, W. (1990). *The electronic text: Learning to write, read, and reason with computers.* Englewood Cliffs, NJ: Educational Technology Publications, Inc.

Finkel, L., McManus, J., & Zeitz, L. (1989). *Microsoft Works through applications.* Gilroy, CA: Computer Literacy Press.

Flake, J.L., McClintock, C.E., & Turner, S.V. (1987). *Fundamentals of computer education.* Belmont, CA: Wadsworth Publishing Company.

Harris, R. (1990). *Understanding desktop publishing.* San Francisco: Sybex.

Heinich, R., Molenda, M., & Russell, J.D. (1993). *Instructional media and the new technologies of instruction* (4th ed.). New York: Macmillan Publishing Company.

Kearsley, G. (1990). *Computers for educational administrators: Leadership in the information age.* Norwood, NJ: Ablex Publishing Company.

Merrill, P.F. *et al.,* (1992). *Computers in education* (2nd ed.). Boston, MA: Allyn and Bacon.

Miller, H. (1988). *An administrative manual for the use of microcomputers in the schools.* Englewood Cliffs, NJ: Prentice-Hall.

Misanchuk, E.R. (1992). *Preparing instructional text: Document design using desktop publishing.* Englewood Cliffs, NJ: Educational Technology Publications, Inc.

Microsoft Corp. (1989). *In and out of the classroom with Microsoft Works.* Redmond, WA: Microsoft Press.

National Project on Computers and College Writing. (1989). *Computers and college writing: Selected college profiles.* New York: The Instructional Resource Center, City University of New York.

Nogales, P. & McAllister, C. (1987). *AppleWorks for teachers.* Wilsonville, OR: Franklin, Beedle & Associates.

Presley, B. & Freitas, B. (1990). *An introduction to computing using Microsoft Works: Macintosh Version 2.* Pennington, NJ: Lawrenceville Press.

Turner, S. & Land, M. (1988). *Tools for schools: Application software for the classroom.* Belmont, CA: Wadsworth Publishing Company.

Ubelacker, S. (1992, March). Keyboarding: The universal curriculum "tool" for children. In N. Estes & M. Thomas (Eds.), *Proceedings of the Ninth International Conference on Technology and Education, 2* (pp. 808-810). Paris, France: Morgan Printing.

Walkenbach, J. (1991, June). Equipping your PC for high-quality sound production. *PC Today, 6* (5), 32-38.

Williams, R. (1990). *The Mac is not a typewriter.* Berkley, CA: Peachpit Press.

Williams, R. & Nelson, K. (1991). *The little Mac book.* Berkeley, CA: Peachpit Press.

Willing, K.R. & Girard, S. (1990). *Learning together: Computer integrated classrooms.* Markham, Ontario, Canada: Pembroke Publishers.

Wresch, W. (1987). *Practical guide to computer uses in the English-language arts classroom.* Englewood Cliffs, NJ: Prentice-Hall.

PART II

INTEGRATED TELEPHONY

The concept of electronic communication technology is not a new one. The telephone, for example, has been in existence for more than 125 years. Yet, recent innovations such as the merger of computer and telephone technologies have provided possibilities for new educational strategies. In particular, communications for distance learning have been enhanced through the expansion of traditional correspondence courses into distant electronic classrooms. Electronic classrooms and electronic universities are proliferating worldwide, linking students to teachers and data-based resources in remote locations. Part II will present information on some recent telephone adaptations used in the educational setting, including electronic mail, facsimile, online databases, electronic bulletin board systems, voice mail, and audiotex.

Chapter Five presents and compares two means of primarily print communications (but carried over telephone lines), which are electronic mail and facsimile technologies. While electronic mail depends on the computer with a telephone connection, facsimile technology can function independent of computers.

Chapter Six introduces and compares online databases and electronic bulletin board systems. Both means of communication can exist independent of each other; however, more telecommunications services are interconnecting online databases and electronic bulletin boards with electronic mail systems to create an interactive text-based, computer-driven communication environment.

Chapter Seven introduces conversant technology, focusing upon audiotex and voice mail. Becoming more popular in education, new prototypes and start-up systems are growing in popularity throughout schools in the United States. One reason for the high interest in conversant technology is the opportunity for 24-hour communication and multilingual accessibility connecting students, teachers, parents, and administrators through special message units.

5

Chapter Five:
Computer-mediated Communications and Facsimile

What are computer-mediated communications and facsimile?

Computer-mediated communications (CMC) and **facsimile (fax)** transmission are two electronic methods for sending and receiving instantaneous written communication in textual form. CMC, sometimes referred to as telecomputing, is composed of electronic mail (**e-mail**) and **computer conferencing**. Both CMC and fax are competing technologies that can be compared to a hybrid of two commonly used, traditional communication systems, which are telephoning and mailing letters; however, no operators, stamps, or letter carriers are ever needed. Some sources claim that fax has the competitive edge over e-mail. Is this true in the educational setting? A comparison of these technologies follows.

What is e-mail?

In the past, if you needed to send a letter or exchange a research paper, you would physically take it or mail it to the individual. If you are using a microcomputer now without a communications network, you might exchange information via a computer floppy disk. This communications system is commonly called sneaker net. If, on the other hand, you have a computer linked to other computers through a LAN, mainframe, or a modem, you can send and receive messages called e-mail. E-mail or electronic mail, also commonly referred to as paperless mail, transmits primarily textual data one character at a time on a computer to a particular individual or group. Each message is created by the sender on a computer keyboard and displayed on a computer monitor. In addition, each message can be stored in the computer and read by the receiver on another linked or networked computer. As a result, through e-mail, colleagues can be contacted instantaneously without ever leaving your classroom or office.

How is e-mail transmitted?

As discussed in Chapter Two, a LAN connects microcomputers together and allows the sharing of peripherals (e.g., printers). In addition, when special communications software is added, a LAN can be a transmission system for e-mail. Typically used for the internal distribution of messages within an institution, e-mail on a LAN is usually limited to a two-mile radius of interconnected computers. Because of distance limitation, LANs generally do not need a telephone connection with telecommunications requirements.

If, however, you want to transmit e-mail over a long distance, sometimes called modem networking, you would generally need a modem, telecommunications software, and a long distance telephone line. E-mail is sent directly to a specific individual or group by dialing the telephone number connected to the receiver's modem. What must be purchased to set up this system?

If you wanted to purchase all the necessary components for a long distance e-mail system using a modem, you might first check to see what components your school already has. Many schools now have at least one microcomputer with the capacity to set up an e-mail system. Next, you would need a modem and communications package. In designing an e-mail system using a modem, the key element is compatibility of the sender-receiver devices. Particularly, it is imperative to match **transmission speeds** and **handshaking protocols**. What does this mean?

First, **transmission speeds** are the transfer rates or speeds of modems. Presently, in educational settings this speed varies from a very slow 300 bits per second (30 characters per second) to a very rapid 9600 bits per second (960 characters per second). The common **bps** or **bits per second** transmission speeds used in schools today are 1200 bps and 2400 bps. It is important to remember that as the speed of the modem increases, so does its cost. But, conversely, as both the modem speed and cost increase, the time spent on sending each message decreases, since you are paying less for a long distance call.

For example, a telephone call from Los Angeles to New York City at the lowest night rate is approximately 15 cents per minute. If you were to send a five-page, doubled-spaced letter, research paper, or any type-written communication at a speed of 1200 bps, it would take only one minute at a cost of 15 cents. In comparison, at 2400 bps, you could send a 10-page paper for the same cost, and if you had a 9600 bps modem, you could send a 20-page paper for only 15 cents.

Another concern is the handshaking protocols. In order for one computer to "understand" when the other computer is ready to accept the e-mail message, a signaling technique is used. The most commonly used handshaking method is XON/XOFF, and the most popular flexible file transfer protocol is KERMIT.

What is telecommunications or modem software?

An essential modem networking e-mail component is the **telecommunications software** package. Like any collection of software applications packages, a variety of options exist. For example, several communications packages work with direct connect auto-dial modems. This means that you can create a directory of your commonly dialed telephone e-mail numbers and then, by highlighting your selection from the menu, the computer will automatically dial that number.

Another example is the 80-column width provided on the computer monitor. Word processing is best done on an 80-column display, which means your typed text appears on the screen as it would on an 8.5-inch typical page. However, some communications software packages only produce a 40-column display, which is less easy to read.

How can e-mail be transmitted on a mainframe system?

As might be expected, most e-mail systems using modems can be expensive since you are paying the long distance telephone toll costs. Yet, there are e-mail systems specifically designed for educators which are free of charge to individual users. But, of course, the institution that owns the required mainframe does pay an initial fee. One e-mail system designed for higher education researchers is called BITNET. A second system for all-level educators is called Internet. Once you have the basic equipment in this e-mail system, there are no long distance costs to individual users.

What is BITNET?

As mentioned, BITNET is designed to link universities and colleges worldwide. To join the network, you must have access to a mainframe computer, obtain a mainframe account, and have a colleague's BITNET e-mail address. This address usually consists of no more than eight characters specifying the sender plus no more than eight characters designating the location of the receiver. For example, if you were sending e-mail to an educator in Krakow, Poland, then the eight-character account might be a condensed version of the receiver's name, such as **gosikolb**, and the address would begin with PL for Poland and KR for Krakow. The remaining four characters would identify the exact location within Krakow. Thus the final BITNET user account and address would be: **gosikolb at plkrry66**.

In comparison, an American educator's account and address from Trenton State College in New Jersey might look like **pbrock @ tscvm**. The sender is Pat Brock from Trenton State College using a vax mainframe machine. Notice the "@" symbol replaces the at on an English language computer keyboard.

On most mainframes systems, you, as the sender, will need a password so that only you can access your e-mail messages. Through this technique, the messages and text communications can be sent and received privately by you unless some unauthorized person discovers or is provided your password. Accessing passwords illegally, not only in BITNET, but in any modem network or LAN, is common practice for the notorious individual called a **hacker**.

What are Internet and NREN?

Although BITNET is generally of interest to primarily college and university professors, the largest worldwide computer network in education, connecting more that 5,000 **subnetworks** or smaller networks with more than 300,000 computers, is Internet. Because of Internet's extensive use, the United State Congress has funded a new expanded bandwidth network called the National Research and Education Network (NREN.) Not only does this system connect schools, but also, governmental institutions, commercial companies, and military branches. What are some subnetworks for education? Samples include KIDSLINK and KIDSNET both directed to student interests, whereas EDPOLYAN (educational policies), ACSOFT (academic software), TRIE (Technology Resources in Education), and JADIST (an electronic Journal of Distance Education) are for teachers.

What is UUCP?

Although most educators are familiar with BITNET and Internet, there is another worldwide e-mail system called **UUCP** or Unix to Unix Copy. Unlike BITNET this e-mail system was developed for the operating system called UNIX. This means that only computers that run the UNIX Operating Systems have been used. However, advances are currently being developed to interconnect IBM, UNIX, Apple, and MAC computer systems.

What is computer conferencing?

So far this discussion on CMC has focused on sending e-mail messages to individuals or groups. Suppose, though, you would like to have an interactive computer-based conversation with several parties simultaneously. This technique is called **computer conferencing**. Computer conferencing is the use of computer networking to facilitate group work and private individual interaction among participants in geographically diverse locations. Through a powerful host computer and its sophisticated software, one or more networks can be connected. Educators and students can link electronically to exchange or discuss ideas, share information, and even complete course assignments. Although not a new concept, computer conferencing currently is growing in popularity. There are several reasons for this increase: (1) more computers are available in educational settings and homes, (2) computer costs have decreased, and (3) educators and students are learning to use computer networking.

Most beginners in computer conferencing have no idea where to find online conferences. One suggestion is to access a commercial service such as *CompuServe*, *Prodigy*, *Delphi*, *GEnie*, or the *AT&T Learning Network*. Another idea is to use a free network (no surcharge) such as BITNET or Internet. By attending a conference or seminar on educational technologies, reading a telecommunications article, or speaking to a computer-knowledgeable colleague, you might learn about other educational networks that exist on regional, statewide, national, and international levels. Regardless of the network you choose, there is commonly an Electronic Bulletin Board System (BBS) which lists upcoming conferences with information for online discussion groups. (See Chapter Six for more details.)

What is time shifting?

If you are unable to view a television program at a particular time, with the use of a VCR you can tape the show and view it at a more convenient time. If you telephone a friend and he is not at home, you might leave a message on his answering machine so he might listen to it at a convenient time. Similarly, with CMC, particularly e-mail, if you send a message and the receiver is not there, your e-mail can be sent and stored in a host computer system. The recipient of the message can retrieve the message at a later time. A response, in turn, can be sent and stored in the same manner. This process, independent of time and space, is called **asynchronous communication** or **time shifting**.

In summary, e-mail as a paperless communications system is growing more popular in education. The use of LANs, modem networking, and mainframe systems in educational settings should continue to proliferate.

Since fax technologies are now becoming more common in school settings, what is their role in school telecommunications?

What is fax?

Another high-tech way to send or receive messages is by using fax. **Fax** or **facsimile**

transmission has merged telephone technology with the photocopy machine. A fax can be compared to the instantaneous mailing of text plus graphics (including photocopies of photographs) to anywhere in the world for the cost of a telephone call. Unlike computer-based e-mail, in which one character is sent at a time, fax transmissions send data composed of light and dark tones of the original document. This means that besides typed messages, hand-written and hand-drawn messages can also be sent. No computer, communications software, or modems are needed, thus reducing costs drastically. The user need have only a telephone and a fax machine.

An important concern in purchasing a fax machine is being certain it is classified as a "Group 3" or possibly "Group 4." As with an e-mail network using microcomputers, the equipment must be compatible. Fax machines face the same problem, but it has been resolved with the use of international standardization of transmission. Currently four international standards have been developed for fax transmissions: Groups 1 and 2 are slow and becoming outdated quickly. Transmission rates on Group 2, for example, permit only 3 pages per minute. Group 3, which is the transmission standard, can send a document in 12 seconds to one minute, depending upon text and graphics combinations as well as print resolution quality. Group 4 transmissions use **Integrated Services Digital Network** or **ISDN**, which is revolutionizing the use of telephones and fax machines. In ISDN technology all data sent and received will be digitized. Data will be transmitted much more rapidly than current e-mail and fax rates of speed, thus decreasing long distance costs and transmission time.

As with any technology there are considerations to address prior to purchase. Which options of facsimile transmissions best suit your educational needs? Do you prefer thermal or regular paper? (some 80% now use thermal paper.) What minimum and maximum size of document do you want to transmit? Do you want a statement regarding the length of time your message took to be sent? These are just a few of the decisions that have to be made by the purchaser. Of course, the more options required, the more expensive the fax machine.

Another benefit of a fax machine over e-mail is the issuing of a transmission report by the fax. At the completion of your message, a statement is printed from the machine that lists the telephone number you faxed, the transmission time, and the number of pages in your message. Of course, e-mail can be hard copied if you have a printer.

A relatively new system for sending and receiving faxes is called a **PC/Fax**. A PC/Fax uses a microcomputer, fax modem, and appropriate fax software. With a PC/Fax, you can send and receive faxes directly from your computer. The benefits of using a PC/Fax include: (1) with networked microcomputers, one PC/Fax system can serve all of the connected microcomputers; (2) with a laptop computer, your fax goes with you; and (3) faxes can be sent between computers without ever having to be printed on paper. Possible problems with this system, though, are that the cost of fax hardware is increased if you do not already have a microcomputer, and the increased need for hard disk storage capacity.

How do you use CMC and fax technologies?

All CMC systems use word processing features for message creation. Most e-mail systems display menu options with various functions such as create a message, send a message, and reply to a message. For modem networking, the receiver's telephone number is dialed, the message to be sent is typed, and then a key is pushed to send the e-mail. For mainframe systems, menus also guide the users and request particular data such as the account number of the user.

To fax, the sender places the hard copy message in a slot on the fax machine, telephones the receiver's number, watches the paper "read" through the machine, and waits for a hard copy transmission paper sheet to appear. One "hands-on" experience will show the ease with which each technology can be learned.

In summary, currently both e-mail systems and fax machines are being used by many educators. However, teachers tend to use e-mail systems more than administrators for projects such as "electronic pen pals" and computer conferencing basically because they have access to computers. On the other hand, most fax machines, located in school offices, are more often used by administrators than teachers and other educational staff members. As more fax machines become available in teachers' rooms, media centers, and classrooms, more teachers and students will be using them. Overall, fax transmissions are easier to use, combine both text and graphics, and, generally, cost less initially than e-mail systems. But, in contrast to e-mail, a fax text transmission cannot be fed directly into a word processing applications package for editing. Why is this an important consideration?

Again, it is essential with any technology to consider your needs before purchasing any hardware or software. For example, if you are editing a newsletter or a publication, it is more efficient to receive an article by e-mail since the text is received within your computer. If, however, you receive the article for editing from a fax transmission, then you must type the document into your computer before you can make the editing changes.

What are the advantages of CMC and fax in education?

Basically there are three advantages in using these technologies in place of mailing a letter or telephoning your message:

First, immediate transmission of your message occurs. There is no need to rely on mail carriers or telephone operators to assist with sending and receiving information.

Second, confirmation of your message is acknowledged by the receiving computer or fax machine. You need not rely on certified mail or an answered phone. Of course, telephone answering machines are available in many situations, but your message is limited to a designated short period of time; whereas, you have no time limits in transmitting messages on e-mail or fax.

Third, both parties need not be present simultaneously to send and receive the electronically transmitted message. Thus, electronic communication in either medium is very efficient.

What are some specific uses for CMC and fax in education?

There are many specific uses of e-mail and computer conferencing models, but few examples of fax in educational settings. As previously stated CMC has an academic audience of teachers and students, while fax communications is generally relegated to administrators and higher education faculty members, particularly in international education or business departments.

For organizational purposes, elementary and secondary school models of CMC will be examined first. College, university, and research examples will follow. Lastly, this section will conclude with e-mail and computer-conferencing models of interest to all educators.

• The Cougar Valley Elementary School in Silverdale, Washington has a school population of 500 students with access to 200 computers plus the advantage of having one telephone per classroom. With easy access to computers and telephones, one of the new technological activities includes electronic mail. Teachers in the school are part of a school-wide e-mail network system, which connects them with other colleagues. Resources can be shared, questions answered electronically, and student record information and class schedules accessed via e-mail messages to and from the administration offices.

• *National Geographic Kids Network* is a hands-on and online telecommunications-based program to encourage learning in science and geography for grades 4-6. Through this program learners from at least 24 countries can collect and conduct local scientific experiments (off the computer) and then compare their data (on the computer) with other student scientists around the world. Research topic units include: *Too Much Trash? What Are We Eating?* and *Solar Energy.* Using easy screen icons, students can plot global addresses, write letters, select data graphs to review, record information in a data notebook, and send or receive messages. Figure 5.1 shows students from Arlington, Virginia working on a pH paper to test the acidity of household liquids. The students perform experiments, make scientific observations, collect data, and share findings with teammates around the world.

• Another e-mail educational usage is the *AT&T Learning Network.* By linking geographically distant elementary and secondary students, this system creates

Figure 5.1. Students doing off-computer science experiments will send their findings via the National Geographic Kids Network worldwide. *(Courtesy of National Geographic Society)*

"Learning Circles" through electronic mailboxes. Offerings include such programs as "Classroom Connections" (cross-curricula projects), "Mind Works" (whole language creative and expository writing), and "Energy and the Environment" (science, social studies, and current issues). An *AT&T Learning Network Newsletter* is available as well.

• *Interactive Communications & Simulations* or *ICS* is another sample of a CMC system. ICS is the most wide-ranging since it is suitable for elementary through college students. Developed by a team of University of Michigan professors, this system organizes participants around theme modules. These include 1990s Earth Odysseys (Columbus in Perspective and Eastern Europe in Flux), Arab-Israeli Conflict Simulation, and an International Poetry Guild. The main purpose of each semester-long module is to involve students globally in sharing opinions and facts through computer conferencing. This type of e-mail and computer conferencing use is often referred to as **instructional gaming**.

• A widely used network for the e-mail exchange of student writing is called *Free Educational Electronic Mail* or *FrEdMail*. Its primary objective is to transmit batches of student work overnight from one location to another. **Nodes** or distant networked computers are programmed to automatically dial phone numbers and exchanges messages. Besides e-mail, electronic bulletin boards provide on-screen data for teachers to review. (See Chapter Six for more information on electronic bulletin boards.)

• Since 1992 TECHNET, the California State University system's computer network, has provided a link between higher education and the private business sector. Through TECHNET college students access real-world business problems, which they then resolve by developing solution scenarios and send this information via computer networking.

The following are examples of CMC models on the college and university levels. There are several well-known computer conferencing networks that have been developed and used at the university level for many years.

• In the 1970s The University of Michigan created the Confer system, which was tied to the Michigan Terminal System or MTS. During this same period of time, the New Jersey Institute of Technology developed another conferencing system, called the Electronic Information Exchange System or EIES. The University of Northern Iowa and the University of Virginia use CAUCUS, which requires a UNIX operating system. CoSy is used at the University of Guelph in Canada and the Open University in Milton Keynes, England.

• Through Harvard University in Cambridge, Massachusetts, an electronic mail system has been established to assist new elementary and high school teachers. The *BTCN* or *Beginning Teachers Computer Network* is a project conducted with recent graduates from the Harvard School of Education who are teaching in various locations throughout the United States. Besides the opportunity to participate in ''forums'' or on-line discussions via an e-mail modem network system, first-year teachers can request private conversations regarding educational problems and concerns from educational ''experts'' or experienced teachers. In the first year of the project, half of the e-mail messages were private in nature.

• For educational researchers, two networks are particularly useful. They are the Educational Research List on BITNET and the Educational Research Forum on *CompuServe*. The Educational Research List on BITNET is free to faculty members who are connected through a mainframe computer at their institution. The Educational Research List was developed primarily to list employment opportunities and news from Washington regarding educational matters. Besides e-mail communications with colleagues, users can also access the National Science Foundation, which sponsors an interactive list to discuss grant regulations and policies.

• *Compuserve*, in comparison, is a commercial nationwide network available for a service fee to the general consumer. However, the Educational Research Forum and other resource forums are directed specifically to educators and contain three services: (1) e-mail, (2) organizations of articles in databases called Libraries, and (3) computer conferencing. For example, the American Educational Research Association or AERA and the Office of Educational Research and Improvement or OERI list employment opportunities, grant competitions, and other data of educational concern.

In addition, *CompuServe* provides a variety of e-mail and computer conferencing forums to general educators at any level of teaching. These specific forums include, for example: (1) the Education Forum for exchange of ideas regarding teaching materials and methods, (2) the Foreign Language Forum with an area focusing on Bilingual Education, and (3) the Science and Math Forum, which makes available hundreds of software programs and suggestions for scientific experiments.

• Another example of e-mail usage for all educators is a service developed by the ALA, the American Library Association, called *ALANET*. There are over 1,000 ''mailboxes'' or contact points in more than 1,000 locations in American libraries, associations, and offices of suppliers. Besides an e-mail system for users, ALANET provides bulletin boards, newsletters, and announcements.

• Also, e-mail is used for all educators in contact with editors or columnists of technology magazines. Rather than write and mail your questions or comments, you can more easily correspond through e-mail. For example, if you wanted to "Talk to EL" or *Electronic Learning*, you can use one of the following online services: *CompuServe, AppleLink,* or *Online America.* For a e-mail contact with *PC World,* use *America Online, CompuServe,* or *MCI Mail*; and for *Byte,* use *BIX.* Details are provided in each issue.

• A final example of e-mail appropriate for a wide range of educators is NASA Spacelink. Teachers and students can not only access space-related information from electronic databases (see Chapter Six), but also can ask questions about current NASA programs, activities, and any historical or astronaut data. Although the response is not immediate, I have found that all of my queries have been answered no more than 24-hours later.

What are some CMC and fax problems and solutions?

The first problem identified by some educators is a lack of equipment or nonaccessibility to these technologies. A solution to this problem is to examine the hardware currently available in the school setting and estimate the amount of additional equipment that is required to develop e-mail or fax opportunities. Educators who are interested in using these technologies in their teaching settings should approach administrators with specific educational plans for teaching/learning usages and, in turn, request access to the technologies.

The second problem is the lack of knowledge and training in educational telecommunications. By reading current journals and publications, attending conferences, participating in workshops, visiting educational settings with e-mail and fax in use, and developing purposes for technology use in curriculum planning, educators can deepen the knowledge base and skills necessary to integrate e-mail and fax into their classroom and instructional methodologies. But, as with any technology, a support system is required. If an on-site technician or expert is not available, then a support service hotline should be accessible to all educators.

The third problem is the cost of long distance charges when using modem networking e-mail or fax machines. "School time" is prime time for high telephone transmission costs. However, there are at least six solutions to reducing and monitoring the toll charges. First, if possible, use a free BITNET, Internet, or UUCP e-mail network. Second, program the telephone or fax to send your message late at night when telephone transmission rates are least expensive. Third, develop an "in-house" e-mail network where there are no or very limited telephone calls. Fourth, decide in advance your message content so that you can send it rapidly and decrease long-distance charges. Fifth, keep specific records of telephone calls and limit or eliminate those costs which seem too high. Sixth, use a "toll restricter" on your modem to limit calls to specific toll call areas. Lastly, research the possibility of **packet switching** in your area. Using this technology, modem networks can be reached by calling a local access number, thus bypassing the need for long distance telephone calls.

Decision-making Guidelines: CMC and Fax

1. Objective: Why use e-mail, computer conferencing, and fax in your educational setting?

2. Integration: How will e-mail, computer conferencing, and fax be integrated in current or future curriculum areas, such as social studies, science, or reading/language arts?

3. Cost: What will be the initial start-up costs and estimated long distance charges?

4. Location: Where will e-mail, computer conferencing, and fax machinery be placed?

5. Security: How will "authorized users" be identified? How will time usage and transmission costs be monitored?

6. Equal Access: Will all educators and students be provided the opportunity to use these technologies? If not, what will a fair access policy entail?

7. Responsibility: Who will supervise, monitor, and keep records on the e-mail, computer conferencing, and fax machine usage?

8. Updating: Who will determine when new e-mail, computer conferencing, or fax long distance sites may be added to the estimated budget costs?

9. Training: Who, when, where and how will educators and students be taught to use e-mail, computer conferencing, and fax machines?

Summary

This chapter has presented information on e-mail, computer conferencing, and fax technologies. Although all forms of electronic communication are adaptable to the educational setting, e-mail and computer conferencing are currently more widely used by teachers and students, while fax technologies are more often used by administrators. However, with the growth of distance learning settings and telecourses, fax machines are becoming more common for sending information to students in remote classroom locations.

Recommended Periodicals

BYTE

Collegiate Microcomputer

Distance Education

Educational Technology

Educational Technology Research & Development

Electronic Education

Electronic Learning

Learning Tomorrow: Journal of the Apple Education Advisory Council

MacWorld

Media and Methods

Online Access

PC Today

PC World

Prospects: Quarterly Review of Education

Special Education Quarterly

Telecommunications

The Computing Teacher

Resources

ALANET System Manager. American Library Association, 50 E. Huron Street, Chicago, IL 60611. (312) 944-6780.

America Online. Quantum Computer Services, 8619 Westwood Center Drive, Vienna, VA 22182. (800) 827-6364.

AT&T Long Distance Learning Network. AT&T, 295 North Maple Ave., Room 6234S3, Basking Ridge, NJ 07201. (800) 367-7225; (201) 221-8544.

Beginning Teachers Computer Network. Diane E. Beals, Research/ Technical Assistant, Beginning Teachers Computer Network, Harvard School of Education, Cambridge, MA. 02138. (617) 495-1000.

CompuServe. 5000 Arlington Centre Blvd., PO Box 20212, Columbus, OH 43220. (800) 848-8990.

Crosstalk. Digital Communications Associates, Inc. 1000 Alderman Dr., Alpharetta, GA 30202. (800) 348-3221.

Delphi. 1030 Massachusetts Ave., Cambridge, MA 02139. (800) 544-4005.

Dialog. 3460 Hillview Ave., Palo Alto, CA 94304. (800) 334-2564.

FrEdMail Project. PO Box 243, Bonita, CA 91902. (619) 475-4852.

GEnie. Box 02B-C, 401 N. Washington St., Rockville, MD 20850. (800) 638-9636.

GTE Education Services. World Classroom Product Manager. 8505 Freeport Parkway, Suite 600. Irving, TX 75063. (800) 634-5644.

Institute for Global Communications. 3228 Sacramento St., San Francisco, CA 94115. (415) 923-0900.

Interactive Communications and Simulations. School of Education, University of Michigan, Ann Arbor, MI 48109. (313) 763-6716.

Learning Link. Learning Link National Consortium. 1790 Broadway, 16th Floor, New York, NY 10019. (212) 708-3056.

Long Distance Learning Network. AT&T, PO Box 716, Basking Ridge, NJ 07920. (800) 367-7225.

Mass LearnNet. Massachusetts Corporation for Educational Telecommunications (MCET). 38 Sidney St., Suite 300, Cambridge, MA 02139. (617) 621-0290.

NASA Spacelink. Spacelink Administrator, NASA Marshall Space Flight Center, Mail Code CA21, Marshall Space Flight Center, AL 35812. (205) 544-0038.

National Geographic Kids Network. National Geographic Society, PO Box 98019, Washington, DC 20036-4688. (800) 368-2728.

News Access. Teachable Tech. 2179 Hannah Lane, Tucker, GA 30084. (404) 939-4596.

NYCENET. NY City Board of Education. Computer Information Services, Intermediate School #25, 34-65 192nd St., Flushing, NY 11358. (718) 935-4040.

Personal Sharing Information Network Project (PSINet). IBM Educational Systems, PO Box 2150, Atlanta, GA 30055. (800) IBM-2468.

Prodigy. PO Box 8129, Gray, TN 37615. (800) 776-3449.

SchoolLink. Radio Shack Education Division, 700 One Tandy Center, Fort Worth, TX 76102. (817) 390-2967.

TECHNET. Ray Haynes, California Polytechnic State University, San Luis Obispo, CA. 93401 (805) 756-1418.

Unison Education Network. Unison Telecommunications Service, 700 West Pete Rose Way, Cincinnati, OH 45203. (513) 723-1700.

References

Barron, A.E. & Orwig, G.W. (1993). *New technologies for education.* Englewood, CO: Libraries Unlimited, Inc.

Beals, D.E. (1991, April). Computer-mediated communication among beginning teachers. *Technical Horizons in Education Journal, 18* (9), 74-77.

Beyda, W.J. (1989). *Basic data communications: A comprehensive overview.* Englewood Cliffs, NJ: Prentice-Hall.

Blurton, C. & Kelly, M. (1992, March). The global classroom. In N. Estes & M. Thomas (Eds.), *Proceedings of the Ninth International Conference on Technology and Education, 3* (pp. 1223-1225). Paris, France: Morgan Printing.

Cannings, T.R. & Finkel, L. (1993). *The technology age classroom.* Wilsonville, OR: Franklin, Beedle & Associates Inc.

Crowley, M.L. (1989). Organizing for electronic messaging in the schools. *Computing Teacher, 16* (7), 23-26.

Eskridge, S.W. & Langer, M.A. (1992, March). Pacific-Link: Using electronic conferencing to provide support to new teachers. In N. Estes & M. Thomas (Eds.), *Proceedings of the Ninth International Conference on Technology and Education, 2* (pp. 632-634). Paris, France: Morgan Printing.

Fishman, D. & King, E. (1990). *The book of fax: An impartial guide to buying & using facsimile machines.* Chapel Hill, NC: Ventana Press, Inc.

Haynes, R. (1993, March). Students solve real problems for business via TECHNET. *T.H.E. Journal, 20* (8), 62-64.

Hazari, S.M. (1990). Using e-mail across computer networks. *Collegiate Microcomputer, 8* (3), 210-214.

Laughon, S. & Kulikowski II, S. (1992, March). Using global educational networks: Topics from Internet. In N. Estes & M. Thomas (Eds.), *Proceedings of the Ninth International Conference on Technology and Education, 3*, (pp. 1238-1240). Paris, France: Morgan Printing.

Lewis, P.H. (1992, August 2). Dialing for data. *The New York Times Education Life*, 4A, p. 41.

Northern Telecom. (1991, March). *Using the telephone to expand the classroom: A guide to teacher and classroom telephony*. Northern Telecom.

Pollack, A. (1991, Sunday July 14). A quirky loner goes mainstream. *The New York Times Business Section 3*, 1 & 6.

Pollard, C. & Pollard, R. (1992, March). A framework for maximizing the use of telecommunications technologies in education. In N. Estes & M. Thomas (Eds.), *Proceedings of the Ninth International Conference on Technology and Education, 2* (pp. 632-634). Paris, France: Morgan Printing.

Quarterman, J.S. (1990). *The matrix: Computer networks and conferencing systems worldwide*. Bedford, MA: Digital Press.

Waggoner, M.D. (Ed.). (1992). *Empowering networks: Computer conferencing in education*. Englewood Cliffs, NJ: Educational Technology Publications, Inc.

Willis, J.W. (1987). *Educational computing: A guide to practical applications*. Scottdale, AZ: Gorsuch Scarisbrick, Publishers.

Wishnietsky, D.H. (1991). Using electronic mail in an educational setting. *Phi Delta Kappan Fastback No. 316*. Bloomington, IN: Phi Delta Kappa.

6

Chapter Six:
Online Databases and Electronic Bulletin Board Systems

What are online databases and electronic bulletin board systems?

Online Databases or **DB**s and **Electronic Bulletin Board Systems** or **BBSs** are both communication networks that connect you to massive amounts of stored information in remote locations. To use either one of these two communication networks, you will need a microcomputer, telephone line, modem, and special telecommunications software packages to view text on your computer screen. While you can only *receive* information from a DB, a BBS allows you to send information as well. It is important to know that there are generally two transmission cost factors: (1) a service fee for data access, and (2) long distance telephone charges.

Together with e-mail, DB and BBS are computer telecommunication systems growing in popularity among educators. From the first appearance of online services in the 1970s, when the use of information-retrieval databases for researchers was the primary focus, dial-up modem users are now **downloading** (printing the data from one's microcomputer screen) more than just research-oriented information. In fact by 1990 more than 10,000,000 computer users worldwide were using electronic bulletin boards. So, what exactly are DBs and BBSs? The following presentation describes these communications systems in more detail.

What is an Online DB?

An Online Database or DB is a collection of related information that can be accessed quickly, generally through a microcomputer that is connected via telephone lines to a powerful computer at a remote location. Through a menu system you can search specific databases and select items from the database, which will then appear on your microcomputer screen. If you have a printer, you can download and make a hard copy of the information you would like to read. As stated earlier, an online database is a one-way communication process. You can only receive information and not generally **upload** (send information) to the mainframe computer from which the database originates.

Figure 6.1. Accessing a DB from a Microcomputer.

Figure 6.1 shows a student accessing a database on her computer and deciding which data she will download to her printer.

What is a BBS?

An Electronic Bulletin Board System or BBS needs the same hardware and software as online databases in order to access information. However, bulletin boards, unlike electronic DBs, allow you to both receive and send messages through a menu system in a two-way telecommunication format. Many messages are sent to a **System Operator** or **SysOp**, who sets up and "posts" these messages on the bulletin board screens; or you may transmit messages to other BBS users. If you don't like the public posting of messages on a BBS, then you can use electronic mail or e-mail.

What might you find on a BBS? Common offerings are public domain software information, question and answer technical advice, computer games, and contests. Who might want to use a BBS? Any Special Interest Groups or SIGs with the appropriate hardware and software might use BBSs. Who might SysOps be? They can be members of formal organizations or hobbyists who have the necessary hardware and software. If you are interested in becoming a SysOp and setting up a BBS, one way is to contact *Galacticomm*, which is a company marketing all the hardware and software you will need to begin a multi-user online BBS. An excellent article to read for a detailed description of planning and setting up a BBS is one by Frisbie *et al.* in *Educational Technology*.

What are integrated online services?

Although some telecommunications systems offer solely or primarily e-mail, DBs, or BBSs, integrated online services combine all components. For example, *Prodigy* and *CompuServe* offer a wide range of services including topical bulletin boards for specialized information, e-mail capabilities, and databases. It is important to note that there can be add-on costs to regular consumer-product charges when using integrated online services.

What are the advantages of DBs and BBSs in education?

There are several primary advantages in using online DBs and BBSs. First, large databases can be accessed relatively easily by microcomputers in the educational setting or at home. The most common commercial online DBs and BBSs include *CompuServe, Prodigy, GEnie*, and *Delphi* information services. Included in these products are data on personal investing, marketing, news and information, airline travel schedules, homelife databases for varied family member interests, and educational encyclopedias. Other online services growing in popularity, are *AT&T Learning Network, BIX, Dialog, General Videotex Corporation, Learning Link, NASA Spacelink, NewsNet, Quantum Computer Services*, and *WorldClassroom*. Each service offers a variety of selections with different pricing structures and service charges.

A second advantage is the convenience of information retrieval. There is no need to find your way to a library and review volumes of books to locate specific data. Instead you can get online by simply following directions to access the database from your microcomputer whether in your classroom, office, or at home.

A third advantage is the availability of massive amounts of print information that you can download onto your printer. Whether you are downloading an article from an encyclopedia or uploading information to display on an electronic bulletin board, you are easily "in touch" with data relevant to your needs and interests.

A final advantage is that both DBs and BBSs serve as educational resources for educators. With a BBS link to a Special Interest Group or **SIG**, you will be able to ask questions and receive assistance with technology problems from other teachers who are on the system.

What are some specific uses of DBs and BBSs in education?

Online databases, bulletins board systems, and electronic mail are often combined within commercial and non-commercial services. The following descriptions provide a sample of the many electronic systems in educational settings today:

• *Apple Global Education Network* or *AGE* is an international project involving more than 150 schools in 25 countries. Developed by Apple Computer, Inc., both teachers and students interact electronically when conducting research, writing games, or role playing, for example.

• DIALOG is a well-used vendor of more than 400 databases. Information is categorized in fields including medicine, law, engineering, and the arts.

• *DOW JONES NEWS SERVICE or DJNS* is a database service in which the subscriber can access over 30 menu-driven databases. Examples of available databases include News (Associated Press), Books (Magill Book Reviews), OAG (Online Airline Guide), and Weather (Accu-Weather, Inc.)

• *FrEdMail (Free Education Mail)* is a BBS with more than 90 bulletin boards designed by teachers. Using FrEdMail, teachers throughout Canada and the United States can send and receive information on topics of interest.

• *National Geographic Kids Network* is a computer-communications system that provides hands-on science and geography experiences for students from grades four through six.

• *NASA Spacelink*, sponsored by NASA, is an electronic information service available to individuals interested in the American Space Program. Data are accessed from a computer at the Marshall Space Flight Center, Huntsville, Alabama. Not limited to schools in the United States, Canadian schools can also seek space technologies data. Students, in particular, find that the databases, e-mail, and bulletin board network are valuable informational resources for learners from elementary through college levels.

What are some DB and BBS problems and solutions?

There are three major concerns addressed by educators regarding the use of electronic systems, which are (1) the cost factor, (2) lack of telecommunications standardization, and (3) need for instruction simplification.

First, the use of DBs and BBSs can be a relatively heavy initial expense with ongoing costs. Not only are telecommunications software and modems required (as well as the additional cost of a microcomputer and printer if they are not already available), but also the charge of adding additional telephone lines in the schools to use specifically for electronic services via modems. Along with the installation charges are the long distance rates for "prime time" electronic access.

What are some ways educators address the high-cost concern? The following suggestions are provided: First, install only one dedicated telephone line for the necessary hardware and software to a shared area, such as the media center, for example. In this way the cost per line will be distributed among a larger number of learners. Second, to eliminate abuses in the unapproved usage of long distance telephone lines, telephone companies can provide information on safeguarding against unauthorized uses. Third, purchase a high speed modem (9600 BPS is best for educational purposes, rather than a 1200 or 2400 BPS) so more data can be sent to your printer faster, thus eliminating longer connection times to remote electronic services and bringing about lower costs for long distance calling charges. Fourth, begin with a service that offers free services, for example, *NASA SpaceLink* and *FrEdMail*, or perhaps a commercial service like *Prodigy* with a set monthly or annual fee but with no hourly rate. But, remember, the toll charges are still ongoing. Last, but not least, is to seek grant monies or support subsidies from local telecommunications or electronic industries. Possibilities for special funding resources exist, but it takes time and energy to complete applications according to deadlines. Thus, through some research and initiative, it might be possible for your school district to make the education/industry connection for advancing technological learning.

A second problem identified was the variety of Disk Operating Systems (DOS) or **platforms** and telecommunications software packages to link the microcomputer and modem to remote computers. Since there is no standard software, hardware-specific networks are used. For example, *PSI Net* serves IBM equipment and *AppleLink* serves Apple computer users. To eliminate a problem of access, educators contact electronic services they plan to use prior to the purchase of specific hardware and software. If, however, the computer basics are already on-site, then be certain to find the services compatible to your machinery.

Third, although many software communications packages are "relatively" easy, it is important to understand that the process does vary according to the electronic service requested. Manuals should accompany each electronic service, which should be studied prior to online "cost per minute" usage. Also, simple online menus and quick reference sheets are sometimes provided and are necessary especially for new users.

Not only seek ease of initial access but also check to see how many of the following recommended functions are available on your selected service and how easy they are to learn prior to connecting online: (1) status and tracking functions tell the user if he or she has e-mail messages; (2) management reports tally time accumulation on the online activity; (3) directories list data pertaining to online conferences; (4) online search possibilities enable the user to find selected data; (5) customization provides personalization and organization of displays; and (6) online, real-time meetings involve users in text conversations on computer monitors.

Decision-making Guidelines: DBs and BBSs

1. Objective: What DBs and BBSs are available for educational purposes and why are they important to incorporate within the educational setting?

2. Integration: How will these applications be used within the present curriculum? Are they best for social studies, science, research, or other subject areas?

3. Cost: What will be the initial cost of modems and dedicated telephone lines? What will be the hourly or monthly fee for the commercial service that interests and is valuable to you and your students? How much will the long distances charges be? Will there be a "cap" on expenditures established in advance?

4. Location: Which computer or computers will have access to the these telecommunications applications? Will DBs and BBSs be available in classrooms, computer labs, administrative offices, media/library centers, or in the educators' homes for professional use?

5. Security: How will access to these applications be monitored? Who will be responsible to see that use is kept within budget guidelines?

6. Equal Access: Will both educators and students be provided access to DB and BBS usage? Will particular classes or grade levels only have access? What policy measures will be established?

7. Updating: Who will be designated as the person responsible to research, compare, and recommend new DB and BBS services?

8. Training: Who will be trained to use these applications? When and where will the training occur? Will there be special time and financial or in-kind benefits offered to the trainees?

Summary

This chapter has described two special computer-based telecommunication systems, which are online databases and electronic bulletin board systems. While DBs are designed for users to receive information, BBSs provide the opportunity to both receive and send data publicly. Both telecommunications systems are used in many schools, particularly as components for distance learning.

Recommended Periodicals

BYTE
Collegiate Microcomputer
Compute
Computers and Education
The Computing Teacher

Educational Horizons

Educational Technology

Electronic Learning

Information Technology and Libraries

Journal of Computer-Based Instruction

Journal of Computer Information Systems

Journal of Computing in Teacher Education

Journal of Research on Computing in Education

PC Magazine

PC Week

Online

Online Access

Tech Trends

Telecommunications

T.H.E. Journal

Resources

America Online. Quantum Computer Services, 8619 Westwood Center Dr., Vienna, VA 22182. (800) 227-6364.

Accu-Weather. 619 W. College Ave., State College, PA 16801. (804) 237-0309.

AppleLink Personal Edition. 20525 Mariani Ave., Cupertino, CA 95014. (800) 545-5047.

AT&T Long Distance Learning Network. 295 N. Maple Ave., Basking Ridge, NJ 07920. (201) 221-2253.

BIX. Three Blackstone Street, Cambridge, MA 02139. (800) 544-4005.

BRS Information Technologies. 1200 Route 7, Latham, NY 12110. (800) 345-4277.

CompuServe. CompuServe, Inc. PO Box 20212, Columbus, OH 43220. (800) 848-8199.

DELPHI. 1030 Massachusetts Avenue, Cambridge, MA 01238. (800) 695-4005.

DIALOG. Dialog Information Services, Inc., 3460 Hillview Ave., Palo Alto, CA 94304. (800) 334-2564.

Dow Jones News/Retrieval Service. PO Box 300, Princeton, NJ 08543. (800) 552-3567; (609) 520-8349.

FrEdMail (Free Education Network). 4021 Allen School Road, Bonita, CA 92002. Modem: (619) 475-4852.

General Videotex Corp. Three Blackstone Street, Cambridge, MA 02139. (800) 544-4005.

GEnie. 401 North Washington Street, Rockville, MD 20850. (800) 638-9636.

Learning Link National Consortium. Link Net Inc., Central Education Network, 1400 E. Touhy Ave., Des Plains, IL 60018. (708) 390-8700.

NASA Spacelink. NASA Marshall Space Flight Center, Huntsville, AL 35812. (205) 895-0028.

National Geographic Kids Network. National Geographic Society Educational Media Division, Dept. 1001, Washington, DC 20036. (202) 775-6580.

NewsNet. 945 Haverford Rd., Bryn Mawr, PA 19010. (800) 345-1301.

Prodigy. Prodigy Services Co., 445 Hamilton Avenue, White Plains, NY 10601. (800) 776-3449.

Quantum Computer Services. 8619 Westwood Center Dr., Vienna, VA 22182. (800) 227-6364.

SpecialNet. GTE Education Services, 8505 Freeport Parkway, Suite 600, Irving, TX 75063. (800) 634-5644.

TI-IN Network. Satellite Transmitted Academic Resources, 100 Central Parkway North, Suite 190, San Antonio, TX 78232. (800) 999-8446.

References

Andres, Y., Jacks, M., & Rogers, A. (1989). *Telesensations: The educators' handbook to instructional telecomputing.* Bonita, CA: FrEdMail Foundation.

Banks, M.A. (1991). Are online services delivering? *Byte Special Issue: Outlook '92, 16* (11), 123-132.

Bowen, C. & Peyton, D. (1990). *The complete electronic bulletin board starter kit.* New York: Bantam.

Dvorak, J. (1990). *Dvorak's guide to PC telecommunications.* New York: McGraw-Hill.

Frisbie, A., Repman, J., & Price, R.V. (1991, April). Establishing an electronic bulletin board. *Educational Technology, 31* (4), 41-43.

Glossbrenner, A. (1990). *The complete handbook of personal computer communications* (3rd ed.). New York: St. Martin's Press.

Grunward, P. (1991, October). Telecommunications in the classroom. *The electronic school: Innovative uses of technology in education. A supplement to The American School Board Journal and The Executive Educator,* 4-11.

Harasim, L. (1989). *Online education.* New York: Praeger.

Hudspeth, D. (1990). The electronic bulletin board: Appropriate technology. *Educational Technology, 30* (7), 23-26.

Hunter, B. & Lodish, E. (1989). *Online searching in the curriculum.* Santa Barbara, CA: ABC-Clio, Inc.

Kurshan, B. (1991, April). Creating the global classroom for the 21st century. *Educational Technology, 31* (4), 47-49.

Lynch, E.A. (1991, May). Student use of online information retrieval systems — a basic skill for the 21st century. In G. McKye & D. Trueman (Eds.), *Proceedings of the Twelfth Educational Computing Organization of Ontario Conference and the Eighth International Conference on Technology and Education* (pp. 488-490). Toronto, Ontario, Canada: C.G.F. Executive Services.

Mason, R. & Kaye, A. (1989). *Mindweave: Communications, computers, and distance education.* New York: Pergamon Press.

Office of Technology Assessment. (1989). *Linking for learning.* Washington, DC: Government Printing Office, Document 052-003-01170-1.

Roberts, N., Blakeslee, G., Brown, M., & Lenk, C. (1990). *Integrating telecommunications into education.* Englewood Cliffs, NJ: Prentice-Hall.

Waggoner, M.D. (Ed.). (1992). *Empowering networks: Computer conferencing in education.* Englewood Cliffs, NJ: Educational Technology Publications, Inc.

Watson, B. (1992). The wired classroom: American education goes online. In J.J. Hirschbuhl & L.F. Wilkinson (Eds.), *Computers in education* (5th ed.) (pp. 180-184). Guilford, CT: The Dushkin Publishing Group, Inc.

Weigel, E. (Ed.). (1992, Spring). Remember: NASA teacher tools continually available! *Educational Horizons, 1* (2), 12.

Weiner, R. (1991, October). Online schools make writing real! *The electronic school. A supplement to The American School Board Journal and The Executive Educator,* 17-19.

7

Chapter Seven:
Conversant Technology

What is conversant technology?

Conversant technology is a relatively new use of telephone communications which includes **audiotex** and **voice mail**. Both conversant technology usages are designed for touch-tone (push button) rather than rotary dial (round dialing) telephones. In the past decade, tens of thousands of retail businesses, offices, and government organizations have installed these new technologies. You probably have already used both communication forms in your everyday life and have never realized it. However, both audiotex and voice mail are only beginning to appear on the school scene.

Generally, audiotex and voice mail are similar interactive telephone services that can use 800 or 900 area code exchanges. Through these exchanges you can connect to a computerized or automated operator who provides information from a computerized data base. Using remote software, voice response systems, and a touch-tone telephone, you can, for example, call for airlines "free-of-charge" on an 800 number, seek your daily horoscope reading on a "pay-per-call" 900 number, or seek the results of sports scores on a 976 "local pay-per-call" number.

An example of an 800 "toll-free call" is NASA's U.S. SPACE CAMP. A caller dialing 1-800-63-SPACE receives the following message:

Thank you for calling the U.S. Space and Rocket Center.

If you are calling for our Reservations Department or for Space-mail Information, press one.

If you are calling for Space Camp Information, press two.

If you are calling for Tour and Group Information, press three.

If you are calling for information about Attractions or Tickets, press four.

If you are dialing from a rotary phone, please hold and the operator will assist you.

As you realize, more television commercials are providing 900 exchange service information. Costs vary greatly from $1.00 to many dollars for the first minute. Since many audiotex information services require more than one minute of user time, automated service companies are finding lucrative markets in the unsuspecting consumers who are not aware of the high costs of some audiotex services. Too often callers assume since an 800 number is free of charge, so is the 900 number. This is not the case at all.

In comparison, voice mail, which is sometimes called automated answering systems or voice messaging units, also uses a generated computer response voice, a computerized data base, and a touch-tone telephone. To use voice mail, you simply call a specific phone number to seek particular information. Your call is answered and you are given a vocal menu of choices. You then push the correct touch tone number, which provides you a connection to requested information, whether it's a collection of movie reviews or weather reports.

In addition to listening to information on voice mail, you can also leave a message to a particular person in a designated storage area or **electronic mailbox**, similar to a telephone answering machine. An important point to note is that electronic mailboxes are password protected, which means that your messages are private.

What are the advantages of conversant technology in education?

Telephoning is one of the fastest ways to communicate with others. But telephoning can also be an inefficient use of time if you cannot contact the caller directly. You must then either call back at another time, or leave your message (limited to a pre-set response time) on an answering machine, assuming there is one available. If you do leave your message and your friend, colleague, parent, or administrator returns your call, you might not be at home, and the caller then must leave his brief message on your answering machine. This frustrating cycle, referred to as telephone tag, can repeat itself many times before sufficient time and access is provided for communication to occur.

With voice mail, you can send a detailed message, which is stored in the receiver's private electronic mailbox box. Or, someone can call you and leave a message in your mailbox. Here's an example. Suppose, you want to call your colleague, Erin Dullea, to compare notes on some new educational technology you have in your school. You know she's teaching in class when you have time to call, so she will be unable to receive the call. With voice mail, you would call and might hear the message "Welcome to Woods Road School. If you want to leave a message for Ryan Patrick, press one. If you want to leave a message for Jamie Rivera, press two. If you want to leave a message for Erin Dullea, press three (... and so on)." So, you press three and leave your message. When Erin listens to her "mail," she can then contact you. (See Figure 7.1.)

Figure 7.1. Student Using Voice Mail.

What are some specific uses of conversant technology in education?

Conversant technology is a service that is becoming more common in the educational setting. The following examples provide you with an idea of the current uses in education:

• *Compu-Call* is a service that provides educators with a "quick and easy" communication link with parents. This program stores natural-sounding voice messages to be sent to particular residences at selected times. For example, through the use of data-based file management, computerized callers termed **electronic truant officers** can contact parents if children have not arrived at school. If needed, *Compu-Call*, with the teacher or administrator's guidance, can arrange meetings with parents when absenteeism becomes excessive. On a more positive note, educators can call parents and leave informational messages pertaining to Open House dates or other special events.

• *900 Support, Inc.* is a service for users of Novell Netware, a network system for computers. By telephoning 1-900-Pro-Help, individuals are provided an on-line support service answering questions about the system. Currently more than 1,000 callers per month use *900 Support, Inc.*

• *Microsoft*, the large software company, also uses conversant technology. Through an 800 number, software owners can call for simple "routine" assistance between the hours of 9:00 A.M. - 5:00 P.M. Pacific Time. In comparison, more complex questions require callers to use a 900 number at specific per minute charge. The special service is called *On-Call* and is available from 6:00 P.M. until 6 A.M. Pacific Time.

• Literary Book Guild members can use conversant technology. By dialing a 900 number, the caller is asked to choose from a menu of six contemporary authors. The selected author will then present the caller with a preview of his or her book that is available for purchase through the service called *Home Preview*. Any time of the night or day a caller can simply telephone and listen to the recorded messages which change every two weeks. The cost is 50 cents for the first minute and each minute thereafter. Presently this service is provided to more than 500,000 Literary Guild members.

What are some specific examples of conversant technology in education?

• Educators at Inman Middle School in Atlanta, Georgia utilize this new telephone technology to communicate with parents. By dialing a number, parents can "find out what's happening in the school." During any 24-hour period of time, parents dial the special school number and wait for a computerized voice menu guiding them to the teachers to whom they wish to listen. Teachers are assigned special-code single or double-digit numbers, and parents can choose the teacher(s) of choice to hear, for example, what was studied in class or what homework was assigned. Since it is voice mail, parents can also leave messages for the teachers.

• A similar service is called *Message Line*. According to J. M. Henderson, former Superintendent of Schools, Montgomery Public Schools, New Jersey, voice mail was installed to meet some reoccurring communications needs. For example, callers "tied-up office telephone lines" when the possibility of winter snow day school closings or early dismissals arose. However, information concerning inclement weather days is just one current use of the system. Electronic mailboxes are available for each school within the district so that callers can be informed about upcoming events 24 hours per day. Parents can also leave messages for particular teachers, and teachers can leave messages regarding homework assignments.

• A third example of conversant technology is used by the educators in Greenbriar Middle School, Greenbriar, Tennessee. Parents can telephone the special number and listen to a recording of the school calendar, athletic event dates and times, and cafeteria menus.

• A fourth example of the specific use of voice mail in education can be seen at the Jefferson and Willard Elementary Schools in Spokane, Washington. *The PhoneMaster Notification System* (*PNS*) from U.S. Telecom International, Inc. in Joplin, Missouri, is a popular phone notification system in which parents and teachers can "exchange information about classroom happenings." A voice card and software were inserted into a DOS-compatible computer with a hard disk. A printer and a single-line telephone were added to complete the communications system. By touch-tone dialing, parents can access many menus, including Parent Teacher group information, school holidays, and the very frequently used "Homework Hotline." Recording their messages in less than a minute per day, teachers list homework assignments for parents to access. Other features that *PhoneMaster* offers include the following options: messages can be programmed to be left on answering machines, attendance calls can be made automatically by the system, up to 90 calls per hour can be completed by the voice mail system, and printouts of received phone calls plus student identification numbers and birthdates can be system-generated.

• At Egan High School in Egan, Minnesota, in addition to listing sporting events, messages from parents to teachers and teachers to parents, an interesting use for the system includes administrative reminders to the staff members regarding forthcoming meeting schedules. By sending out the message to a "list" or database of telephone numbers, the administrator's announcement is automatically routed to all the numbers on the list; band members were informed of new uniform arrivals through a recorded message; and lost football equipment was found through this messaging system. To enhance the message network, teachers can check for voice electronic mail through their microcomputers, where messages can be heard as well as seen on the monitor. When the message is received by the teacher, the message note disappears.

According to Jerold Bauch, director of the Betty Philips Center for Parenthood Education at Vanderbilt University, at least 25 school systems in eight states are using these new electronic mailboxes. Studies show that half of the parents who have access to the schools' voice mail systems telephone for information or to leave messages every day. Bauch predicts that voice mail someday will be as regular as report cards. Research results on the effects of the systems are available through the university.

On the college or university level, voice mail can be used by students in many schools to register for courses, find campus information, or contact faculty members for appointments. Professors can also request information for grant funding through voice mail systems. For example, to receive information on the Fulbright Scholarship Program, it is possible to request applications through a voice mail network. By telephoning, the caller is directed through a verbal menu system to more efficiently connect to the proper source. After listening to the message queries, simply leave a message in the electronic mailbox. Of course, the traditional detach-and-mail information form is still available.

What are some conversant technology problems and solutions?

There are five basic problems identified by educators in using audiotex and voice mail. First is the sense of impersonal contact with the parent, administrator, or colleague; the "human touch" is absent. True, "live" communication is missing, but message-leaving and information-gathering is possible 24 hours per day without both caller and receiver being present. There are very few educators who want to be available 24 hours a day, seven days a week to speak to parents or administrators. Voice mail, in particular, allows the lines of parent-teacher communications to be more open on a daily basis rather than at the end of report card marking periods. Many parents also realize the busy schedule of educators and might hesitate to call daily unless there are extenuating circumstances. Thus, these new telephone-computer based technologies can enhance school-community communications without adding more teacher time and responsibilities.

A second problem is the cost of the systems. Prices vary according to system size, hardware components, and capabilities. To address this concern, analyze the needs of the school plus the budget cap for the project. Seek a system which can be expanded as funding permits. For example, using a microcomputer-based system can be less expensive than a PBX or Private Branch Exchange system. Also, the choice of software varies in price and capability. A simple package is the *The Complete PC's Complete Answering Machine*. A more expensive package is *The Complete Communicator* with 999 password protected mailboxes. For more information on voice mail, contact any voice mail company, for example, DataQuest, Northern Telecom, Octel, AT&T, or Rolm.

A third problem is a concern for parents who are non-English speaking. Of course, telephone messages can be recorded in several languages and a voice menu selection can provide the non-English speaking parent an avenue for understanding. For example, an introductory message might be multilingual, with directions in the menu selection for a message totally in the caller's language of choice.

The last problem is the quality of voice reproduction. For anyone who has used several systems of audiotex or voice mail, noticeable differences can be "auditorally" observed in the duplication of the human voice. Since voice digitization requires a large amount of computer memory, a process called **compression** condenses the amount of memory space required to store messages. However, speech compression translates into poorer quality of voice reproduction. The more expensive PBX-based voice mail systems have the best "human sound" quality, whereas the PC-based systems have slightly less quality in voice reproduction. An important consideration in audiotex or voicemail system selection is the "human" quality of digitized speech patterns.

Decision-making Guidelines: Conversant Technology

1. Objective: Is there a need to better communicate with teachers, administrators, parents, and the community through a 24-hour electronic service?

2. Integration: How will conversant technology be introduced and used within the educational system?

3. Cost: What system will be used? What will be the cost of installation? Will there be any ongoing costs? From where will the funding come?

4. Location: Where will the system be placed to be used by members of the school system?

5. Security: What assurances will be made that only authorized educators will use the system?

6. Equal Access: Will educators be provided the opportunity to leave messages for parents? Who will record the events, cafeteria menus, or updates of messages to parents? Will you provide students with opportunities to record messages, or will adults only be provided access?

7. Responsibility: Who will be held accountable to select and assist in recording messages? Who will be responsible to see that teachers receive incoming messages daily?

8. Updating: Who will be responsible to consider and make recommendations for enhancements that can be added to the basic system?

9. Training: Who will be instructed to use the system? When and where will the training take place?

10. Voice Quality: What is the acceptable level of digitized vocal patterns in the sending and receiving of computerized messages? Is PC system quality adequate? Should a PBX system be considered?

Summary

This chapter has discussed conversant technology with a focus upon audiotex and voice mail. Currently, both telephone-based systems are gaining popularity in educational settings. System users can more efficiently receive and send messages without the problems of ''telephone tag'' or ''tied-up telephone lines.''

Recommended Periodicals

Educational Technology
Electronic Education
Electronic Learning

PC Week

Tech Trends

Technology & Learning

Telecommunications

T.H.E. Journal

Resources

AT&T EasyLink Services. 55 Corporate Drive, Room 14C54, Bridgewater, NJ 08807. (908) 658-6352.

Bauch, Jerold, Director of the Betty Philips Center for Parenthood Education. Box 81, Dept. BHG, Peabody College of Vanderbilt University, Nashville, TN 37203. (615) 322-8080.

Compu-Call. Associated Computer Technologies, Inc., 3237 NW 27th Ave., Gainesville, FL 32605. (904) 373-4382.

Fulbright Scholarship Program. Council for International Exchange of Scholars, 3007 Tilden St., NW, Suite 5M, Box GPOS, Washington, DC 20008-3009. (202) 686-7877.

Message Line. United Telephone Service, Chambersburg, PA. (717) 245-6144.

U.S. Space and Rocket Center/U.S. SPACE CAMP. 6225 Vectorspace Blvd., Titusville, FL 32780 or One Tranquility Base, Huntsville, AL 35780. (800) 63 SPACE.

References

Elmer-DeWitt, P. (1989, May 22). "Hello! This is voice mail speaking: The new phone systems are fast, efficient, and a pain in the neck." *Time, 133* (21), 98.

Esters, S.D. (1991, February). Dialing up profits. *Black Enterprise, 21,* 37.

Nickens, J.M. & Bauch, J.P. (1989, March). Computer-based communication between schools and homes. In J.H. Collins, N. Estes, W.D. Gattis & D. Walker (Eds.), *Proceedings of the Sixth International Conference on Technology and Education, 1* (pp. 449-452). Orlando, FL: C.E.P. Consultants, Ltd.

Noll, A.M. (1986). *Introduction to telephones and telephone systems.* Norwood, MA: Artech House, Inc.

Northern Telecom. (1991, March). *Using the telephone to expand the classroom: A guide to teacher and classroom telephony.* Publication No. ES 9102.

PC Week. (1991, March 11). Today NetWare, tomorrow the world, *8,* 119.

Publishers Weekly. (1991, March 1). Literary Guild lists 900 book ordering with author contributions, *238* (11), 18.

Seymour, J. (1991, April). PC-based voice mail: The price is right. *Today's Office, 25* (11), 12, 14, & 16.

Sheier, R.L. (1990, October 28). Sign of the times: Microsoft extends 900 lines to BASIC users. *PC Week, 196* (43), 196.

The Economist. (1988, November 11). After the tone .... *313,* (7628), 87.

T.H.E. Journal. (1991, May). New phone system gets educators and parents 'talking,' *18* (10), 48, & 50-52.

Verespe, M.A. (1988, October 2). No more telephone tag. *Industry Week, 238* (19), 68.

PART III

EDUCATIONAL RADIO AND INSTRUCTIONAL TELEVISION

Numerous electronic telecommunication systems are used in education today, creating "electronic pathways" for communication, particularly educational radio and instructional television. Both mass media technologies provide educators and students with opportunities for distance learning experiences. Part III will present both one-way and two-way radio and television technologies that enhance the teaching/learning process.

Chapter Eight presents a currently little used, but readily available technology — educational radio. Discussions introduce aspects of broadcast radio, interactive radio, shortwave radio, and amateur radio.

Chapter Nine covers the definitions and delivery systems of Instructional Television (ITV). Topics such as Telecourses and Teleconferencing are included. The chapter also provides descriptions of audio teleconferencing, audiographics teleconferencing, and videoconferencing.

8   Chapter Eight:
Educational Radio

Educational Radio

Radio is most commonly recognized as the audio transmission of broadcast programming. However, radio can also be an interactive medium, allowing for the exchange of information between participants in different locations. Although not classified as a new technology, radio is a rediscovered resource used in educational settings today. Various types of radio exist, including broadcast radio, interactive radio, shortwave radio, and amateur radio.

What is broadcast radio?

Broadcast radio is direct AM or FM audio transmission of licensed scheduled programming. **AM** or **amplitude modulation** signals travel greater distances than FM, but sound quality is inferior to signals on **FM** or **frequency modulation**. With the advent of new technologies, for example, AM stereo and digital radio signals, broadcast quality will further increase. Even though radios are a common technological resource (there are more than two radios for every man, woman, and child in the U.S.A.), radio is still not commonly used in many classrooms today. Why not?

There are two reasons pertaining to education: (1) the competition of television and (2) the limited number of educational programs. Prior to the advent of TV, radio broadcasting was a popular resource for education in the 1930s and 1940s. Broadcast radio programming included, for example, "School of the Air." Many teachers and students in Ohio, Wisconsin, Kansas, Michigan, Minnesota, New York, Indiana, and Texas integrated broadcast radio programs into their classrooms.

By the late 1940s, television was introduced, which transmitted both audio and video information simultaneously. General popularity for educational radio programming as an educational resource began to decline. Today, broadcast radio is still used in certain geographically-isolated areas especially in less developed countries, where distance learning is a pedagogic necessity.

What is interactive radio?

Traditionally, interactive radio has meant simulated interactivity between the audience and the broadcaster. In educational settings, this technology generally presents radio lessons in a question-and-answer format. For example, after the "radio teacher" asks a question, a short time period is provided for verbal learner response. Although the radio teacher does not actually hear the students' responses, the correct answer is given to the learners via the radio. In this simulated interactive environment, students guided by their own classroom teacher or adult supervisor are kept auditorially alert in the fast-paced drill and practice programming design.

Once used in rural parts of the United States, interactive radio is now popular in countries such as South Africa, Nicaragua, Bolivia, Papua New Guinea, and Kenya, where students are taught subjects including mathematics and English language learning. Various research studies have demonstrated that interactive radio in specific areas is not only successful as a supplemental resource but also as a delivery system for core curriculum. Currently, interactive radio programming in France has added an additional dimension. Radio France Internationale, the Alliance Francaise, and Hachette Publishing Company have collaborated to develop a series of instructional radio broadcasts to correlate with hard copy materials for distance learning.

What are shortwave and amateur radio?

Every educator has used an AM or FM radio — probably daily. You might even own a multiband radio, which allows you to also access shortwave stations. However, very few educators are familiar with shortwave and amateur radios, which can be valuable resource technologies in the classroom.

What is shortwave or world band radio?

Shortwave or **world band radio** is a device on which you receive multilingual transmissions from at least 160 nations and more than 1,000 licensed broadcasting stations worldwide. At least one-half billion people listen to shortwave radio broadcasts once a week. With the advent of portable sets and now even world band radio for your car, more individuals have the opportunity to listen to international broadcasts.

Presently this shortwave technology, whether in a stationary location or in a vehicle, is the best source of reliable English-language newscasts received 24 hours per day.

In appearance, a shortwave radio looks and responds much like a typical AM or FM radio. Both batteries and plug-in varieties are available. Physical size and costs vary. However, unlike the common AM or FM radio with a limited broadcasting range, a shortwave radio can pick up or **receive** programming around the globe. Why is this so?

The variety in broadcast transmissions depends upon the nature of radio waves, which are similar to light waves. Traveling at the speed of light, radio waves are measured in two ways: by **frequency** and **wavelength**. Low frequency signals have a long wavelength and high frequency signals have a short wavelength. What's the difference?

When a medium to long wave signal is sent from a transmitter, it radiates out in all directions over distances similar to a light bulb emitting light. Medium to long wave signals travel along the earth's surface and are called **ground or surface waves**. This type of broadcast transmission signal used by AM and FM radio programming is called **point-to-point communication**. It cannot reach listeners beyond a few hundred miles.

In comparison, high frequency waves for shortwave radio act differently, reaching listeners continents apart. To transmit international broadcasts worldwide, shortwave radio signals are reflected by different layers of the upper atmosphere or the **ionisphere** between 60 to 300 miles from the earth's surface. This reflection process is similar to a mirror reflecting light. The shortwave transmitter concentrates the radio signal into a narrow beam similar to the lightbeam of a flashlight. This radio signal originates at an earth-based station, is sent up to the ionisphere, and then is "bounced back" to another site on earth for the listener to receive. Sometimes, though, the signal is bounced several times from the earth to the ionisphere before reception occurs. These **skips** can cause fade-in, fade-out reception due to a weakened signal.

Although less reliable in program reception and set frequency than medium or long wave transmission, shortwave programming reaches greater distances. Variety in transmission quality, however, depends upon upper atmospheric conditions, time of day, season, geography, and frequency.

For English-speaking listeners, the most popular stations are the BBC, Radio Canada, the Voice of America, Radio Australia, and the English-language service of Deutsche Welle, the German radio network. Of course, broadcasts are available in many languages according to the service. For example, the Voice of America broadcasts in more than 35 languages and estimates its worldwide audience at 130 million listeners.

Since you (like most educators) probably do not own shortwave radio now, but you may want to buy one, it is important to know how to decide which radio is best for you. As with other technologies, there are many models and a very wide price range. You must first decide how and when you plan to use the receiver. Chart 8.1 lists questions and answers that you should ask yourself before making your decision.

Question: Where do I want to use a shortwave radio?

Answer: If you want to use a shortwave radio at home, choose a table-top model. If you want to use it for traveling, choose a lightweight portable model.

Question: How much should I spend for a shortwave radio?

Answer: If you plan to spend a minimum amount ($50.00), choose a simple model with no "extras" (e.g., alarm, headphones, FM band, etc.) If you plan to spend more than $100.00, then your shortwave radio will not only have additional features, but also your reception will probably be better.

Question: Is frequency range coverage important?

Answer: If your answer is yes, then you will be able to receive more stations. A good basic range is 9410 — 15070 kHz. If range is not important to you, you should realize that you will receive fewer stations.

Question: Which station finder style is best?

Answer: There are two styles, Analog and Digital. If you prefer the analog style, which is a dial and pointer, you might find it more difficult to find exact station frequencies. Many shortwave radio users prefer the digital style, which has an easy-to-read numerical frequency display.

Chart 8.1. Questions and Answers About Buying a Shortwave Radio.

What is amateur or ham radio?

Amateur or **ham radio** is global communications. It's a worldwide fraternity of people with common, yet varying, interests, learning about each other and exchanging ideas with every on-the-air contact. Because of this fact, amateur radio has the capability to enhance international relations and understanding as does no other hobby. Where else can you talk to a cattle rancher in Montana, a scientist at the South Pole, or a ham orbiting the earth in a space shuttle? You can do all this without even leaving your school or home, as illustrated in Figure 8.1.

The way communications is accomplished is as interesting as the people of amateur radio. Signals can be sent around the world by using the earth's ionisphere as a reflector. Signals can also be beamed from point to point by mountaintop relay stations. Even orbiting satellites called **OSCARS** (Orbiting Satellites Carrying Amateur Radio) are used to achieve worldwide communication.

Unlike shortwave radios, amateur radios allow you not only to receive information, but also to send information over the airwaves. So, to become a "ham" you need to earn an Amateur Radio License, which is not as difficult as you might think. In the United States, the license has been the traditional way of entering the world of amateur radio.

Figure 8.1. A Ham Radio Operator Using a Computer to Track Satellites. *(Courtesy of the American Radio Relay League)*

You first need to study radio basics. The best source of self-study materials has been developed by the **ARRL** (American Radio Resource League). A manual entitled *Now You're Talking! Discover the World of Ham Radio* incorporates all you need to know to pass the test. (Please see Resources for details.) This test consists of 30 questions covering basic electronic theory and **FCC** (Federal Communications Commission) rules and regulations. In addition, you will be tested on your ability to copy and send Morse Code at five words per minute. Beginning in 1991, as a means of encouraging newcomers, the FCC instituted a Technician Class license. To obtain this license the applicant must pass two written tests consisting of 55 questions, but is not required to demonstrate Morse Code skills. Where can these licensing tests be taken? There is no need to worry about the availability of test sites, since there are at least 6,000 volunteer examiners around the United States alone who can test you. Again the ARRL will be helpful in locating the examiner and testing location nearest you.

What are the advantages of shortwave and amateur radio as compared to AM/FM radio in education?

AM/FM radio equipment is readily available and easy to use. Yet, there are basically three advantages shortwave and amateur radio have over AM/FM radio. First, shortwave radio receives international broadcasts that provide unedited direct links into countries or areas of the world, unlike the limited capacities of AM/FM transmission. This direct global communication is further enhanced through the two-way capabilities of amateur radio. Second, educational and social programming on shortwave and ham radio is offered 24 hours per day unlike many AM/FM radio stations that have limited programming or time restraints. Third, there are no product commercials or advertisements on shortwave and amateur radio, which are common in AM/FM radio programming.

What are specific uses of radio in education?

Broadcast and interactive radio are common elements in a model called The Radio Mathematics Project in Nicaragua. Under the U.S. Agency for International Development, Stanford University conducted a research project to assess the effective and efficient use of educational radio in the field of mathematics. The results of the study were highly positive.

Another example of broadcast radio is a model used in South Africa. The University of South Africa (UNISA) recently developed a large-scale radio research project broadcasting ten instructional programs to students in various geographical locations. Results of the project demonstrated that radio was an excellent means of communication in a third world setting. As a readily available and relatively inexpensive device, radio is a particularly useful information delivery system to a mass audience in diverse locations. A recommendation was made in the final report that both students and teachers should produce and broadcast instructional programming.

Shortwave and amateur radio connect students "live" to places they have studied in geography classes, and at a very reasonable cost. With shortwave, an inexpensive receiver can be purchased for the classroom. Transmissions in languages indigenous to the areas or regions are available (often with English transmission times as well) that present cultural, religious, historic, news, musical, and propaganda-type programming to the listeners. Since the primary purpose of many government-operated shortwave stations is to promote tourism and interest in a particular part of the world, students will be fascinated by the variety of information they receive.

Also, because shortwave and ham radio transmissions are sent according to **Greenwich Mean Time (GMT)** or **Coordinated Universal Time (CTU)**, students learn about world time, map locations, and station distances. By taking these inexpensive electronic field trips, listeners learn to concentrate and to exercise their auditory skills. In addition, language courses are provided on many stations to teach foreign languages to the listeners as well as programming that teaches the listener how to discriminate among different major language groups. But suppose the teacher or student wants only to hear English-language programming? It is easy using shortwave radio.

There are major stations that transmit programs in English. One of the most popular services available since 1932 is *BBC* (British Broadcasting Corporation) *World Service.* *World Service* is heard by more than 30 million English-speaking individuals around the globe. The original program guide for programming was entitled *London Calling*, but as of November 1992, the new *BBC Worldwide* magazine replaces its predecessor. Included in the new program guide are also television broadcast schedules, articles of international interest, and reviews of new books, audio and video cassettes. In addition, this 100-page magazine offers transmission times of regular programs, summaries of series programming, letters to the editor, and frequencies of English-language programming transmitted to nearly 100 countries or areas around the world.

What are some types of programming offered through BBC? For example, the May 1993 issue contains the following samples of information: Monthly radio and television programming schedules, book, video, and audio reviews, special features including "Pirates of the Airwaves" and "Mission to Mars." It is interesting to note that "BBC English" is a teaching program and supplementary magazine containing more than 100 hours of material broadcast to most countries around the world. Beginning to advanced learners can request program note sheets or full coursework through additional cassette tapes simply by contacting BBC World Service. (Please see Resources for more information.)

Two other shortwave stations offer information to further educate shortwave listeners.

They include *Media Network* broadcast by Radio Netherlands and *Shortwave Listener's Digest* from Radio Canada International. (Please see Resources for more details.)

Other English-language services on shortwave radio include Radio Moscow, Voice of America (VOA), Radio Canada International, Deutsche Welle, and Voice of Israel. For multilingual broadcasts United Arab Emirates Radio, Radio Free Europe, and Radio Liberty are popular choices. How would a listener know where to find the frequencies for these services?

There are two sources for information: The first is a free booklet entitled *Time and Frequency Dissemination Services*, which reports geophysical factors such as sunspots which can cause "blackout" or no transmission periods, and others that may affect program transmissions. The second is *Passport to World Band Radio*, which acts as a guide to the 160 listed broadcast locations.

So, while shortwave radio offers a diversified selection of broadcasts, ham radio provides students and teachers direct interaction with licensed operators around the world. Not only do users listen to international transmissions, but also they can partake in interactive dialog. Most ham operators are very altruistic in nature. Not only do they enjoy the camaraderie of international contacts, but also hams are invaluable connections in providing assistance during emergencies (e.g., earthquakes and hurricanes.)

Here are two recent examples of the valuable role hams have played in emergencies. In 1989 two natural disasters occurred in America: One example was the devastating San Francisco area earthquake. When local telephone communications were disconnected, the hams of San Francisco provided transmissions and messages between residents and distressed relatives. The second disaster occurred with Hurricane Hugo. Island nations like the Caribbean and Puerto Rico were devoid of communication to the mainland. Through a network of hams, the shipment of medical supplies, food, and relief necessities was coordinated. More recently, hams were active in the fall of 1992 in communicating with victims and rescue teams during Hurricane Andrew in Florida and Louisiana and Hurricane Iniki in the Hawaiian Islands.

What are some examples of radio usage in education?

While most broadcast radio programming is primarily for entertainment, shortwave radios add current events and cultural elements to enhance learning. Shortwave radio in the USA grew in popularity during the Persian Gulf War as many Americans became aware of the importance of shortwave for current news coverage. Stores were flooded with buyers who wished to listen to the war developments through news stations other than AM/FM radio or cable TV. By the time daily editions of newspapers were published, the news was already part of history. Listeners wanted to hear the most current crises, conditions, successes, and failures the armed forces were facing.

Some classrooms set up learning stations or short wave radio areas that included: (1) a world map to note or pin where transmissions have been received, (2) a log book to record transmission frequencies and reception dates and times, (3) a tape recorder to record interesting programs for use at other times or to play prerecorded tapes from previous programming transmissions, (4) writing material to take notes on incoming programming, and (5) possibly, for reference use, a current issue of *BBC Worldwide* and *Passport to World Band Radio*.

By randomly scanning the frequencies, listeners were able to receive direct transmissions from Iraq or Kuwait and listen to the propaganda being offered in English on some Arab stations. Israeli broadcasts presented their war interpretations and commentary while BBC offered interesting viewpoints from British correspondents. Students or teachers using the short wave radio could receive accounts and opinions of the war situation through many perspectives, bringing an international awareness of world reactions to this unfortunate chapter in global history.

Another example of shortwave usage is illustrated in the case of two Soviet educators who wanted to improve their English while still living in the Soviet Union but hoping one day to visit America. Learning English was a major factor in gaining access as visiting teachers to the USA. Living in an isolated area far from the routes of tourism or English-speaking television programs, their best way to learn the English language was through *BBC World Service* and *Voice of America*, which they did. They became exchange teachers in America.

A final example of an educational use for shortwave is the acquisition of free literature and souvenirs from broadcasting stations. In order to encourage audience listening, many stations will send calendars, brochures, magazines, QSL postcards (similar to ham operator response contact verifications), pins, pennants, stickers, t-shirts, or even coins and stamps if you notify them that you have received their broadcasts. To receive these "freebies," just send information about the following data: station reception location on your radio, topic and time of the broadcast, your address and location. To find the world band station addresses, refer to *Passport to World Band Radio*; and for developing a correct communications form, read *Shortwave Goes to School* for more information. One note of advice: some shortwave and amateur radio responses can take as long as three months, so be patient.

A recent motivation to learn and use amateur radio in the classroom has been created by NASA. In 1990 American astronaut Ron Parise flew aboard Shuttle Mission STS-35 or Space Shuttle Columbia and made contacts with hams and schoolchildren across the USA. He never realized that when he received his Amateur license at the age of 12 that this knowledge and skill would be helpful in his future job training as a college teacher of physics and on through his professional career. One note of advice, though: if you are interested in retransmitting a shuttle message, according to an FCC ruling, you must first receive permission from NASA to do so.

What are some radio problems and solutions?

While the only problem identified in the use of broadcast radio is lack of educational programming, there are at least five problems existing in the use of shortwave and ham radio in the educational setting. These are as follows:

The first problem that exists is the lack of knowledge and awareness of shortwave and amateur radio by most educators. Not a commonly used communications device in classroom settings, these technologies need to be introduced and described to teachers.

If you are one of the many educators who has little or no knowledge about the potentials of shortwave or ham radio, here are two suggestions for you. After some fundamental reading about shortwave and ham radio, visit an electronics store, where a salesperson can demonstrate the product to you. You might be interested in purchasing a multiband radio, which has AM/FM and shortwave capabilities in one set. Try several styles of shortwave and ham radios yourself and develop a basic understanding in the use of these communication devices. You might even be interested in getting a Novice license and become a ham yourself.

Also, if you are interested in ham radio, become a member of the ARRL, and receive a monthly subscription to their publication called *QST*. If you are interested in world band radio, send for free program guides to learn more about broadcasting offerings. An example is *World Harvest Radio Internationale*. (Please see Resources for information.)

The second problem that exists is to determine which radio to purchase. Prior to purchasing a shortwave radio, you should keep several helpful factors in mind: First, decide whether you prefer an analog or digital station finder. Second, it is wise to purchase a device with frequency memory so that you can set a frequency in advance of using your receiver. A minimum memory set should contain at least 36 settings.

What are some popular shortwave radios? Many models include products manufactured by *Sony*, *Radio Shack*, *Panasonic*, and *Magnavox*. The best way to decide on the model that is right for you and your classroom is to try out the products and decide on your budget constraints.

A third problem that exists is the variability of transmission reception. The ideal time for shortwave radio reception is early in the morning, particularly at sunrise, and late at night. Neither is an ideal time for classroom use. There are three alternatives to addressing this problem: (1) Tape the programs to be used later in class, (2) permit the students to sign out the radio for over- night use, and (3) begin a short wave radio club and seek subsidy so that each member might own his/her own shortwave radio to use before and after school hours.

The fourth problem that exists is that shortwave and amateur radio transmissions are strongly influenced not only by daily changes of the sun's position, but by seasonal changes as well. For example, during the spring, with increasing hours of daylight in the Northern hemisphere, higher bands or frequencies, in the range of 15, 17, and 21 MHz, are better. At night, frequencies of 6-11 MHz provide better reception.

The last problem is to recognize and follow the rules for **prohibited transmissions** according to the FCC, which include the following seven items: (1) Acceptance of direct and indirect payment for operating an amateur station, (2) broadcasting, (3) news gathering, (4) transmitting music, (5) aiding criminal activity, (6) transmitting codes and ciphers, and (7) engaging in obscenity, profanity, and indecency.

To ensure that rules are heeded, educators should act as role models as well as advise students regarding these regulatory conditions. Illegal uses of radio transmissions are called **pirating** and **clandestine activities.** On the topic of illegal radio use, shortwave has its share of offenders as well. For example, sometimes you might hear a station broadcasting for donation or "love letter replies," both of which are illegal uses of on-air broadcasting. Scams exist in world band radio as in any field, so be cautious of unauthorized requests.

Decision-making Guidelines: Educational Radio

1. Objective: Why should radio media be used in your setting?

2. Integration: How will radio media be integrated in current or future curriculum areas particularly social studies, science, or language classes?

3. Cost: What will be the initial purchase cost and cost of battery replacements annually?

4. Location: Where will the receiver or ham radio equipment be placed if only one set is purchased?

5. Security: What measures should be taken to ensure that the electronic equipment doesn't "walk away?" What insurance coverage and school policy is formed to permit the loaning of shortwave radios to students?

6. Equal Access: Who will have access to the equipment? How will funding be made available for students who would like to purchase radios?

7. Responsibility: Who will be ultimately responsible for the equipment?

8. Updating: How will funds be budgeted to subscribe annually to shortwave and amateur radio journals and to purchase other support materials?

9. Training: Who will be taught techniques of using shortwave and ham radio? When will this training occur?

Summary

This chapter has discussed a form of communication used in educational settings — the radio. Types of radio media include broadcast radio, interactive radio, shortwave radio (world band radio), and amateur radio (ham radio). While broadcast radio and shortwave radio allow for the radio reception of information only, interactive radio and amateur radio provide the user the opportunity not only to receive data, but also to respond. Amateur radio, unlike the other forms of radio, requires a license for transmission use.

Recommended Periodicals

BBC Worldwide

London Calling

Monitoring Times

Popular Communications

Radio Electronics

Resources

BBC Worldwide. PO Box 76S, Bush House, Strand, London, England WC2B 4PH. (071) 257-2211.

KUSW: Super Power Radio Worldwide. PO Box 7040, Salt Lake City, Utah 84107. (800) 695-8181.

London Calling. PO Box 76S, Bush House, Strand, London, England, WC2B 4PH. (071) 257-2211.

Monitoring Times. PO Box 98, Brasstown, NC 28902. (704) 837-9200.

Passport to World Band Radio. International Broadcasting Services. PO Box 3000, Penn's Park, PA 18943. (215) 794-8252.

QST. The American Relay League, Inc. 225 Main Street, Newington, CT 06111. (203) 666-1541.

Radio Database International. International Broadcast Services. PO Box 3000, Penn's Park, PA 18943. (215) 794-8252.

Sangean America, Inc. 2651 Troy Ave., South Elmont, CA 91733. (800) 232-2929.

World Harvest Radio International. PO Box 12, South Bend, IN 46624. (219) 291-8200.

References

Baig, E.G. (1991, February 4). Tuning in Radio Bagdad: News you can use technology. *U.S. News and World Report, 110* (1), 70.

Barlow, D. (1991, May). Shortwave radio in the classroom. *Education Digest, 56* (9), 10-13.

Barrett, W.P. (1988, August 8). Getting the news abroad. *Forbes, 2,* 104.

Bell, R. (1992, March). Using shortwave receivers to increase global awareness at the elementary level. In N. Estes & M. Thomas (Eds.), *Proceedings of the Ninth International Conference on Technology and Education 3* (pp. 1226-1228). Paris, France: Morgan Printing.

de Saivre, D. (1989, February-March). "Bonne route" ... avec Radio France Internationale ("Have a good trip" ... with Radio France Internationale.) Francaise-dans-le-Monde (223), 50-54. EJ388993.

Heinich, R., Molenda, M., & Russell, J.D. (1993). *Instructional media and the new technologies of instruction* (4th ed.). New York: Macmillan Publishing Company.

Interactive radio instruction: Confronting a crisis in basic education. (1990). Washington, DC: U.S. Agency for International Development and Education Development Center.

Krueter, R.A. (1991, January). Tune in the world: With R-E's EZ shortwave receiver. *Radio Electronics, 62* (1), 6 & 60.

Leinwoll, S. (1988, April). Short wave radio. *Radio Electronics, 59* (3), 78.

Leinwoll, S. (1988, August). Short wave radio: General conditions for July and August. *Radio Electronics, 59* (8), 78-79.

Leinwoll, S. (1988, October). Short wave radio: General conditions and more on fundamentals. *Radio Electronics, 59* (10), 39 & 84.

Leinwoll, S. (1989, February). Short wave radio: Sunrise and sunset affect frequency propagation. *Radio Electronics, 60* (2), 87.

Leinwoll, S. (1989, April). Short wave radio: International frequency coordinating committee. *Radio Electronics, 60* (4), 72-73.

Magne, L. (1990). *Passport to world band radio.* Penn's Park, PA 18943: International Broadcasting Services, Ltd.

Mustoe, M. (1988). *Shortwave goes to school: A teacher's guide to using shortwave in the classroom.* Lake Geneva, WI: Tiare Publications

Radio, the interactive teacher. (1985). Washington, DC: Academy for Educational Development.

Ramirez, A. (1992, August 16). Broadcast blues: Radio stations for sale but buyers hold back. *The New York Times, 141* (4), 7.

Spain, P. (1985, Spring). The fourth r — Interactive radio. *Development Communications Report* No. 49, 13.

Spanswick, S. (1993, February). Receiving loud and clear. *BBC Worldwide,* 4, 68-74.

Stevens, G. (1991, July). Frequency and wavelength: Back to basics. *London Calling, 20* (7), 21.

Stevens, G. (1991, August). International short wave broadcasts: Back to basics. *London Calling, 20* (8), 19.

Stevens, G. (1991, October). Choosing a radio: Back to basics. *London Calling, 20* (10), 17.

van Niekerk, L.J. (1992, July). *The radio UNISA research project.* Paper presented at the Eleventh International Seminar on Staff and Educational Development, University of Glasgow, Glasgow, Scotland.

9

Chapter Nine:
Instructional Television

What is instructional television?

As the predominant audio/visual medium for mass communication today, television as a technology needs little defining. Although many programs offer entertainment, cultural, informative, and educational programming for the general viewing audience, some broadcasts focus on specific educational goals and are directed to educators and students. This form of programming is called **Instructional Television** or **ITV**. As the mainstay of daytime public television stations, ITV provides specific lessons for learners in traditional and non-traditional settings. Some programming, though, requires special equipment and access permission from the broadcasting stations, along with varied delivery systems.

Traditionally television has been a one-way communications technology with the viewer acting as a passive observer. However, new technologies are transforming television into an interactive, two-way communications system. With added electronics, such as telephones and electronic keypads, the student viewer now can interact with the televised instructor.

How is ITV programming delivered to educational settings?

There are seven delivery systems that transmit ITV programming. These systems include: (1) broadcast television including commercial stations and non-commercial or public stations, (2) closed-circuit television, (3) cable television, (4) terrestrial microwave transmission, (5) satellite transmission, (6) common carrier telephone lines, and (7) fiber optics.

What is broadcast television?

Broadcast television is commercial and non-commercial licensed stations that televise free programming. Commercial television is subsidized by advertising and include American network affiliates of ABC, CBS, NBC, and FOX. One of the first instructional efforts made in commercial TV was a show called *Continental Classroom* pioneered by NBC. From 1958 until 1963 daily broadcasts including *Atomic Age Physics* and *Chemistry* provided college credits for viewers.

Although primarily designed for entertainment rather than educational purposes, current commercial TV programming can be adapted to instructional purposes by instructors. Commercial television productions sometimes include contemporary and classic drama, research studies, historical documentaries, and current events programming.

In contrast to commercial television, non-commercial or public television has a non-profit status. Committed to a "free" public audience, the more than 320 American stations are subsidized by federal, state, corporate, and other private funding sources.

Most programming is supplied by a network called the **Public Broadcasting Service** or **PBS**. Generally morning and afternoon broadcasts are dedicated to instructional programming directed towards schools and educational settings, while evening programming is targeted at a general audience. Your Education Services Director at your local PBS station can provide you with exact times and titles of programming. In addition, there is a centralized programming source for elementary and secondary teachers called the *Public Broadcasting System (PBS) Elementary/Secondary Service.*

What is closed-circuit television?

Unlike commercial and public television broadcasting, **closed-circuit television** or **CCTV** is a private, non-licensed delivery system connected by wire. Educators and students can create their own television programming and set schedules without governmental licensing regulations.

Because of direct wiring requirements, transmission distance is usually limited (e.g., between classrooms and a studio). Campus-wide and school-district-wide interconnections can be created, but costs rise as geographic coverage area increases. However, since some educational systems prefer to custom-design and transmit programs without governmental licensing, (e.g. Minnesota and Indiana), some educational institutions are willing to pay the costs to connect schools and colleges hundreds of miles apart.

What is cable television?

Since the first television stations were located in highly populated areas, communities in rural settings had little or no programming reception. This programming access problem was solved by issuing a television license to a television company, erecting a tall common antenna, and transmitting programming to the limited area via cable. Thus, Community Antenna Television (CATV) was developed. Today this television delivery system is more commonly referred to as Cable TV. A wider variety of programming choices on 35 to 50 different channels (soon to be offered up to 500 in some communities!) is offered on Cable TV. Presently, over 70 percent of all schools and colleges subscribe to commercial cable systems.

Unlike other delivery systems, to access cable programming you need to pay an installation charge and a monthly subscription fee. If the subscriber is interested in additional programming, monthly fees are increased. Originally designed for a "narrow-cast" or very specific market, "broad-appeal" programming is now more popular than expected. The primary reason for a wider audience interest is called "aftermarket" programs, particularly recently-released movies.

Cable popularity is due to several reasons: (1) There is a wide variety of programming available from 24-hour news services such as *CNN Headline News* to special educational services such as the *Discovery Channel, The Learning Channel, Channel One*, and *Cable in the Classroom*; (2) improved clarity of video reception; and (3) its potential for interactive programming. Figure 9.1. presents a program from the Discovery Channel called, "The Imagination Machines," which examines the impact of the interactive technology revolution on education.

Unlike commercial or PBS television broadcasts over the airwaves, cable programming needs special cabling connecting your television to the local cable service. Cable program distribution begins at the **head end** or cable company with antenna locations through trunk lines to feeder lines to drop lines. Also, you might need a special box called the **converter box** connected to your television, depending upon the set model.

It is important to realize that those schools or homes with more than one television need more than one cable connection. Also, unlike commercial or public television, cable is not free-of-charge. In many educational settings the installation fee may be waived, but there may be monthly "basic" charges, additional costs for optional programming services or channels, and sometimes service charges, if repair assistance is needed.

Figure 9.1. A Scene from *The Imagination Machines. (Courtesy of Teacher TV and The Discovery Channel)*

What is microwave transmission?

Television signals broadcast in the microwave spectrum of sound (more than 2000 megahertz or MHz) are referred to as microwave transmission. **Terrestrial** or **earth-based microwave transmission** is communicating through the use of **parabolic antennas** called **microwave dishes,** or more simply, **dishes**. These circular electronic devices, commonly placed on roofs and towers of many educational sites, transmit and receive signals within the earth's atmosphere. What this means is that although transmitted programming can extend further than CCTV without direct wiring, the educational reception and transmission location must be in line-of-sight of the transmission tower. If in line-of-sight, the dish can receive or send transmissions. However, if there are physical obstructions like very tall buildings or mountains, microwave frequency signals cannot reach the desired educational locations.

Thirty years ago the Federal Communications Commission (FCC) assisted microwave broadcasting in educational institutions by assigning a specific part of the microwave spectrum (2500-2690 MHz) for only educational purposes. This special assignment is called **Instructional Television Fixed Service (ITFS.)** Currently more than 100 licensed school sites operate several hundred channels on the ITFS spectrum.

ITFS is one of the least expensive private delivery systems for ITV, but there are certain use limitations. For example, while there is no limit to the number of **remote** or distant locations that can receive broadcasts from the ITFS station, interactive responding from remote receiving sites is limited due to the maximum number of six channels. Also, it is important to realize that ITFS is reliant upon terrestrial microwave transmissions and is best suited for flat terrains without tall structures.

What is satellite transmission?

Satellite transmission refers to the use of orbiting devices in space to receive and send signals from earth-based stations. Satellite transmission, also called **satellite television programming** or **Direct Broadcasting by Satellite (DBS)**, began 30 years ago. Presently, commercial, public, and cable delivery systems all use satellite programming for some of their broadcasts.

Each communications satellite (e.g., Spacenet III, Westar V, and Satcom 5) has a special orbit described as **geosynchronous** or **geostationary**, which means the satellite moves at the same speed as the earth's rotation. This technique allows each satellite to stay parallel with a specific area on the earth so that transmission is constant. Because the satellite is orbiting 23,600 miles above the earth surface, the satellite's coverage area or **footprint** could include nearly half of the earth's surface.

Earth-programming stations with dishes transmit signals up to satellites. This process is called **uplinking**. Retransmitted signals are sent to other earth stations. This retransmission process is called **downlinking**. Programming choices are selected on channels called **transponders**. (See Figure 9.2.) If you have a satellite dish receiving transmissions, your earth-station is referred to as **Television Receive-Only** or **TVRO**. Since two concepts, yet to be discussed, called video teleconferencing and telecourses, use both downlinking and uplinking of satellite transmissions, more information on this subject will be provided later in this chapter.

Today it is common to find programming listings in newspapers and television magazines for commercial, non-commercial or cable TV. However, you need to subscribe to a special publication to locate DBS programming. Popular publications include *Satellite Orbit Magazine, Satellite TV Week, STV Magazine, On Sat, Satellite TV Prevue,* and *Satellite Learning List Quarterly.*

An example of programming via satellite generally contains the channel or transponder, specific satellite, time usually on Eastern Standard Time (EST) and dates of program transmission. The term **recurring feeds** is often used and means regularly scheduled programming. Chart 9.1 represents a very small sample of program listings for recurring feeds as published in the *Satellite Educator.*

Figure 9.2. Selecting Transponders for Downlinking.

What are some specifics about satellite systems?

Suppose your school is considering purchasing a satellite television system. What should you know if you are on the planning committee? It is important to have a preliminary understanding of the following terms: First, **Satellite frequency** or transmission signals can be on the C-band, Ku-band, or both. It is important to know the frequency band available to you in your satellite system, since certain programs can only be received through one frequency band location. Second, **specific satellites** carry certain programming schedules. From the many satellites now in orbit, you need to know if you have a **steerable or** a **fixed downlink**. A steerable downlink means that you can adjust your dish direction. In comparison, a **fixed downlink** describes a dish that is only pointed to one specific satellite for programming reception. Be aware that sometimes ''free'' dish equipment from companies will allow transmissions from the company's satellite only. Third, **scrambling** is a method used to ''encode'' many program offerings so that only paid subscribers can ''decode'' and access the transmissions clearly.

Satellite/ Transponder	Time (EST)	Weekday (Monday — Friday) Program
F4/22	8:30 AM	America's Disability Channel
S1/05	10:30 AM	Today's Japan
F1/18	2:10 PM	Contemporary Applied Math
F1/22	5:20 PM	Russian II
S3/11	6:30 PM	CNN (Spanish)

Chart 9.1. Sample of Recurring Feeds for Satellite Programming.

What are common-carrier telephone lines?

A typical electronic device added to television delivery systems that adds interactivity to ITV is the telephone. Common-carrier telephone lines transfer communication data through combinations of copper wire in cables, microwave technology, and fiber optics. Schools can connect sites for ITV by entering into fee- or tariff-based agreements with telephone companies. Costs of agreements vary based on the requested services. Necessary equipment might have to be purchased and installed, as well as a monthly service charge established. Telephone company transmission links can be very expensive. There are three basic ways to conserve on spending: (1) establish a cooperative ITV venture with your school and a telephone company, (2) consider telephone trunk line transmission using a **codec** or code/decode electronic device rather than fiber optic transmission, and (3) compare the price of a leased line versus a pay per minute line.

What are fiber optic cable systems?

The newest advance in cable TV technology is fiber optic cabling. This cabling can transmit television, telephone, and computer data over glass fibers. This new technology converts electrical signals (which are often hindered by electromagnetic interference) into light waves. Light waves can provide more, higher quality television channels, with the potential to transmit voice and data transmissions, which greatly enhances ITV communication. However, as is the case with most new technologies, the cost is high for fiber optic cabling systems. With the eventual decrease in price, it will become a more popular delivery system based on its quality performance and integrated communications capabilities.

What is teleconferencing?

Teleconferencing is the interactive electronic transmission method for real-time, two-way conversations among groups of individuals in different geographical locations. In education this communications system is frequently used in courses for students and staff development for teachers called **distance learning**. There are generally three types of teleconferencing: **audio teleconferencing**, **audiographic teleconferencing**, and **video teleconferencing**.

What is audio teleconferencing?

The least expensive and oldest form of teleconferencing is audio teleconferencing, sometimes simply referred to as audioconferencing. Audioconferencing is a non-visual communications format in which participants can hear, but not see, each other. To communicate you will need a common dial-up telephone line, speakerphones, and directional microphones. An audioconference can be as simple as a conference-call on a telephone line. In contrast, you might want to connect up to 40 participants who can talk to each other at more than three locations. In this case, you will need a more complicated audioconferencing system. In addition to the basic equipment, you will need to include an audio telephone bridge. This bridge is an electronic system, either provided by a telephone company or owned by a school system, that adjusts the audio volume and connects multiple telephones at participating locations.

What is audiographics teleconferencing?

To enhance the non-visual limitations of audioconferencing, audiographics teleconferencing adds the perspective of two-way static image transmission. Usually limited to two interactive locations, audiographics teleconferencing requires at least one telephone line, speakerphones, and a pair of fax machines — one at each participating site. To avoid interruptions and downtime in the audio transmission of information, a second telephone line for fax machines should be added. With this teleconferencing system, hard copy black and white or color illustrations, charts, and photographs can be shared by participants in both locations.

Two new developments are predicted to improve audio teleconferencing, which are: (1) future fax machines will create mailing lists to send rapid faxes to multiple sites, thus increasing the number of remote locations participating in audiographics teleconferences; and (2) video capture cards will be added to microcomputers using color display systems. Via a high-speed modem or fax-modem, these images can be shared by all participants through microcomputers.

What is video teleconferencing?

The most expensive and sophisticated teleconferencing system is video teleconferencing, or simply, videoconferencing. Ideally, full-motion video and audio transmissions are exchanged at various participating sites via a satellite, cable, or microwave network.

More commonly used in education sites today is the one-way television or video and two-way audio videoconferencing system. Besides audio feedback from students by telephone or speakerphone, there is another system in use today. It is sometimes called an electronic non-verbal system, in which students use response keypads to elicit yes-no answers or send more complex alphanumeric messages to the instructor. Regardless of response alternative, the primary reason for selecting the one-way video, two-way audio design is its lower price. In comparison, two-way television and two-way audio is the most desirable videoconferencing system, but the cost of this full video and audio system is beyond most education budgets at the present time.

What do you need to set up a videoconferencing system?

To set up a videoconferencing system in your school, you might want to use one of the oldest and most common delivery techniques, which is satellite videoconferencing. To do so, you will need uplinking and downlinking equipment. If you plan to send transmission signals to a satellite, you will need uplinking hardware. To receive signals from a satellite, you need downlinking hardware. Of course, both transmissions need a satellite dish, which is commonly placed on the roof of a building. (See Figure 9.3.)

Creating an uplink connection is much more expensive. If you are transmitting programming, you need a sound-proof, acoustically designed classroom referred to as a studio classroom, lighting, microphones, audio teleconferencing components, at least one television camera, and an uplink transmitter. In addition, you will need trained professionals and technicians to run the system smoothly. Ideally, participants and educators need training sessions to learn to effectively teach and discuss in this new environment.

In comparison, creating a downlink connection is less expensive. Primary costs include a satellite dish located within the range of satellite transmissions with its related signal-receiving electronics and a professional technician.

Because of economic factors, many schools select only to downlink satellite programming. By adding audio teleconferencing components, students and teachers can actively participate in one of the many videoconferencing programs via satellite. For example, recent programming included "Telecommunica-

Figure 9.3. Satellite Dish Atop a Classroom Building at Trenton State College.

tions: Bringing the World into the Classroom" and "Space Age School Special with Sally Ride." sponsored by PBS Elementary/Secondary School Service. Other popular educational satellite services include the *Discovery Channel*, *Channel One*, and *SCOLA*.

What are telecourses?

Telecourses are class sessions where students and teachers are not in the traditional school classroom settings but are present in at least two different locations. Telecourses are the backbone of a rapidly growing alternative approach to education called **distance learning**. Historically distance learning courses were delivered through radio or home mail correspondence. Currently in some parts of the world, courses are still delivered via radio, but most commonly telecourses are delivered through television and teleconferencing systems.

Ideally, telecourses are two-way audio and two-way video formats. However, due to cost constraints, many telecourses are offered as two-way audio and one-way video sessions. Other means of teleconferencing are also used, including audioconferencing and audiographics teleconferencing to teach learners in diverse locations. In addition, some telecourses are composed of primarily videotaped programming televised at scheduled intervals.

What are educational applications of telecourses?

As previously mentioned, staff development inservice training and recertification programming are available via telecourses. While some viewers watch instructional programs on a voluntary basis, others prefer to earn college credits. Secondary and postsecondary viewers can earn college credits by viewing a sequence of specific programs on a particular subject or course. Often students are required to read accompanying textbooks, study guides, learning exercises, and other academic resources to supplement the learning experience. In addition, some courses use fax, mail, electronic mail, in-person tutors, and instructors/advisors to provide more opportunities for interaction.

If you are interested in earning college credits through a telecourse, contact an educational institution that provides this alternative approach to traditional education. You can find information through many public television stations, your local college or university, or through your reference or media librarian. Depending on your location and delivery system access, there are generally many telecourses offered each semester. Two popular telecourses that might be of interest to you are *Focus on Society* and *Understanding Human Behavior*.

In addition, some school systems lacking qualified specialist teachers to instruct particular required courses (e.g., Russian, Japanese) use satellite downlink programs to meet their needs. When courses are under contract to be delivered to educational sites, they are referred to as **contract courses**.

How do you videotape a television program?

Sometimes an ITV program, telecourse, or teleconference is inconvenient or impossible for you to view during its scheduled time. So, you decide to videotape it. First of all, be certain that you are permitted to videotape a program rather than purchase or rent it. It is wise to take copyright restrictions seriously. To help educators with legal videotaping rules and regulations, PBS offers a guide entitled *Copyright: Staying within the Law* by Tom Flavell.

Next, you must follow the written directions included with your VCR for videotaping. Generic directions applicable to most VCR players are displayed in Chart 9.2.

---

1. Be certain that you have a VCR tape with sufficient time to record the program. Tapes are generally VHS 1/2-inch format, 30-160 minutes at standard speed. Label them immediately so that you do not forget what show you are taping. Include the title of the program, length of time needed to view the program, and the program date.

2. Read the proper use and longer wear explanations enclosed in your VCR tape package. For example, avoid storing the tapes in excessively hot, dusty, or strong magnetic field areas. Also, always place the cassettes in their sleeves and store in upright or vertical position.

3. Before you begin to actually program, review the control panel of your VCR player with the illustrations in your manual. Be able to locate the various controls or buttons discussed in the directions.

4. Be certain to check in a program listing the exact length of the program to be taped. Set the time to begin taping and end taping.

5. Before taping your intended program, try setting your VCR player to record a sample program. (Don't forget to install the tape cassette!) Check your results.

Chart 9.2. Generic Directions for Videotaping Television Programming.

If VCR taping is still a mystery to you (as it is to many teachers), one electronic option for you to consider is called *VCR PLUS+*. This small hand-held, remote device allows you to record a television program in one short step. To use this product you must use a TV listings schedule with special coded programs. Beside each program listing there is a three to seven digit number which you must type into the keypad to identify the show you want to record.

What are the advantages of ITV in an educational setting?

There are six primary advantages of instructional television, whether one-way or two-way transmission: First, most learners are "seasoned TV viewers" prior to attending formal education classes. Watching television is a popular activity and students easily adapt to this alternative delivery system in education. Studies have revealed that students:

> ... comprehend more of what they see on television than what they read or hear
> on the radio — and they remember it longer (Adams *et al.*, 1990).

Second, as the Cable Alliance for Education (CAFE) encouraged the use of educational programs in schools, teachers, too, seeing the potential value of television in the classrooms, were seeking more educational programming to enhance their curricula.

Third, not only can more varied courses be offered at the college level to a more diverse student population at off-campus sites, but also to elementary and high school students in very rural or isolated parts of the country.

Fourth, homebound students or teachers who cannot physically attend classes or discussions can participate from remote locations provided they have the necessary electronic equipment.

Fifth, ITV can provide real-time presentations of current events and "live" worldwide audio-visual learning experiences.

Sixth, teachers geographically dispersed can electronically share ideas and concerns with other educators without leaving their local schools, thus eliminating travel time and commuting costs.

What are some specific uses of television in education?

The following examples are just a few of the many specific uses of instructional television:

• The Boston Public Schools introduced a *Math for the 90's* professional development program via cable television. Through a "distance learning" approach elementary and middle school teachers received four hours of televised math, during which time a two-way audio telephone connection permitted opportunities for questions and commentary from remote sites. At the completion of each four-hour session, a "live" teacher-leader at each location provided more hands-on opportunities for the inservice participants.

• The Eastern Iowa Community College District for the past five years has used the *TIE System* for two-way interactive telecommunication among its three colleges. All campus sites are connected via a microwave link providing both audio and visual contact. This system transmits not only credit and non-credit college courses, but also council, faculty, and committee meetings among distant counterparts.

• The *Kids Interactive Telecommunications Experience by Satellite* or *KITES* was created in 1988 at the University of Lowell College of Education in cooperation with Digital Equipment Corporation and the Massachusetts Corporation for Educational Telecommunications. During one audio-video teleconferencing program, an elementary school class from Massachusetts discussed global issues and concerns with students in Germany.

• *NASA Select* is NASA's television service available to teachers. Daily broadcasts include educational and informational programs (which may be videotaped by the viewer). Programming is accessible either through local cable network or by microwave dish.

• *NASA Satellite Videoconferencing for Educators* program. In 1987, NASA Educational Affairs began a videoconferencing series directed to elementary and secondary educators entitled "Update for Teachers." Each one-hour program includes two-way audio and one-way video transmission. Future plans for this system include a Teacher-in-Space lesson from the Shuttle with students asking questions to the orbiting "teacher" and interactive videoconferencing from the proposed Space Station Freedom.

• The Oregon Health Sciences University School of Nursing provides a Bachelor's Degree in Nursing to students who live in the rural areas of Oregon. Lecture courses are transmitted via a two-way audio/video network while the clinical component of the degree program takes place in each student's community.

• *The Satellite Educational Resources Consortium (SERC)* offers transmitted "live" instruction to 23 states. A 1989 U.S. Department of Education Star Schools grant provided funding for satellite receivers, televisions, and telephone lines to participating locations. Courses such as Japanese, Russian, math, and sciences were provided to students in remote or small schools that did not have the facilities to directly offer these courses in traditional classroom settings.

• *SUNSTAR* is a network of satellite transmission and receiving sites in Florida. This network consists of 34 downlink sites as well as a C-band uplink and two television stations. During its initial year of operation in 1989-1990, SUNSTAR offered teleconferences on topics such as AIDS, child abuse, and computer training. Since 1990 the network has connected schools and universities in Florida with students in Canada, South and Central America, and Europe.

• *Teacher TV* or *TTV* is a new cable program co-sponsored by The Learning Channel and the National Education Association. Directed specifically to innovative teachers, programming concepts present practical information, innovative resources, and teaching techniques concerning such topics as business and education, technology in the classroom, peer coaching, intergenerational learning, and teacher preparation. Figure 9.4 illustrates an example of a program. Produced in cooperation with the National Education Association, Teacher TV focuses on educators in their classrooms all over the United States.

• *Ti-In Network, Inc.* is a Texas-based instructional system using satellite transmission from the GTE Spacenet II satellite. Venture capital and a federal grant of $6.5 million financed its creation in 1985. To join the network, an annual subscription fee is required plus the start-up costs for the equipment and installation. Each subscribing school receives the broadcast signal on a satellite dish, and the programming is viewed through a television monitor. Two-way audio is available but actual interaction is limited as the number of participants increases. Courses such as Trigonometry, Research and Technical Writing, and Computer Math are available for students. Not only for students, the Ti-In Network also provides staff development programs such as Introduction to

Figure 9.4. *Technology in the Classroom*, a Teacher TV program. *(Courtesy of the Learning Channel)*

Models of Teaching, Writing Across the Curriculum, and Teacher Evaluation: Pre-observation, Observation, and Scripting.

• *The Whittle Educational Network*, developed by Whittle Communications, has three programming components. "Channel One" is a daily 12-minute advertiser-supported news broadcast; "The Classroom Channel" offers schools with 250 hours of non-commercial educational programming annually; and "The Educators' Channel" provides programming relevant to teachers.

What are some ITV problems and solutions?

There are several problems cited by educators. The following seven concerns are most frequently identified and addressed: First, the initial setting up of an educational or instructional delivery system, particularly a satellite system with both uplink and downlink capabilities, can be expensive. Educators commonly seek federal grants or develop funding ventures with resources from industry or telecommunication companies. Another commonly used solution is the formation of an educational consortium in which participating schools share costs and facilities.

Second, "distance learning" can be viewed as a threatening concept to some educators. More students in remote classrooms need fewer instructors. However, many teachers are learning to accept this alternative delivery system of instruction, especially for the physically-challenged, mature, or full-time employed. Distance learning is, indeed, servicing a more diverse population. To minimize the "threat" of machines-taking-teachers'-jobs, contracts are being written and approved by educational associations to limit the rebroadcasting of videotaped courses.

Third, some ITV programming or downlinked teleconferencing does not match the teacher's schedule. So, some teachers prefer to videotape ITV programming to view at teacher-selected time periods rather than alter their schedules to fit the live cable or satellite broadcasts. Although some networks permit taping, such as CNN Newsroom, others require special permission.

Fourth, many educators see instructional or educational television as passive rather than active learning experiences. To counteract this opinion, lesson plan ideas are available from many networks that encourage the use of a broadcast as a "jumping-off place" for class discussions, a motivational strategy in introducing a new concept or fact base in a unit, lesson, or a classroom learning station, or as a summary of a previously taught concept. Teachers themselves create uses for television broadcasts by integrating the program content within their curriculum planning.

Fifth, as ITV programming increases, questions arise as to the effectiveness of this new television-based teaching methodology. However, Diane Morehouse (1986) in *Minnesota Technology Program Findings* has demonstrated that the level of student interaction is similar in both IATV classes and traditional, on-site classes. She also found that achievement seems not to be based on the medium of instruction, but, in fact, is a reflection of the student group and/or the quality of the teaching methods.

Sixth, educators need to identify a successful method for testing and material distribution to students. Some ITV educational systems deliver materials by courier, fax, or electronic mail.

Seventh, some ITV participants sense a lack of personal student-teacher or human face-to-face contact. To address this concern some schools arrange for the on-screen teacher to visit the sites once a week; others organize conferences with instructors and parents of younger students. In addition, some educational consortia address impersonalization by limiting the number of enrolled students and remote sites receiving programming.

Decision-making Guidelines: Instructional Television

1. Objective: Why should ITV (including telecourses and teleconferencing) be used? How will the curriculum be enhanced?

2. Integration: Should class schedules be changed to meet broadcast schedules, or should videotaped programs be used? Is permission needed to tape network broadcasts?

3. Cost: How much funding is provided in the budget for ITV? If funding does not permit closed circuit, cable, microwave transmissions, or satellite programming, can commercial and public broadcasts be available to teachers?

4. Location: Will every classroom have access to at least one television? If not, where will the on-loan equipment be stored?

5. Security: Who will be designated as responsible for the delivery system equipment, where will the electronics be placed, and how will they be secured?

6. Equal Access: If one television per classroom is not practical, how will sharing the equipment be determined? On a first-come-first-serve basis, rotational, or by advanced planning submission requests?

7. Updating: Who will be responsible to recommend new equipment pieces or a more costly delivery system network? Who will seek funding for such an effort?

8. Training: How will teachers be taught to use the new delivery systems? Will there be release time or stipends for training sessions?

Summary

Television is the most popular audio-visual educational technology today. This chapter presented one-way and two-way or bi-directional television commonly referred to as Instructional Television (ITV). Delivery systems were discussed. Additional topics highlighted in this chapter were telecourses and teleconferencing.

Recommended Periodicals

American Journal of Distance Education
Educational Horizons
Educational Technology
Electronic Learning
Electronic Media
Electronics
Journal of Broadcasting and Electronic Media
Media and Methods
Orbit
Popular Communications
Satellite Dish Magazine
Satellite Educator
Satellite Times
Satellite TV
Satellite TV News
STV Magazine
Technology & Learning
Tech Trends
TVRO Technology
TV Satellite Videoworld
VHF Communications

Resources

ACTV, Inc. 1270 Avenue of the Americas, New York, NY 10020. (212) 262-2570.

Agency for Instructional Technology (AIT). PO Box A, Bloomington, IN 47402. (800) 457-4509.

Association for Educational Communications and Technology (AECT). 1025 Vermont Ave., Suite 820, NW Washington, DC 20005. (202) 347-7834.

AT&T Learning Network. PO Box 4012, Bridgewater, NJ 08807. (800) 367-7225 Ext. 4158.

C-SPAN in the Classroom. 400 N. Capitol Street, NW Washington, DC 20001. (800) 523-7586.

Cable News Network. Turner Educational Services, 1 CNN Center, Atlanta, GA. (800) 344-6219.

Children's Television Workshop. 1 Lincoln Plaza, New York, NY 10023. (212) 595-3456.

Copyright: Staying within the Law: A Resource Guide for Educators. PBS E/SS, 1320 Braddock Place, Alexandria, VA 22314-1698. Fax (703) 739-8495.

Corporation for Public Broadcasting (CPB). 901 E. St., NW Washington, DC 20036. (202) 879-9600.

The Discovery Channel. 7700 Wisconsin Avenue, Bethesda, MD 20814-3522. (301) 986-1999.

Educational Resources Center. Thirteen/WNET, 356 West 58th Street, New York, NY 10019. (212) 560-6613.

International Television Association (ITVA). 6311 N. O'Connor Rd., Suite 230 LB-51, Irving, TX 75039. (214) 869-1112.

KITES (Kids Interactive Telecommunications Experience by Satellite). Dr. John LeBaron, University of Lowell College of Education, One University Ave., Lowell, MA 01854. (508) 934-4621.

The Learning Channel. 7700 Wisconsin Ave., Bethesda, MD 20814-3522. (800) LEARNER.

Learning Link. LinkNet, 1400 E. Touhy Ave., Suite 260, Des Plaines, IL 60018. (708) 930-8700.

Mind Extension University. 9697 East Mineral Ave., Englewood, CO 80112. (800) 777-6463.

NASA Select. NASA: National Aeronautics and Space Administration, Washington, DC 20546. (202) 358-1533.

National Distance Learning Center. Owensboro Community College, 4800 New Hartford Rd., Owensboro, KY 42303. (502) 686-4556.

Public Broadcasting System. PBS Elementary/ Secondary Service or Adult Learning Satellite Service, 1320 Braddock Place, Alexandria, VA 22314. (703) 739-5038.

Satellite Educational Resources Consortium (SERC). Marketing Director, PO Box 5000, Columbia, SC 29250. (800) 476-5001.

Satellite Educator. Satellite TV Week, PO Box 308, Fortuna, CA 95540. (707) 725-6951.

Sony Corporation of America. Conference & Satellite Systems Business and Professional Group, 3 Paragon Dr., Montvale, NJ 07645. (201) 930-7194.

Square One: Children's Television Workshop. School Services, Dept. PMM 191, One Lincoln Plaza, New York, NY 10023. (212) 595-3456.

Teacher TV. The Learning Channel, 7700 Wisconsin Ave., Bethesda, MD 20814-3522. (212) 475-8030.

Television Associates, Inc. 2410 Charleston Rd., Mountain View, CA 94043. (415) 967-6040.

TI-IN Network. 100 Central Parkway North, Suite 190, San Antonio, TX 78232. (800) 999-8446.

VCR Plus+. Gemstar Development Corporation. 709 E. Colorado Blvd., Suite 221, Pasadena, CA 91101. (800) 432-1VCR.

Videoconferencing Systems, Inc. 5801 Goshen Springs Rd., Norcross, GA 30071. (404) 242-7566.

The Weather Channel. 2600 Cumberland Parkway, Atlanta, GA 30339. (404) 434-6800.

The Whittle Educational Network. 706 Walnut St., Knoxville, TN 37902. (800) 445-2619.

References

Adams, D., Carlson, H., & Hamm, M. (1990). *Cooperative learning and educational media: Collaborating with technology and each other.* Englewood Cliffs, NJ: Educational Technology Publications, Inc.

Barker, B. *et al.* (1989). Broadening the definition of distance education in light of the new telecommunications technologies. *American Journal of Distance Education, 15* (4) 20-29.

Bates, B.J. & Siczo DeJong, A. (1991, Spring). Channel diversity in cable television. *Journal of Broadcasting and Electronic Media, 35* (2), 159-166.

Baylin, F. & Gale, B. (1986). *Satellites today: The guide to satellite television* (2nd ed.). Indianapolis, IN: Howard W. Sams & Co.

Bronk, R. (1992, March). The Whittle Educational Network: Building a technological highway. In N. Estes & M. Thomas (Eds.), *Proceedings of the Ninth International Conference on Technology and Education, 1* (pp. 70-71). Paris, France: Morgan Printing.

Chaffin, E. (1991, March). Classroom TV: What's available to schools: A comprehensive listing of educational programs and services offered by cable channels, PBS, and other stations. *Electronic Learning* (10), 16.

Chung, J. (1991, January). Televised teaching effectiveness: Two case studies. *Educational Technology, 31* (1), 41-47.

Conway, C.F. (1991, May). Math for the 90's: Teletraining project. In G. McKye & D. Trueman (Eds.), *Proceedings of the Twelfth Educational Computing Organization of Ontario Conference and the Eighth International Conference on Technology and Education* (p. 376). Toronto, Ontario, Canada: C.G.F. Executive Services.

Cyrs, T.E. & Smith, F.A. (1990). *Teleclass teaching: A resource guide* (2nd ed.). Las Cruces, NM: Center for Educational Development, New Mexico State University.

Descy, D.E. (1991). Two-way interactive television in Minnesota: The KIDS network. *Tech Trends, 36* (1) 44-48.

Digital learning using digital fiber optics; Applications, technologies, and benefits. (1991, February). Publication Number: ES 9101, Northern Telecom.

Freidel, J. & Kabat, E.J. (1991, May). Enhancing learning through teacher education and technology. In G. McKye & D. Trueman (Eds.), *Proceedings of the Twelfth Educational Computing Organization of Ontario Conference and the Eighth International Conference on Technology and Education* (p. 377). Toronto, Ontario, Canada: C.G.F. Executive Services.

Gilbert, J.K., Temple, A., & Underwood, C. (Eds.). (1991). *Satellite technology in education.* New York: Routledge.

Grant, A. & Waterman, D. (1991, Spring). Cable television as an aftermarket. *Journal of Broadcasting and Electronic Media, 35* (2), 179-187.

Gudat, S. (1988, March). Satellite network helps keep rural schools open. *Phi Delta Kappan, 69* (7), 533-534.

Heinich, R., Molenda, M., & Russell, J.D. (1993). *Instructional media and the new technologies of instruction* (4th ed.). New York: Macmillan Publishing Company.

Holmsberg, B. (1989). *Theory and practice of distance education.* New York: Routledge.

Johansen, J.H., Collins, H.W., & Johnson, J.A. (1990). *American education: An introduction to teaching.* Dubuque, IO: Wm. C. Brown Publishers.

Johnson, L.N. & Tully, S.M. (1989). *Interactive television: Progress and Potential.* Bloomington, IN: Phi Delta Kappa Educational Foundation.

Kamil, B.L. (1991, May/June). Comprehensive teaching with cable television. *Media and Methods, 27* (5), 25-26.

Keegan, D. (1990). *Foundations of distance education* (2nd ed.). New York: Routledge.

Kitchen, K. & Kitchen, W. (1988). Two-way interactive television for distance learning: A primer. *Technology Leadership Network Special Report.* Alexandria, VA: National School Board Association.

Klivans, J.D. (1991). *Teaching at a distance over interactive television*: Augusta, ME: University of Maine.

LeBaron, J. (1989, September). KITES: Kids interactive telecommunications experience by satellite. In J. LeBaron (Chair), Symposium conducted at the *Third International Conference of Interactive Technology and Telecommunications*, University of Maine.

Lochte, R. (1993). *Interactive television and instruction: A guide to technology, technique, facilities design, and classroom management*. Englewood Cliffs, NJ: Educational Technology Publications, Inc.

Long, M. & Keating, J. (1988). *The world of satellite TV* (5th ed.). Winter Beach, FL: Mark Long Enterprises, Inc.

McFarland, M. (1992, March.) Distance learning using an educational network. In N. Estes and M. Thomas (Eds.), *Proceedings of the Ninth International Conference on Technology and Education 3* (pp. 1155-1156). Paris, France: Morgan Printing.

Matheny, J.F., Larsen, E.J., & Clower, K. (1990, March). SUNSTAR: Florida's network of satellite transmission and receiving. In N. Estes, J. Heene, & D. Leclerqc (Eds.), *Proceedings of the Seventh International Conference on Technology and Education 1* (pp.72-73). Brussels, Belgium: CEP Consultants, Ltd.

Morehouse, D. (1986). *Minnesota Technology Program Findings*. St. Paul, MN: Minnesota State Department of Education.

Nixon, W.D. (1990, March). NASA distance learning projects for education. In N. Estes, J. Heene, & D. Leclerqc (Eds.), *Proceedings of the Seventh International Conference on Technology and Education 1*, (pp. 74-76). Brussels, Belgium: C.E.P. Consultants, Ltd.

Ostendorf, V.A. (1990, November/December). Shopping for a satellite curriculum. *Media and Methods, 27* (2), 103 & 138.

Pinsel, J.K. (1988). *Distance learning: A summary of telecommunication efforts involving education service agencies and others*. Arlington, VA: American Association of Educational Service Agencies.

Pollard, C. & Pollard, R. (1992, March). Technologically-mediated instruction systems: Teaching alternatives. In N. Estes, & M. Thomas (Eds.), *Proceedings of the Ninth International Conference on Technology and Education, 2* (pp. 905-907). Paris, France: Morgan Printing.

Shandle, J. (1989, October). Videoteleconferencing breaks into the open. *Electronics, 62,* 87-89.

Solomon, G. (1991, March). Distance learning: A Georgia high school receives live televised instruction via satellite — and it works. *Electronic Learning, 10,* 12.

Spring, J. (1990). *The American School 1642-1990*. White Plains, NY: Longman.

Study of school uses of television and video, 1990-1991 school year. (1992). Washington, DC: Corporation for Public Broadcasting.

Tiene, D. (1993, May). Channel One: Good or bad news for our schools. *Educational Leadership, 50* (8), 46-51.

Verduin, J.R. & Clark, T.A. (1991). *Distance education: The foundations of effective practice*. San Francisco: Jossey-Bass.

Wall, M. (1986, March). Technological options for rural schools. *Educational Leadership, 43* (6), 50-52.

Walters, S.C. (1991, May/June). Satellite education: First generation and beyond. *Media and Methods, 27* (5), 24-25.

Weigel, E. (Ed.). (1992, Spring). Remember: NASA teacher tools continually available! *Educational Horizons, 1* (2), 12.

Willis, B. (1993). *Distance education: A practical guide.* Englewood Cliffs, NJ: Educational Technology Publications, Inc.

Willis, B. (Ed.). (1994). *Distance education: Strategies and tools.* Englewood Cliffs, NJ: Educational Technology Publications, Inc.

Zigerell, J. (1991). *The uses of television in American higher education.* New York: Praeger.

PART IV

NEW TECHNOLOGIES FOR INSTRUCTION

New technologies for instruction are finding their way into educational settings. Teachers and students are being empowered by new electronic resources, which enhance presentations, provide more individualized learning, and access massive sources of sound and text data, plus "image banks" of thousands of maps and fine art collections. With the deluge of new technologies, it is important not only to know what exists, but also to have a basic understanding of how they are used in the classroom.

While *microcomputers* were new to the 1980s, *multimedia* is the wave of the 1990s. Multimedia is an umbrella concept describing multisensory technology incorporating various combinations of text, animation, sound, video, and graphics. Within each multimedia system, a microcomputer provides the opportunity for user interaction and decision-making. Part IV describes technologies used in schools today, and presents some new technologies which may influence the educational settings of tomorrow.

Chapter Ten presents Compact Disc Technology. The chapter covers CDs and CD-ROMs and introduces the newest innovations, which are WORM, rewritable optical discs, CD-I, CDTV, DVI, QuickTime, VIS, Photo CD, and CD + MIDI.

Chapter Eleven explores Videodisc Technology. The various levels of videodisc interactions and formats are explained.

Chapter Twelve introduces Desktop Computer Music with an emphasis on Musical Instrument Digital Interface or MIDI.

Chapter Thirteen discusses Multimedia and Hypermedia. Included is a preview of some educational technologies of tomorrow.

10 Chapter Ten: Compact Disc Technology

What is compact disc technology?

Developed for greater storage capacity and clarity of sound reproduction, **Compact Disc** or **CD technology** is replacing the traditional analog encoding of sound (used on records or videotape cassettes) with a digital or numerical representation. Through the concentrated energy of a beam of laser light, information is placed in tiny pits onto the sensitive layer of a thin metal master disc surface. To hear the digitized sound, a laser and photodetector generate the electrical signals which ultimately drive the loudspeakers. This process is called simply **optical data storage**. There are three main reasons why optical discs are increasing in popularity: (1) durability, since grease, dirt, fingerprints, and scratches are minimized by a clear coating protecting the disc surface; (2) high capacity of data storage since, for example, graphic data stored on one CD is equivalent to data stored on 550 floppy disks; and (3) enhanced sound clarity for music CDs.

What are CDs and CD-ROMs?

CDs and CD-ROMs are the most common compact disc technologies in education today. Although they are both CD technologies, there are two major differences between them. First, CD (sometimes referred to as CD-A or CD-Audio) stores and plays music. In comparison, CD-ROM (or Compact Disc-Read Only Memory) stores and plays primarily text and graphic images. Second, CDs do not need to be used with computers, but CD-ROMS do.

The CD is recognized as a high-fidelity audio disc. First introduced in 1982, this approximately five-inch diameter storage medium for music and sound is now rapidly replacing long-playing records for three reasons: (1) digitally encoded and stored music has very little added sound distortion; (2) a beam of light which does not scratch the surface of the disc replaces the phonographic needle; and (3) one CD can hold at least 60 minutes of music. (See Figure 10.1 for an illustration of a CD.)

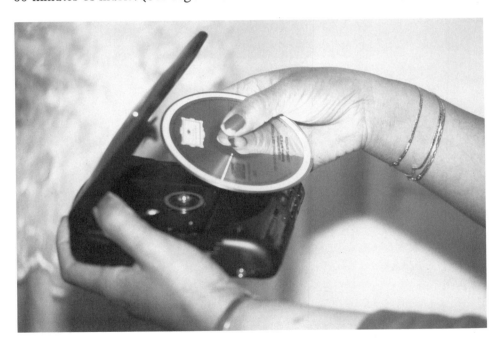

Figure 10.1. CD and its Player.

Shortly after the introduction of the audio CD, a spin-off of the compact disc technology was easily and inexpensively adapted for use in microcomputer systems: **CD-ROM or Compact Disc-Read Only Memory** provided a massive storage medium for text and graphics (more than one-half billion characters of information) are read by CD-ROM drives. (See Figure 10.2.)

Figure 10.2. Microcomputer with CD-ROM Drive.

Since CD-ROMs store such a large amount of data, a relatively large indexing system is also necessary. Sometimes the index and related files can require as many as 275 million characters. However, there is still much storage space left.

It is important to remember that traditional CD technologies are primarily storage mediums. Besides the use of CDs for music, the data stored on CD-ROMs most commonly include electronic reference materials, visual databases, and software collection lists. As a storage medium, a CD-ROM can hold more than 650 Mb of data, which is equivalent to 250,000 pages of text. So, while both CDs and CD-ROMs were designed to "play" the music or "read" the data already commercially digitized on the discs, no changes in the music or data can be made by the user. (See Figure 10.3.)

What are some new developments in CD Technologies?

There are at least four categories of new developments in CD technologies, which include: (1) recording, (2) incorporating animation and video, (3) storing photographic images, and (4) combining CD technology with MIDI. (See Chapter 12 for more information on MIDI.)

First, the original "read-only" capability of CD technology is changing. Now **CD-WORM** (Write Once-Read Many) allows you to write but not erase your data. Another development called **rewritable optical discs** permits you to write, erase, and also rewrite on CD-ROMs. Both are available to a limited degree in the commercial market.

Second, a new CD technology provides the capability for CD-ROMs to store animation and video motion on a variety of storage and delivery platforms. In the past, data images, video, and sound took up enormous amounts of computer storage space. Now a process, called **video compression** has been developed to reduce video files to a

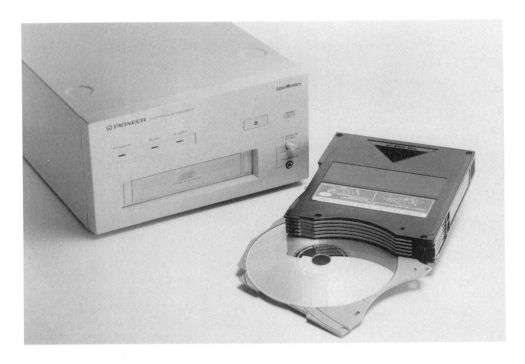

Figure 10.3. CD-ROM and CD-ROM Changer.

manageable size for storage. The following discussion presents some of the newest designs, including **CD-I** (Compact Disc-Interactive), **CDTV** (Commodore Dynamic Total Vision), **DVI** (Digital Video Interactive), **QuickTime**, and **VIS** (Video Information System).

What is CD-I?

CD-I was developed in 1986 by Philips and Sony for an interactive video, audio, and computer system. CD-I uses a standard CD disc which is inserted into a player with a built-in computer processor connected directly to a television. By using a mouse or remote control unit, you can interact with on-screen images.

There are four important factors in CD-I technology: (1) a worldwide standard has been developed so that a CD-I disc will play on any CD-I player in the world; (2) CD-I is not a technology or hardware device which is added to a computer system, but is instead a self-contained unit; (3) CD-I players can play both CD-I and CD discs; and (4) a compressed video format is used.

What is CDTV?

Similar to CD-I, CDTV by Commodore is a stand-alone unit that can connect to a television. Using Commodore Amiga computer technology, a CD and CD-ROM player add to the graphics, sound, and video capabilities of the microcomputer. CDTV interaction is controlled by a mouse or remote control unit. A limitation with CDTV is that only one-quarter screen motion video currently is available.

What is DVI?

Another development in CD technology using the techniques of digitization and compressed video is DVI. A special technique created by Intel Corporation decompresses the video on a computer and allows up to 72-minutes of full/motion video to be stored on a CD-ROM. In addition, DVI can also store digital formats of text, audio, and graphics.

Like CD-I, DVI is relatively easy to use. You need to attach the electronic component to a television or VCR monitor. Although DVI has a user friendly appearance (like a videogame with a mouse and a remote control), it is really a powerful computer-based electronic storage and access system usable internationally. (See Figure 10.4.)

Like CD-I, DVI has already established a worldwide standard. Because of this fact, proponents of DVI predict that by the year 2000, DVI chips will be standard features on many personal computers. Currently, because of the high costs of this CD technology, and the scarcity of commercial applications, most schools do not use DVI.

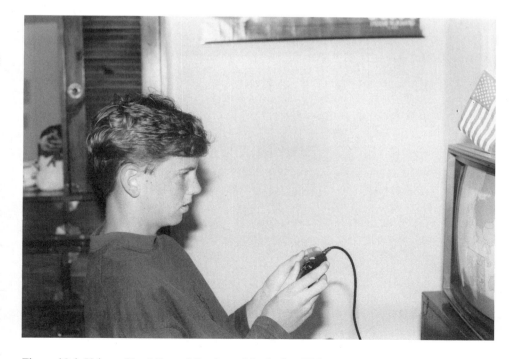

Figure 10.4. Using a Hand Control Device to Manipulate Video Images.

What is QuickTime?

QuickTime is a new video compression technique developed by Apple Computer to save motion video on a Macintosh (with 2 Mb of RAM and a System 6.07 or above) computer drive. Similar to CDTV, only a small window (about one-quarter of the screen) displays the video image. It is important to note that a high-density floppy disk can hold only a few seconds of QuickTime motion video. To resolve this problem, a CD-ROM or large-capacity hard drive is also recommended for the system.

What is VIS?

VIS was released in 1992 by Tandy Corporation and Microsoft. This technique is similar to CD-I and CDTV. Connected to a standard television, a computer provides participant interaction which is controlled by up to two remote control units. However, like QuickTime and CDTV, motion video appears on only one-quarter of the screen. An interesting point to note with this CD technology is that a VIS game and information can be saved on a small credit card-size cartridge.

What is Photo CD?

Photo CD (Photographic Compact Disc) was developed by Kodak to store photographic images on CD. Now pictures taken with a camera can be developed and placed on a compact disc. The CD is then played on a Photo CD or CD-I player and viewed on a television screen.

How do you care for optical storage discs?

Whether you are using a CD disc or a videodisc (see Chapter Eleven), both technologies are optical medium storage devices and although durable, need special care. Chart 10.1 lists tips for optical disc care.

What are the advantages of CD technology in education?

First, as microcomputers expand in power and memory potential, the demand for data storage capacity increases. Replacing magnetic storage mediums such as audio cassettes and floppy disks, CD technology provides a medium for the storage of digitized audio and video information. Because of the benefits of digitization, product variety, and storage capacity of CD technologies, proponents predict that by the year 2000 probably 90% of software purchased for schools will be presented on CD technology media rather than computer diskettes.

Another advantage of CD technology over more traditional storage mediums is its massive text and graphics storage capacity increased by the development of new data-compression techniques, which permits the storage of more data within a limited area. It is difficult to imagine, but true, for you now to hold an entire encyclopedia or a copy of *Books in Print* in two fingers of one hand via CD-ROM technology.

```
1. Always grasp the disc by the edges or by the
center hole and one edge. Try not to touch the
metallic surface.
2. As with computer disks, store optical discs in a
standing position away from heat sources, excessive
humidity, and freezing temperatures. For example, do
not store them along window sills.
3. With a clean cloth dampened with water, wipe the
disc in a circular direction before each use. If the
disc becomes very soiled, use a very mild diluted
detergent to wipe the disc surface. Never use
alcohol, static-prevention sprays, or record-cleaning
products.
4. If your disc becomes cracked, do not use it. You
could ruin the disc player.
```

Chart 10.1. Tips for Optical Disc Care.

Using multidisc drives is another advantage of CD technology. Players called **jukeboxes or carousels** can hold and randomly access selections from a maximum of six discs. If you have CD technology, you can then connect or daisy-chain up to eight multidisc drives together. A daisy-chained multidisc drive design would provide you access to tens of thousands of multimedia lessons on the total of 48 CD-ROMs.

The next advantage of CD technology is the quality of data storage. Since neither disc is embedded with the traditional record grooves, the platter surface appears perfectly smooth. Also, with no reader head or stylus pressing on the physical surface of the disc, the data cannot be "worn out" or damaged by long-term wear. Thus, compact discs are relatively durable when compared to more traditional mediums of data storage.

Another advantage of CD technology is the rapid and random access of tremendous quantities of recorded disc information. So, not only can you choose what data you want but also in what sequence you want the data to be accessed. This option provides flexibility in selecting text, images, graphs, video, sound, and musical programs.

The final advantage of CD technology, particularly with CD and CD-ROM, is that the original contents cannot easily be changed after manufacture, whether intentionally or accidentally. For this same reason archival records are safely stored without fear of illegal data entry.

How is CD technology used in education?

It is predicted that as this decade continues, the CD and CD-ROM markets are likely to "grow dramatically" due to the following factors: standardization of equipment, lower costs, more vendors for these technologies, and better performance. CD-ROMs are expected to be a major factor in the future distribution of data, reference works, and multimedia software. With the advent of WORM, rewritable compact discs, CD-I, CDTV, DVI, QuickTime, VIS, Photo CD, and CD + MIDI, a more varied selection of CD technology will be discovered and utilized in everyday classroom settings rather than in only prototype demonstrations.

In education there are many uses of CD-ROMs, including instructional and simulation software, and reasonably-priced databases, encyclopedias, directories, and bibliographic references. To make CD technology more attractive to school settings, network licensing can be purchased so that one software product can be used on many computers. This process, of course, not only provides more users more opportunities to use CD technology, but also decreases the cost of the product per microcomputer station.

Audio CDs, which are growing in popularity in the home setting and up-scale vehicle sound systems, have a more limited, but growing, use in the educational setting. Originally relegated to music-related curricula, CD technology can be added to Multimedia systems. (See Chapter Twelve and Chapter Thirteen for further information.)

A popular general application of the CD-ROM in the elementary and high schools is its use as an encyclopedia. The educator or student types in the desired "search word" or "key word" to research. A list of articles containing the key word appears on the computer screen and, after a few commands, the text of listed articles, and perhaps even graphics such as maps or pictures, may appear. In addition, you might want to use **electronic searching** as a research tool.

What is electronic searching?

Probably, at one time or another, you will need to research an area of interest or concern. In the past, locating keywords listed in large reference volumes and then tracing their original articles for review was a tedious and laborious process. The electronic CD technology has eased the process greatly.

A common CD-ROM research application in high schools and colleges is the use of a database called ERIC or Educational Resources Information Center. Sponsored by the US Department of Education, ERIC is a network of 16 clearinghouses specializing in different educational areas. Included in the ERIC database are document citations from *Resources in Education* (RIE) and a file of 750 professional journal citations from *Current Index to Journals in Education* (CIJE).

To do a CD-ROM ERIC search you type in keywords on a computer terminal. The CD-ROM will "electronically" scan its database of resources and then list the article citations and abstracts on the screen for you to review. If you would like a copy of the information, you simply print it out via the printer. For example, I searched the string of keywords "teleconferencing and computers" on ERIC CD-ROM and within 30 minutes I read and printed 40 citations, each with 21 categories of information, including descriptors, such as title, year of publication, author, abstract, and year of publication. If I were to do a traditional search, the process probably would have taken at least five hours — that is, if all the volumes were available in the library!

Another library CD-ROM revolution is the installation of electronic card catalogs. Rather than search through rows of organized file card catalogs, you access your requested information through a computer screen. You may even be able to find out if the book you are looking for is on the shelf, checked out, or available in another branch library, again all through the microcomputer and CD-ROM. In some library systems, printers are available to provide a hard copy of your data. If you're interested in more CD-ROM library applications, an excellent source for information, including cataloging services, public access catalogs, indexes, and databases, is *The CD-ROM Handbook*. This source provides the current or future user a wealth of information.

An interesting current trend for educational marketing is the joint partnership of CD-ROM hardware and software. This process is called **CD-ROM Bundling**, which means upon purchase of a specific CD-ROM player, a package of software is available for a very reduced price. If you are seeking a "good deal," the bundling marketing concept might be good for you to investigate.

What are some specific uses for CD technologies in education?

Currently, the most common use of the CD-ROM is as a text-retrieval package, with instructional and simulation packages soon to begin an explosive era of growth. To provide you with a better understanding of the storage capacity and potential educational uses of CD-ROM packages, the following sample products are described:

• *Bookshelf,* the first CD-ROM application disc developed by Microsoft Corporation, is popular with students and educators who need to write papers, essay assignments, or articles for publication. The following reference books are included on the one CD-ROM disc: *The American Heritage Dictionary; Roget's II: Electronic Thesaurus; The World Almanac and Book of Facts; Bartlett's Familiar Quotations; The Chicago Manual of Style; Houghton Mifflin Spelling Verifier and Corrector; Forms and Letters; US Zip Code Directory; Houghton Mifflin Usage Alert;* and the *Business Information Services Directory.*

• *Books in Print Plus* and *Books in Print Plus with Book Reviews Plus* are databases containing more than 750,000 titles. More than 20,000 new listings are added annually.

• *CD-ROM Science and Technical Reference Set* is a database of 7300 articles from the *McGraw-Hill Concise Encyclopedia of Science and Technology* plus 98,500 terms and 115,500 definitions from the *McGraw-Hill Dictionary of Scientific and Technical Terms.*

• *Compton's MultiMedia Encyclopedia* contains 32,000 articles plus 15,000 images, maps, and graphs, 60 minutes of sound, music and speech, 45 animated sequences, 800 full-color maps, 5,000 charts, and a complete on-line *Merriam-Webster Intermediate Dictionary.* (See examples of this encyclopedia in Figures 10.5 and 10.6.)

• *Discis Books* offers children's books on CD ROM. Reading the basic text is enhanced by actual voices, sound effects, and music. By using a mouse peripheral, pronunciation of individual words as well as isolated syllables and in-text explanations are available to the reader. Some selections are also available in Spanish, French, and Cantonese.

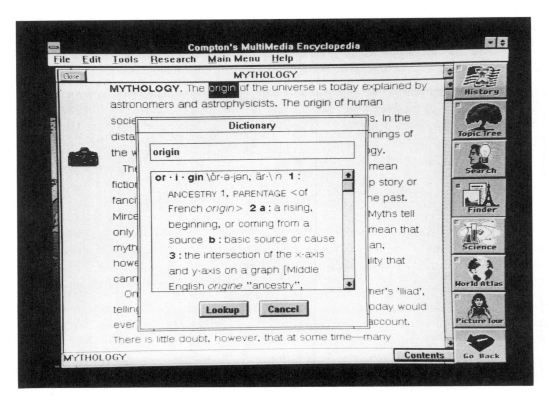

Figure 10.5. The *Compton's MultiMedia Encyclopedia* uses an online dictionary. If the word "origin" in this mythology article is unfamiliar, a "window" can be opened, giving the word's pronunciation, use, and definition. (*Courtesy Compton's MultiMedia Encyclopedia*)

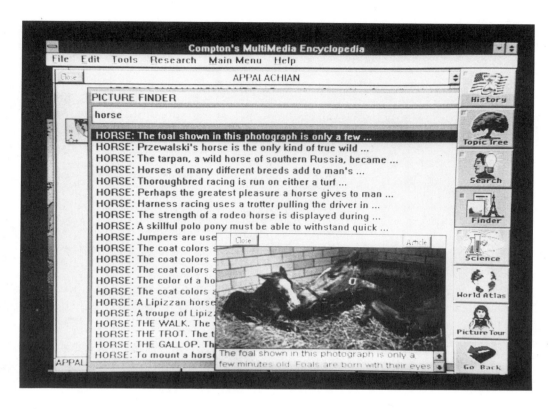

Figure 10.6. Users of *Compton's MultiMedia Encyclopedia* and *Compton's Interactive Encyclopedia* can call up photographs that correspond to captions through the picture finder menu on the right. (Courtesy *Compton's MultiMedia Encyclopedia*)

• *Dissertation Abstracts Ondisc* is a CD-ROM edition of the large-sized volume entitled *Dissertation Abstracts*. This database is used primarily for college or university research and is updated annually.

• *Fast Past* is a history database on CD-ROM which contains several thousand articles. The student or educator can type in a topic, year, and world location, and the retrieval program will produce a historic fact which incorporates all three criteria.

• *The First National Item Bank and Test Development System* is a CD-ROM product that incorporates more than 80,000 validated test questions which assess at least 10,000 learning objectives for grades K-12 in 38 subject areas. Tests can be supplemented with graphic enhancements and can then be developed by the teacher or administrator, and sent to Tescor, Inc. for "test scanning" correction.

• *Geodisc* is a collection of accurate geographic databases which include roads, railroads, elevations, boundaries, etc. The series contains a USA Atlas as well as individual states, which provides for state level to city block detail. A Windows/On the World (WOW) application program permits the user to personalize lessons by creating text, graphics, and symbol overlays.

• *LaserQuest* is a four CD-ROM database containing records of 4.6 million library books, visual materials, maps and manuscripts housed in more than 1000 libraries. Search keywords or descriptions include such categories as titles, authors, and identification numbers. Supplemental discs of 150,000 new titles are available bimonthly.

• *Mammals: A Multimedia Encyclopedia* by the National Geographic Society combines still photos, text, audio, and video on a CD-ROM.

• *PC Software Interest Group (PC-SIG)* produces a CD-ROM that includes thousands of shareware programs and templates for MS-DOS computers. Products such as databases, spreadsheets, utilities, games, PC-Write, PC-File and PC-Talk are available for PC-SIG users.

• *Picture Atlas of Our World* was developed by the National Geographic Society and IBM Educational Systems. High-resolution maps and cultural information are contained on this recently released CD-ROM.

• *SilverPlatter Information, Inc.* offers several CD-ROM databases including ERIC, PsychLIT (Psychological Abstracts), Sociofile (Sociological Abstracts), A-V ONLINE (information on 300,000 audiovisual materials, videos, films, filmstrips and other media, LISA (abstracts of the world's literature), COMPU-INFO (12,000 computer product listings), and CHEM-BANK (source of information on hazardous wastes).

• *The Visual Dictionary* by Facts on File, Inc. contains a database of graphic images of common objects with both English and French labels.

Other new CD technology incorporating animation and motion video are also appearing on the market. The following list includes examples of these products:

• *Children's Musical Theater* by Sonic Images allows the user to watch and listen to an animated animal band perform, participate as one of the musicians or vocalists, and modify any of the four included melodies. This product is designed for CD-I technology.

• *Palenque* is a program developed by the Bank Street College of Education for use with DVI technology. It is an educational application in which the user explores a Mayan archeological site. A multimedia database provides video, audio, text, and pictures of the Mayan culture and its ancient writing as well as data pertaining to the regional rain forest.

• *Playing with Language* from Syracuse Language Systems emphasizes language and reading development through the use of VIS technology.

• *The Treasures of the Smithsonian* program by Philips Interactive Media of America is designed for CD-I technology. In this package hundreds of exhibits that are found at the Smithsonian Institute are accessible on compact disc.

• *World's Vista Atlas* developed by Applied Optical Media offers a combination of the exploration of the earth and its people via maps, text, graphic images, and more than 1,000 photographs. In addition, examples of 61 foreign languages are spoken and a variety of ethnic music is accessible. This program is used with CDTV technology.

What are some CD technology problems and solutions?

Although there are advantages to using CD technology in the educational setting, there are also some problems. The following discussion will present the most commonly identified problems as well as suggestions by educators for addressing them:

First, although you and your colleagues are familiar with audio CDs, you may know little about CD-ROMs or extended innovations. The best way to resolve this problem is to learn either formally or informally how and why to use the technology. Formal introductory small-group training sessions are recommended, but "hands-on" experience is the best teacher. If you would prefer to learn alone, then seek CD-ROM tutorials that you can use. Many CD-ROM collections include either an "electronic" tutorial on the disc or printed tutorial. If you are more comfortable learning from someone else, find a knowledgeable person to answer questions during the tutorial process. Sometimes placing the CD-ROM player or workstation near a librarian in a media center is a solution. If, however, actual retrieval databases are not accessible to you, then microcomputer simulations can be used.

A second problem of CD technology usage is determining the best location for hardware placement. Ideally, every classroom should have CD technology, but, since most schools begin with one CD system, the best location is one that is central and accessible to all administrators, teachers, and students. Generally, that site is the library or media center.

A third problem is the high cost of the initial investment for hardware. Although less than the cost of a personal computer, CD technology is an added expense to any school budget. However, if you can identify CD technology as a good investment, since it is cost-effective, space-saving, or time-saving, then funding may be available. It is important to know that as CD technology is mass-marketed, the price of hardware is decreasing. Another method providing for the saving of money is to create a networking system of user stations. Software packages are available that provide network-based, multi-user access to CD-ROM databases. These packages run on CD-ROM servers and microcomputers with attached CD-ROM drives.

A fourth problem of CD technology is that data cannot be updated, since CD-ROMs are, as the name states, "read-only" memories. Yet, a process does exist to update to a current disc. Your CD product needs to be registered with the manufacturer and then, for a small price, a more current disc can be purchased to replace the outdated CD-ROM. This "upgrade" solution is a common one in education.

A fifth problem recognized by educators is the lack of standardization in the CD technology. As with computers that run under a variety of disk operating systems, many CD technology products are not compatible. However, standardization for all CD technologies is on the horizon.

Decision-making Guidelines: CD Technologies

1. Objective: What is the reason for the purchase of the CD technology?

2. Integration: How will the new technology be incorporated meaningfully into the current curriculum?

3. Cost: How much funding initially will be needed?

4. Location: Where will the hardware be placed?

5. Security: How will the CD equipment and discs be protected from theft or misuse?

6. Equal Access: How and what will assure educators and students equal access and opportunities to this new technology?

7. Responsibility: Who will be responsible to see that the CD systems are working properly?

8. Updating: Who will determine when CD technology should be replaced because the data are outdated?

9. Training: Who, when, where and how will teachers and students be trained to use the CD technology?

Summary

In this chapter, compact disc technologies were described. New CD technologies were presented including, WORM, rewritable compact discs, CD-I, CDTV, DVI, QuickTime, VIS, Photo CD, and CD + MIDI. Regardless of compact disc technology variety, all CDs are optical data storage mediums, are digitally recorded, are approximately five inches in diameter, and are durable, long-lasting mediums for information.

Recommended Periodicals

Audio
BYTE
CD-ROM End User
Digital Audio and Compact Disc Review
Educational Technology
Green CD Catalog
High Fidelity
Laserdisc Professional
MacUser
Macworld
Media & Methods
MPC World
Online
Online Access
Optical Information Systems
Opus
Ovation
PC Computing
PC Magazine
PC Week
References Services Review
Special Libraries
Stereo Review
Technology & Learning
T.H.E. Journal

Resources

Applied Optical Media Corporation. 18 Great Valley Parkway, Malvern, PA 19355. (215) 889-9564.

Bookshelf. Microsoft Corporation, 16011 NE 36th Way, Redmond, WA 98073-9717. (206) 828-8080.

Books in Print Plus. Bowker Electronic Publishing, 245 West 17th Street, New York, NY 10011. (800) 232-3288.

Britannica Software, Inc. Britannica Centre. 310 S. Michigan Ave., Chicago, IL 60604. (312) 347-7155.

Broderbund Software, Inc. 17 Paul Dr., San Rafael, CA 94903. (415) 382-4400.

CD-I Information Bureau. 5700 Wilshire Blvd., Suite 475, Los Angeles, CA 90036. (213) 930-2882.

CD-ROM Resource Group, Inc. 500 South Pearl St., Denver, CO 80209. (303) 733-3068.

CD-ROM Science and Technical Reference Set. McGraw-Hill Book Company, Consumer Group, 11 W. 19th St., New York, NY 10011. (212) 337-5026.

CD Technology, Inc. 766 San Aleso Ave., Sunnyvale, CA 94086. (408) 752-8500.

Compton's Interactive Encyclopedia. 2320 Camino Vida Roble, Carlsbad, CA 92009. (800) 862-2206.

Compton's MultiMedia Encyclopedia. 2320 Camino Vida Roble, Carlsbad, CA 92009. (800) 862-2206.

Discis Books. Discis Knowledge Research, Inc., 45 Sheppard Ave. East, Toronto, Ontario, Canada M2N 5W9. (800) 567-4321.

Dissertation Abstracts Ondisc. University Microfilms International, Electronic Publishing, 300 N. Zeeb Road, Ann Arbor, MI 48106. (800) 521-0600.

Eastman Kodak Company. 343 State St., Rochester, NY 14650. (800) 242-2424.

Fast Past. Interage Research, Inc., 7619 N. Rogers, Chicago, IL 60626. (312) 764-1892.

The First National Item Bank and Test Development System. Tescor, Inc., 461 Carlisle Dr., Herndon, VA 22070. (800) 842-0077; (703) 435-9501 in VA.

Geodisc. Geovision, Inc. 270 Scientific Dr., Norcross, GA 30092. (404) 448-8224.

Icom Simulations, Inc. 648 South Wheeling Rd., Wheeling IL 60090. (800) 877-4266.

Intel Corporation. PO Box 7641, Mt. Prospect, IL 60056. (800) 548-4725.

LaserQuest. General Research Corporation, Library Systems, PO Box 6770, Santa Barbara, CA 93160-6770. (800) 235-6788.

Microsoft Corporation. One Microsoft Way, Redmond, WA 98052. (206) 882-8080.

National Education Center for Educational Media. 4314 Mesa Grande SE, Albuquerque, NM 87108. (800) 468-3453.

Palenque. Bank Street College of Education, 610 W. 112th St., New York, NY 10025. (212) 222-6700.

PC-Software Interest Group (PC-SIG). PC-SIG, 1030 East Duane Ave., Sunnyvale, CA 94086. (408) 730-9291.

Philips Interactive Media of America. 1111 Santa Monica Blvd., Los Angeles, CA 90025. (231) 473-4136.

Picture Atlas of Our World. National Geographic Society, 17th and M Sts., Washington, DC 20036. (800) 368-2728.

QuickTime Tools. Claris Corporation, 5201 Patrick Henry Dr., Santa Clara, CA 95052. (408) 727-8227.

SilverPlatter Information, Inc. 100 River Ridge Dr., Norwood, MA 02062. (800) 343-0064.

Sony Corporation of America. 1 Sony Dr., Park Ridge, NJ 07656. (201) 930-1000.

Syracuse Language Systems. 719 E. Genesee St., Syracuse, NY 13210. (315) 478-6729.

Tandy Multimedia PC Family. Tandy Corporation/Radio Shack, One Tandy Center, Fort Worth, TX 76102. (800) 243-2015.

The Visual Dictionary. Facts on File, Inc., 460 Park Ave. South, New York, NY 10016. (212) 683-2244.

References

Bailey, C.W. Jr. (1990). Intelligent multimedia computer systems: Emerging information resources in the network environment. *Library Hi-Tech, 8* (1), 29-41.

Barron, A. & Baumbach, D.J. (1991). *Optical media: What every educator needs to know about the new technologies.* Orlando, FL: The UCF/DOE Instructional Technology Resource Center, School of Education, University of Central Florida.

Barron, A. & Baumbach, D. (1990, June). A CD-ROM tutorial: Training for a new technology. *Educational Technology, 30* (6), 20-23.

Barron, A.E. & Orwig, G.W. (1993). *New technologies for education.* Englewood, CO: Libraries Unlimited, Inc.

Becker, H.J. (1991, February). Encyclopedias on CD-ROM. *Educational Technology, 32* (2), 7-20.

Brewer, B. & Key, E. (1988). *The compact disc book: A complete guide to the digital sound of the future.* New York: Harcourt Brace Jovanovich, Publishers.

Bowers, R. (1989). Getting serious about the information age. *Optical Information Systems, 9* (3), 131-134.

Bruder, I. (1991, September). Guide to multimedia: How it changes the way we teach and learn. *Electronic Learning, 11* (1), 22-23.

Byrom, E. (1990, Summer). Hypermedia (multimedia). *Teaching Exceptional Children, 22* (4), 47-48.

Demarais, N. (1988). *The CD-ROM handbook.* Westport, CT: Meckler Corporation.

D'Ignazio, F. (1989). *The Scholastic guide to classroom multimedia.* New York: Scholastic, Inc.

Frentzen, J. (1989). Text retrieval for CD-ROMs comes of age, *PC Week, 6,* 95.

Galbreath, J. (1992, April). The educational buzzword of the 1990s: Multimedia, or is it hypermedia, or interactive multimedia ... ? *Educational Technology, 32* (4), 15-19.

Galbreath, J. (1992, June). The coming of digital desktop media. *Educational Technology, 32* (5), 27-32.

Gayeski, D.M. (1992, May). Making sense of multimedia: Introduction to Special Issue. *Educational Technology, 32* (5), 9-13.

Gretsch, G. (1991, February). *Multimedia Information Delivery.* Paper presented at Mac on Campus Conference, New Brunswick, NJ.

Grunin, L. (1989). Software review: PC-SIG library offers thousands of programs for less than 50 cents each. *PC Magazine, 8,* 48.

Heinich, R., Molenda, M., & Russell, J.D. (1993). *Instructional media and the new technologies of instruction* (4th ed.). New York: Macmillan Publishing Company.

Holtz, F. (1988). *CD-ROMs: Breakthrough in information storage.* Blue Ridge Summit, PA: Tab Books Inc.

The International CD-ROM report *INNOTECH.* (1990, October), 2 (1), 3.

Kratzert, M. (1989, November). *An examination of the role of reference librarians in the light of new technology.* Paper presented at the California Library Association Meeting, Oakland, CA.

Loveria, G. & Kinstler, D. (1990, Fall). Multimedia: DVI arrives. *BYTE IBM Special Edition, 15* (11), 105-108.

Lynch, P.L. (1991). *Multimedia: Getting started. Apple technology in support of learning.* Sunnyvale, CA: PUBLIX Information Products, Inc.

McQueen, H. (1990, March). Networking CD-ROMs: Implementation considerations. *Laserdisc Professional, 3* (2), 13-16.

Machrone, B. (1989). The future of the CD-ROM, *PC Magazine, 8,* 67.

Martin, J. (1990). CD-ROM: A cost effective text-management solution. *PC Week, 1,* 82.

Mulligan, D. (1991, February). *Introduction to teaching using the geology/geoscience Macintosh network.* Paper presented at Mac on Campus Conference, New Brunswick, NJ.

Multimedia Review. (1991, June). *Technical Horizons in Education Journal, 18* (11), 30-33.

Oley, E. (1989). Information retrieval in the classroom. *Journal of Reading, 32* (7), 590-597.

Orwig, G.W. & Baumbach, D.J. (1991). *CD-ROM: What every educator needs to know about the new technologies.* Orlando, FL: UCF/DOE Instructional Technology Resource Center, College of Education, University of Central Florida.

Philbin, P. & Ryan, J. (1988). ERIC and beyond: A survey of CD-ROMs for education collections. *The Laserdisc Professional, 1* (4), 17-27.

Pournelle, J. (1991). Jukebox computing: A sextet of CD-ROMs on-line makes for lively computing, *Byte, 16,* 73.

Rash, W., Jr. (1990). CD-ROM to the rescue. *Byte, 15,* 77.

Rose, P. (1989). Software review: CD-ROM science and technical reference set, *PC Magazine, 8,* 200.

Rubinyi, R. (1989). New technologies for distance education: A needs assessment at the delivery site. *TDC Research Paper No. 4,* St. Paul, MN: Minnesota University at St. Paul.

Schroeder, E.E. (1991). Interactive multimedia computer systems, *ERIC Digest.* Syracuse University, Syracuse, NY: ERIC Clearinghouse on Information Resources.

Schwier, R. & Misanchuk, E.R. (1993). *Interactive multimedia instruction.* Englewood Cliffs, NJ: Educational Technology Publications, Inc.

Seymour, J. (1990). Forecast '91: Will the CD-ROM market finally explode? *PC Week,* (7), 47.

Somerson, P. (1990). Free and easy: CD-ROM applications, *MacUser, 6,* 21.

Trotter, A. (1992). Schools gear up for 'hypermedia' — A quantum leap in electronic learning. In J.J. Hirschbuhl & L.F. Wilkinson (Eds.), *Computers in Education* (5th ed.). Guilford, CT: Dushkin Publishing Company.

Van Horn, R. (1991). Educational power tools: New instructional delivery systems. *Phi Delta Kappan, 72* (7), 527-533.

Walkenbach, J. (1992). CD ROM drives: 680 MB or bust! *PC World, 10* (5), 88-103.

Wilson, K. & Tally, W. (1991). Classroom integration of interactive multimedia: A case study. *Technical Report No. 16,* New York: Center for Technology in Education, Bank Street College of Education.

11

Chapter Eleven:
Videodisc Technology

What is videodisc technology?

Videodisc technology is an electronic storage and retrieval system that uses a player to access a massive amount of video and audio information from a **videodisc**, which is also referred to as a **laserdisc**. (To illustrate storage capacity, for example, one videodisc can store images that can otherwise be contained in 1,300 carousel slide trays.) Like a CD-ROM, a videodisc is a durable optical data storage medium. Unlike its 5-inch compact disc competitors (e.g., CD-I, DVI, CDTV, and VIS), a 12- or 8-inch videodisc is not digitized, but rather uses analog signals similar to a videocassette tape (VCR) system. Because of this analog video similarity, the videodisc will be compared to the traditional videotape.

How do videodisc and videotape technologies compare?

Videotape technology has been used in educational settings for at least two decades. In comparison, the concept of videodisc technology was introduced in 1970, but did not appear in education until the early 1980s. Videodisc advocates claimed that videodiscs would quickly replace videotapes. However, several of the first videodisc formats were not very successful. The most recent one uses a format called an optical reflective disc, which does offer competition for a videotape. Currently, though, videotape systems are still more commonly used in classrooms.

Since most educators are very familiar with videotapes and VCRs, it is helpful to compare this technology to videodisc systems. There are similarities between videodiscs and videocassette tapes. For example, both need software (a videotape or videodisc) and a player with a TV-type monitor. Also, both technologies use a video camera and editing procedures to produce video content material on a videotape or on a videodisc. In addition, both sets of video images are stored in **frames**, which in the "play" mode, move at 30 frames per second creating motion.

However, there are some major differences. First, when a videotape is recorded, it can easily be re-recorded. Once video images are produced on a videotape and the tape is sent to a mastering studio to produce a videodisc, the images on the videodisc cannot be re-recorded or altered.

Second, although both technologies store and read material by frames, the storage methods differ. On a videotape, images and sound are stored in a linear ribbon-like sequence as on an old 16 MM film. In comparison, a videodisc stores and reads material on frames which are 54,000 concentric circles per side (108,000 images on both sides) of the disc. Since there so many frames, they are further categorized into **chapters**. To create motion, frames can be accessed at 30 frames per second, which provides for 30 minutes of video per disc side.

A third difference is each technology's accessing information style. While a videotape is played from beginning to end, it is possible to scan forward or reverse to select a particular frame to view. Usually, though, a trial and error search is used to locate a specific frame with an image that appears "fuzzy." In comparison, each of the 54,000 videodisc frames (per side) is numbered. So by using a barcode reader or a computer, it is easy to locate and isolate a selected frame. In addition, each frame has a very sharp image.

The final difference pertains to the audio component. While a videotape has one sound track, a videodisc has two. Both videodisc tracks can be played simultaneously for stereo sound or played individually. For example, on a videodisc, it is possible to store an English audio version on one track and a Spanish audio version on the second audio track.

To summarize the comparison of videotape and videodisc characteristics, see Chart 11.1.

Video Format: **Videodisc**

Characteristics:

Medium: Optical data storage

Sizes: Two sizes: 12- or 8-inch silver-colored platter

Advantages: (1) Large storage capability of 54,000 still or motion images, or audio per disc side, (2) rapid random access of stored data, (3) durable, no wear medium plastic, (4) CD-quality sound, (5) longer shelf life than a videotape

Disadvantages: (1) Costly original production of disc, (2) limited number of software products, (3) videodiscs cannot be re-recorded

Educational Use Status: Increasing in education

Video Format: **Videotape**

Characteristics:

Medium: Magnetic-tape storage

Sizes: Three sizes: (1) 3/4-inch which is uncommon in education; (2) 1/2-inch VHS or Beta, with VHS being more common than Beta in education; and (3) 8 mm, the newest compact format

Advantages: (1) Many software products, (2) tapes can be re-recorded, (3) educators are very familiar with VCR technology

Disadvantages: (1) Quality of taped programming deteriorates with use, (2) slow access of stored data

Educational Use Status: Currently very common in education

Chart 11.1. A Comparison of Videodisc and Videotape Characteristics.

How do you find information on a videodisc?

Both videotapes and videodiscs store information. However, because the videodisc is a massive storage device, a rapid retrieval system is necessary to access data efficiently. So, there are three ways to find your information in a videodisc system: (1) by frames (individual images), (2) by chapters (categorized images), and (3) by time (elapsed playing time). So sought information can be identified, isolated, and retrieved for viewing with the assistance of a computer, and a remote control with a SEARCH button or a barcode reader.

What are CAV and CLV formats?

Videodiscs have two standard formats: **CAV (Constant Angular Velocity)** and **CLV (Constant Linear Velocity)**. Basically in this chapter the CAV videodisc has been discussed since it is more commonly used in education due to its interactivity possibilities. Whether you are accessing still images or full motion video, you can "freeze" the specific point you would like to view on your screen or "step" each frame in slow motion. For example, some diving coaches use CAV videodiscs to examine the step by step progress of athletes' complex dives. As mentioned, the image will be sharp, unlike the point at which you stop the moving image on your VCR.

In comparison, the CLV format contains as much as 60 minutes of video on each disc side, and for this reason the CLV format is also called "extended play." However, there are three differences between CLV and CAV. As compared to CAV, the CLV format has limited use in educational settings. With CLV (1) you cannot select a specific image in a "freeze" frame, (2) you cannot move forward and backward frame by frame, and (3) you cannot rapidly access desired portions of the videodisc.

So, as videodiscs begin to become more popular in educational settings, you will find the CLV videodisc or laserdisc format used more for viewing movies from a beginning-to-end sequence. Currently CLV videodiscs are used in some classrooms but are more often used in home settings. Your local video store may have CLV videodiscs, usually referred in the commercial consumer market as laserdiscs, to rent or purchase.

What are the levels of videodisc interactivity?

Although all video formats provide color, motion, and sound, not all video formats are truly interactive. In educational settings there are three types of videodisc players based on user control. As an educator, you should be familiar with these following levels of user interactivity:

Level I has the least interactivity and is sometimes referred to as manual control interactive video. Since there is no microcomputer within the system, you must use a barcode reader or a remote control keypad to access selected information.

• Level II includes a disc player equipped with an internal microcomputer. Computer programs are encoded onto the videodisc by the production company. However, interactivity is limited to true-false or multiple-choice response formats. Since many educators prefer a more varied question and answer format, Level II videodiscs are not commonly used in classrooms today. This level is popular, though, with training programs in industry.

• Level III requires a videodisc player plus external microcomputer system. Although most expensive of the three levels, Level III is the most flexible since it provides opportunities for interactivity and creativity. In this level you can do all the tasks in Level II, and additionally, you can store student records, use branching (non-linear) techniques, and store/retrieve databases on the computer.

It is important to note that both Levels I and III need one monitor to display computer information and another monitor to display visual (movies, slides, etc.) sequences. Also printers generally are not needed within any level of the system.

Although various degrees of interactivity occur at all levels, only Level III is truly an interactive videodisc. However, in educational settings today Level I and Level III are both used. Seventy-five percent of today's schools with videodisc technology use levels that require only a videodisc player and remote control hardware. With this simple Level I configuration, a microcomputer is not necessary. Instructors can easily add videodisc-enhanced experiences with remote control content pacing, or utilize a barcode scanner on barcode strips attached to lesson plan materials to quickly access particular frames. However, with the addition of a microcomputer, interactivity provides a more individualized pacing and control of most appropriate, response-dependent instruction or sequence viewing.

What are barcode readers?

Barcode readers are simple devices that read "zebra-stripe" codes similar to the UPC codes you find on packaging in many stores today. In education a barcode reader is generally a hand-held, wired device that you use to scan a series of information bar lines. Each set of lines identifies a particular frame on your videodisc so that during a lesson you can easily and quickly locate selected information. Currently barcodes are printed in many new textbooks or lesson plans that include videodiscs as part of their resource package. If you do not have a barcoding system available to you now and you would like to add barcodes to your lesson plans, it is possible to purchase a barcode program that will enable you to integrate your lessons with videodisc technologies. Two samples include *Bar'n'Coder* for the *Macintosh* and *LaserBarcode Tool Kit* for MS-DOS microcomputers, both manufactured by *Pioneer Electronics Corporation*.

If you have never used a barcode scanner before, you might need some practice to make the device work properly. Chart 11.2 offers you tips to make barcode reading or scanning successful.

1. Hold the reader like a pen at a perpendicular angle to the barcode strip.

2. You must scan or pass the barcode reader across the strip from left to right. Be certain to start far enough to the left and continue far enough to the right to get an accurate reading. You know the reading has been done when you hear a beep.

3. When you are scanning, be certain to press and hold down the button on the top of the barcode reader. This technique is similar to "dragging" open a pull-down menu on a microcomputer screen with a mouse.

Chart 11.2. Tips for Using Barcodes.

Is it possible to create your own videodisc?

Yes, it is possible to create your own videodisc. Basically you will need to plan and develop a high-quality videotape. This videotape is then sent to an optical recording company to transfer the taped version to videodisc format. You should know that this development process can be complex as well as costly (in the tens of thousands of dollars) and that you will need the help of a professional team. However, if you have the financing from your educational institution or from a granting source, you and your team can create an interactive videodisc customized to your specific needs.

The following four stages will help you to plan your final videodisc product:

1. Form a design and production team. Personnel should include at least one subject expert, curriculum designer, programmer, script writer, and graphics designer. Discuss and set your design plan, budget, and schedule. Decide on your level of videodisc interactivity (I-III) and format (CLV or CAV). Seek videodisc mastering company standards, requirements, and recommendations. Write and edit the script, develop sequence flowcharts, storyboards, and artwork, and videotape your program. This stage should cost approximately 45% of your budget.

2. Edit your videotape. Add enhancements to your product such as film, slides, sound effects, or music. Be certain to seek copyright permission for the use of any non-team photos, stock footage, or musical pieces. You might consider reviewing public domain sources and requesting special "deals" for educational projects. Send a copy of your videotape with completed production forms to the mastering and replication company of your choice. This stage should cost approximately 40% of your budget.

3. At this stage your video is sent to the mastering and replication company and is processed according to your specifications. You should request a "check disc" for review. If you have any questions for this stage, it is important to contact the customer support and technical service departments available for post production details. This stage should cost 5% of your budget.

4. You receive the videodisc. Check your disc and make certain that everything on the disc is correctly ordered and timed. Next you develop your interactive elements. If you have chosen Level I interactivity, at this stage you create a barcoding system. If you have selected Level II or Level III interactivity, then you can use an authoring technique to control your program. **Authoring** is a computer language software that allows you to control the time and presentation of your content. This final stage should cost approximately 10% of your budget.

Two very helpful sources on videodisc production include *3M's Optical Recording Laser Videodisc Post Production Guide* or *Pioneer's From Media to Multimedia: Empowering your Videos with Interactivity*. See Resources for details.

What are the advantages of videodiscs in education?

In today's TV society, many learners are visually oriented. If you are familiar with television or VCR technology, then you can understand how the videodisc is one new technology that takes advantage of this trend. The following list contains advantages of videodisc usage as compared to traditional mediums:

1. Using this interactive medium, you must be an active participant (passive observing is not possible) in the individualized, self-paced environment.

2. Rapid retrieval of mass amounts of stored information on this durable medium allows for easy access.

3. Videodisc technology is one means of combining elements of what amounts to older audiovisual technologies (e.g., the 16 MM projector, slides, film loop projector, etc.) into one electronic device.

4. The best quality in sound, animation, and video are provided through the laser videodisc, which allows more motivating tutorials with optional touch screen monitors.

5. Videodiscs require a lot less storage space than their traditional counterparts, films or VCR tapes.

How are videodiscs used in education?

Videodiscs are growing in popularity in the educational setting. More and more elementary through college faculty and administrators are purchasing and integrating this relatively new technology into the curriculum, not only as instructional assistance for students, but also as in-service opportunities for teachers. There are three basic categories for the use of videodiscs in education today: (1) images and sounds can be stored in archive collections, replacing the need for expensive photography and art books or sets of slides required for specific curriculum resources; (2) simulations allow the student to interact with the videodisc environment in place of "real-life" experiences which may be impractical, too expensive, or hazardous; and (3) tutorials are used to teach subject content. Some tutorial videodiscs are correlated with textbooks and workbooks so that a variety of teaching and learning modes can be used. (See Figure 11.1.) Also some educators incorporate videodiscs as supplemental elements to their lessons.

Figure 11.1. Twelve-inch Videodiscs from a Curriculum Series. *(Courtesy of The Discovery Channel)*

What are some specific uses for videodiscs in education?

• *ABCNews Interactive* by Optical Data Corporation is a videodisc teaching tool to assist instructors in the presentation of complex news topics to students. Produced by a team of producers from Nightline, World News Tonight, and other ABC News programs, these videodiscs presently cover three subject areas, including health issues, historical events, and social and political issues. Examples of titles are *AIDS*, *Teenage Sexuality*, *In the Holy Land*, *Martin Luther King, Jr.*, and *The Kremlin: An Interactive Tour*. To extend the use of these videodiscs in the classroom, curriculum-based support materials are available including materials such as a guidebook, authoring tools computer software, and a set-up and operation manual.

• *College USA* by Info-Disc Corporation is a videodisc that presents colleges and universities to prospective students.

• *Discovery Interactive Library* is a set of videodiscs from the Discovery Channel's interactive library focusing upon topics in social studies, science, technology, and natural science.

• *GTV* from National Geographic Society and Lucasfilm, Inc., is a program on American history. Distributed by Optical Data Corporation, GTV consists of two videodiscs and computer software (to adapt videos to suit your needs). More than 40 short video shows on topics such as Native Americans and immigration are directed to students in grades 5 through 12. (See Figure 11.2.)

• *The Living Textbook* by Optical Data Corporation is an earth, life, and physical science videodisc set plus image directory and interactive computer software. Contents include slide images, diagrams, and movie clips plus printed materials for non-videodisc usage.

Figure 11.2. Teacher Helping Students with a GTV Program. *(Courtesy of National Geographic Society)*

• *Rain Forest* is a product for students in grades 6-12 that combines a videodisc and a pair of HyperCard stacks to access chapters including titles such as "Watery World," "Nocturnal Life," and "Forest Canopy." (See Chapter Thirteen for an explanation of HyperCard.) Segments of original film from the rain forests of Costa Rica can be augmented with scripts discussing film segments. Included are preview questions with multiple-choice answers and feedback. An interesting feature is that the second stack of cards will allow students to create their own multimedia presentation by combining informational databases provided on the laserdisc.

• *Space Disc* by Optical Data Corporation is a three-volume, updated study of space exploration which includes videodiscs entitled Voyager Gallery, Planetscapes, and Space Shuttle.

• *Trigland* by Minnesota Educational Computing Corporation (MECC) is an example of Level III videodisc technology designed for direct instruction. Specifically intended for educational settings where a limited number of students are interested in an advanced math course, Trigland provides an individualized or paired setting where learners under math instructor supervision complete the semester-length course. When connected to a computer, videodisc concept presentations are complemented by computer-generated applications as well as student progress monitored electronically.

• *Windows on Science* by Optical Data Corporation is a collection of video-based curriculum programs on Earth, Life, and Physical Science for upper elementary, middle, and high school students. Recommended by the Texas State Department of Education, *Windows on Science* is the first video-based program approved in a state textbook adoption decision where this instructional technology competed with the traditional textbook medium. Another location using this videodisc program is the Hualapai Indian Reservation in Peach Springs, Arizona. Within a project called TNT (Tradition and Technology), the process-oriented program integrates the language and culture of the Native American with new technologies. (See Figure 11.3.)

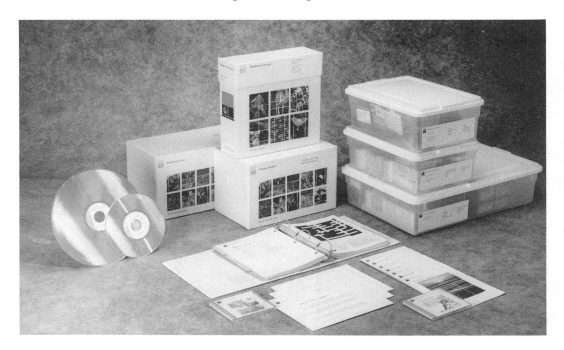

Figure 11.3. Videodisc-based Basal Curriculum Set for *Windows on Science. (© Peter Loppacher, 1991, used by permission)*

What are some videodisc problems and solutions?

Although there are many advantages to using videodisc technologies in the educational setting, there are some problems. The following discussion will present the most commonly identified concerns, with suggestions from educators for addressing them:

First, as with any new technology, there is a cost factor involved. Basically you will need a laserdisc player and compatible microcomputer plus, of course, the videodiscs. If you are a first-time laserdisc buyer, you might find a special price that will include a reduced price for hardware. To assist in initial expenses, seek financial support from local industry, grants, and hardware donations. You might contact educational technology companies and volunteer to be a participant in a research project. Your services could be compensated with temporary if not permanent hardware and software basics.

Second, too little in-service or pre-service "hands-on" training is available for educators in the use of videodisc technology. To compensate for this need, self-motivated, and sometimes self-taught educators are acting as motivating role models who, in turn, informally or formally teach other colleagues.

Third, Level I videodiscs are not interactive, but some educators would like them to be. Now it is possible to convert a Level I videodisc to a Level III videodisc through a process called **repurposing**. Basically repurposing is adding computer software that has been designed by the original manufacturer, another company, or even by the teacher. For the educator to repurpose a videodisc, it is necessary to use an **authoring tool** such as *HyperCard* for the *Macintosh*, *TutorTech* for the *Apple II* family, and *LinkWay* for the *IBM* and MS-DOS models. Any educator can create computer programs to control new applications. In summary, repurposing is a form of interactive customizing for presentations, lessons, and tests. (See Chapter Thirteen: Multimedia for more information.)

Fourth, it is possible to create your own videodisc. If you have a professional team and sufficient financing, you can develop a customized product, whether it's a public relations informational disc for your school or a curriculum resource to enhance your teaching and learning plans.

Decision-making Guidelines: Videodisc Technology

1. Objective: What is the reason for the purchase of videodisc technology? What levels of interactivity will be used? Will you need both CAV and CLV formats?

2. Integration: How will videodisc technology be incorporated meaningfully into the current curriculum? Or how will the instructional methodology be changed to include videodisc technology?

3. Cost: How much funding will be needed initially? What will be the added expense to connect videodisc technology to existing computers?

4. Location: Where will the videodisc technology hardware be placed in the educational setting?

5. Security: How will the equipment be protected from vandalism or misuse?

6. Equal Access: What policy will be established to permit sharing by all instructors and students? Or will access be limited to grade level area/subjects or specially trained educators?

7. Responsibility: Who will be held accountable to see that the videodisc system is correctly running and maintained?

8. Updating: Who will be responsible to recommend or seek recommendations for future enhancements and videodisc collection decisions?

9. Training: How will educators be trained to use the new videodisc technology?

Summary

This chapter described videodisc technology. Discussions included a comparison of videodisc and videotape characteristics, CAV and CLV format standards, levels of interactivity, and videodisc development.

Recommended Periodicals

BYTE
Educational Technology
Electronic Learning
Laserdisc Professional
Journal of Educational Multimedia and Hypermedia
MacUser
MacWorld
MPC
Multimedia Review
Optical Information Systems

PC Computing
PC Magazine
PC Week
PC World
The Computing Teacher
T.H.E. Journal

Resources

AIMS Media. 6901 Woodley Ave., Van Nuys, CA 91406. (800) 367-2467.

Alarton Press, Inc. PO Box 1882, Boulder, CO 80306. (800) 523-9177.

Applied Learning International. 1751 West Deihl Ave., Naperville, IL 60540. (312) 369-3000.

Barcode Maker. Creative Laser Concepts. 555 Saturn Blvd., Suite B-281, San Diego, CA 92154. (619) 424-5117.

Encyclopaedia Britannica Educational Corp. 310 South Michigan Avenue, Chicago, IL 60604. (800) 554-9862.

From Media to Multimedia: Empowering your Videos with Interactivity. Pioneer Communications of America. Multimedia Systems Division, 600 E. Crescent Ave., Upper Saddle River, NJ 07458. (800) LASER-ON.

Info-Disc Corporation. 4 Professional Dr., Suite 134, Gaitherburg, MD 20879. (800) 648-6422.

Laser Learning Technologies. 3114 37th Place South, Seattle, WA 98144. (800) 722-3505.

Laserworks. 3336 North Clark, Chicago, IL 60657. (312) 327-3636.

Minnesota Educational Computing Corporation (MECC). 6160 Summit Dr. North, Minneapolis, MN 55430. (800) 685-MECC.

National Geographic Society Educational Services. Washington, DC 20036. (800) 368-2728.

Optical Data Corporation. 30 Technology Dr., Warren, NJ 07060. (800) 524-2481.

Optical Recording Laser Videodisc Post Production Guide. 3M Optical Recording Department, 3M Center Building 223-5N-01, St. Paul, MN 55144-1000. (715) 235-5567.

Philips and Du Pont Optical Corporation. 409 Foulk Rd., Suite 200, Wilmington, DE 19803. (302) 479-2514.

Pioneer Communications of America, Inc. 600 East Crescent Ave., Upper Saddle River, NJ 07458. (800) LASER-ON.

Rain Forest. National Geographic Society. 17th and M Sts., Washington, DC 20036. (800) 638-4077.

SEM Video Products, Inc. 2147 East 17th St., Brooklyn, NY 11229. (800) 247-6644.

Society for Visual Education, Inc. Department BM, 1345 Diversey Pkwy., Chicago, IL 60614-1299. (800) 621-1900.

Sony Corporation of America. Intelligent Systems Division, Sony Dr., Park Ridge, NJ 07656. (201) 930-6034.

Smithsonian Laserdisc Collection. Lumivision. 1490 Lafayette St., Suite 305, Denver, CO 80218-2393. (303) 800-0400.

Teaching Technologies. PO Box 3808, San Luis Obispo, CA 93403-3808. (805) 541-3100.

Technidisc, Inc. 2250 Maijer Dr., Troy, MI 48084-7111. (800) 321-9610.

U.S. Video Source. 219 Glenridge Ave., Montclair, NJ 07042. (800) USA-DISC.

VideoDiscovery. 1515 Dexter Ave., N., Suite 400, Seattle, WA 98109. (800) 548-3472.

The Voyager Company. 1351 Pacific Coast Hwy., Santa Monica, CA 90401. (800) 446-2001.

References

Ambron, S. & Cooper, K. (1988). *Interactive multimedia: Visions of multimedia for developers, educators, and information providers.* Redmond, WA: Microsoft Press.

Anderson, C. & Veljkov, M. (1990). *Creating interactive multimedia: A practical guide.* Glenville, IL: Scott, Foresman & Co.

Barron, A.E. & Orwig, G.W. (1993). *New technologies for education.* Englewood, CO: Libraries Unlimited, Inc.

Beer, J. & Freifeld, K. (1992, May). Super tutorials. *PC World, 10* (5), 192-194.

Bergman, R.E. & Moore, T.V. (1990). *Managing interactive video/multimedia projects.* Englewood Cliffs, NJ: Educational Technology Publications, Inc.

Carlson, H.L. & Falk, D.R. (1989). Effective use of interactive videodisc instruction in understanding and implementing cooperative group learning with elementary pupils in social studies and social education. *Theory and Research in Social Education, 17* (3), 241-258.

Cowan, H. & Walker, N. (1990). Graphic history. *Electronic Learning, 10* (2), 30.

Gayeski, D.M. (1992, May). Making sense of multimedia: Introduction to special issue. *Educational Technology, 32* (5), 9-13.

Glenn, A.D. & Sales, G.C. (1990, Spring). Interactive video: its status and future in the social sciences. *International Journal of Social Education, 5* (1), 74-84.

Harter, D.L. (1991, May). Results of a study on a methodology for the diffusion of interactive videodisc technology into a secondary school curriculum. In N. Estes & M. Thomas (Eds.), *Proceedings of the Twelfth Educational Computing Organization of Ontario Conference and the Eighth International Conference on Technology and Education* (pp. 178-180). The University of Texas at Austin, Austin, TX.

Hasselbring, T.S., Sherwood, R., & Bransford, J. (1988). An evaluation of a level-one instructional videodisc program. *Journal of Educational Technology Systems, 16* (2), 151-169.

Henich, R., Molenda, M. & Russell, J.D. (1993). *Instructional media and the new technologies of instruction* (4th ed.). New York: Macmillan Publishing Company.

Hessel, S. (1988). Interactive videodisc and special education. *Optical Information Systems, 8* (4), 190-196.

Hosie, P. (1987). Adopting interactive videodisc technology for education. *Educational Technology, 27* (7), 5-10.

Imke, S. (1991). *Interactive video management and production.* Englewood Cliffs, NJ: Educational Technology Publications, Inc.

Jones, L.L. & Smith, S.G. (1990). Using interactive video courseware to teach laboratory science. *Tech Trends, 35* (6), 22-24.

Kushner, J. (1991, May). HyperCard-driven videodisc presentations. In N. Estes & M. Thomas, (Eds.), *Proceedings of the Twelfth Educational Computing Organization of Ontario Conference and the Eighth International Conference on Technology and Education* (p. 608). The University of Texas at Austin, Austin, TX.

Lynch, P. (1991). *Multimedia: Getting started.* Sunnyvale, CA: PUBLIX Information Products, Inc.

McKendree, J. & Mateer, J. (1992, September). Design and production of interactive video. Paper presented at *The Sixth Annual Conference of Distance Education, Training and Interactive Technologies*, University of Maine.

Nordgren, L.E. & Fry, L.C. (1990). Interactive video "for the rest of us." *Apple Library Users Group Newsletter*, 100-105.

Optical Data Corporation. (1991). *Pocket guide for video disc-enhanced instruction.* Warren, NJ: Optical Data Corporation.

Orwig, G.W. & Baumbach, D.J. (1991). *Laser video discs: What every educator needs to know about the new technologies.* The UCF/DOE Instructional Technology Resource Center, College of Education, University of Central Florida.

Phillipo, J. (1988, November/December). Videodisc players: A multi-purpose audiovisual tool. *Electronic Learning, 8* (3), 50-52.

The PRINTOUT: Special Videodisc Issue. (1991, Spring). The UCF/DOE Instructional Technology Resource Center, College of Education, University of Central Florida, 7 (2), 2-15.

Reed, M. (1991, October). Videodiscs help American Indians learn English and study heritage. *T.H.E. Journal, 19* (3), 96-97.

Sales, G.C. (1989, May). Applications of videodiscs in education. *The Computing Teacher, 16* (8), 27-29.

Schweir, R. (1988). *Interactive video.* Englewood Cliffs, NJ: Educational Technology Publications, Inc.

Schweir, R.A. & Misanchuk, E.R. (1993). *Interactive multimedia instruction.* Englewood Cliffs, NJ: Educational Technology Publications, Inc.

Slike, S.B. *et al.* (1989). The efficiency and effectiveness of an interactive videodisc system to teach sign language vocabulary. *American Annals of the Deaf, 134* (4), 288-290.

Smith, R.A. (1990). Videodisc — The next temptation. *The Computing Teacher, 17* (5), 12 & 13.

Van Horn, R. (1992). Educational power tools: New instructional delivery systems. In J.J. Hirschbuhl & L.F. Wilkinson (Eds.), *Computers in Education* (5th ed.). Guilford, CT: The Dushkin Publishing Group, Inc., 31-36.

Veir, C. (1988). Capitalizing on technological advances to serve rural special education populations. *Rural Special Education Quarterly, 9* (4), 7-15.

The videodisc compendium: 1992-1993 edition. (1993). St. Paul, MN: Emerging Technology Consultants. (Annual Updates)

12 Chapter Twelve:
Desktop Computer Music

What is desktop computer music?

In schools the advent of desktop computer music is changing music education. Using digitized sound with microcomputers, electronic music in classroom settings can be divided into three categories: CD technologies, microcomputer music programming, and Musical Instrument Digital Interface (MIDI). This chapter will emphasize MIDI, since it is now the most creative influence in music education.

First, new optical data technologies, particularly the compact disc or CD (sometimes referred to as CD-Audio or CD-A), enables you to enjoy high-quality sound plus non-sequenced selection of musical pieces on disc. Replacing long-playing records, CDs are more durable and have better sound than records, or audio tapes. One of the newest developments in CD technology is called CD + MIDI. By combining MIDI technology with CD, CD music discs can accompany themselves by your changing of instruments, key signatures, and other MIDI information. Some new CD-ROM products also contain high-quality sound plus the advantage of storing large amounts of information. (See Chapter Ten.) When connected to a multimedia system controlled by a computer, CD sound and large CD-ROM storage capacity can enhance the teaching learning/process, adding a new dimension to text-based resources. See Figure 12.1.

Figure 12.1. This CD-ROM disc not only contains 31,000 articles but also sounds and music, including a composition from Mozart. *(Courtesy Compton's MultiMedia Encyclopedia)*

Second, from the 1970s, microcomputers were introduced to educational settings with BASIC and Logo programming languages the mainstay of instruction. During the same period the **Sound Interface Device** or **SID** chip was added to microcomputers, providing these electronic devices with sounds suitable to musical programming in BASIC and Logo. By writing simple BASIC or Logo programs, even on the limited 64K RAM memory, it was possible to create and control electronic sound. Through a process called Electronic Sound Synthesis, the sounds of a plucking string or fingering the notes of acoustical instruments were created. In addition to musical tones, the microcomputer could also create a variety of sound effects. However, during this period, there were no interfacing standards for combining a synthesizer and a computer. This meant that hardware pieces were incompatible.

Third, in 1983, instrument manufacturers developed **Musical Instrument Digital Interface** or **MIDI**. This industry-wide protocol for exchanging digitally encoded information to control a synthesizer's sound circuitry resolved the problem of non-communication between computers and synthesizers. MIDI is an interfacing standard that permitted various manufactured hardware pieces to be connected together in a series. During the 1980s most synthesizers contained microprocessors to control musical sounds. Less than ten years later, the microprocessors themselves made the musical sounds. With the addition of MIDI, musical keyboards rather than computer keyboards could be connected to the microcomputer. The simplistic sounds made by the computer were enhanced and expanded through the MIDI interface, which translates software commands or instructions into the language that is recognized by the connected peripherals (e.g., drum machine).

What is MIDI?

MIDI is the standard for communicating musical information among musical devices and microcomputers. Simply, musical notes are converted into digital numerical patterns. By connecting a musical keyboard synthesizer to a microcomputer, or adding a special sound card and sound source, you can create complex compositions that can be stored, edited, and played on your microcomputer. In addition, you can control the number and sound of instruments. If you wish to see your composition in musical notation, it is possible to even print your musical score. This process is similar to writing, storing, and printing your documents in word processing. However, in MIDI, sound is stored in addition to text-based documents. Currently MIDI is becoming a more reasonably priced and more common item in electronics shops because of the development of new multimedia microcomputers.

What is needed to develop a MIDI system?

Like microcomputer systems, MIDI systems need hardware and software. Besides your basic microcomputer, hardware components you will need are a synthesizer (keyboard with headphone jacks), an amplifier (sound enhancer such as the school stereo system and standard headphones), and an interface device (allows software to be connected to a "tape synch" multi-track tape recorder or "drum synch," which enables a machine to be synchronized with another MIDI device such as the synthesizer). In addition, you might decide that you would also like to connect other hardware options.

The following five types of software can be used in MIDI educational settings: (1) **Sequencer software**, contains sound data; (2) **music generator software**, stores piano, bass, and drum sounds; (3) **notation software**, changes MIDI data into standard musical notation which can be varied with desktop publishing tools; (4) **educational software**, instructs the student to play and better understand musical concepts; and (5) **entertainment software**, displays color, computer-generated screen images called **fractals**. Fractals are timed to sound emissions.

The most important software type is sequencer software, which offers basic features that enables you to change the tempo and pitch within musical pieces, transpose compositions, and make multi-track recordings. When purchasing sequencer software, you should consider five factors: (1) ease of use; (2) real-time, step-time, and modular programming; (3) number of tracks; (4) quantization; and (5) the ability to print music scores. Ease of use means that the manuals and tutorials should be clearly written with on-screen practice.

Real-time, step-time, and modular programming means that all played music can be stored (in real time) and written one note at a time (step-time). In addition, song fragments can be sequenced separately and then linked together to form a complete composition (modular programming). Regarding the number of tracks, individual tracks vary from four to 64. The ideal number for educational purposes is 16. Quantization means auto-correct where software features correct timing errors. This feature is particularly helpful to beginning composers. Lastly, it is recommended that you be able to make hard copies of musical compositions. You can accomplish this goal if your software has printing capabilities. If not, request the name of a compatible music printing program that you can purchase.

What musical knowledge is needed to learn MIDI?

To fully understand the capabilities of MIDI, you must have a basic understanding of music and sound, including knowledge of pitch, loudness, duration, and timbre, since these elements change sound into music. It is also valuable to understand waveforms and the shaping of sound. Of course, understanding synthesizers and their role in MIDI compositions is valuable as well. Two books that provide a good basic understanding of music fundamentals and MIDI explanations for MIDI novice educators are *The MIDI Book: Using MIDI and Related Interfaces* by Steve DeFuria with Joe Scacciaferro and *Music and the Macintosh* by Geary Yelton.

What are some advantages of desktop computer music in education?

There are at least four advantages for the use of desktop computer music in the classroom:

First, with computer programming and MIDI, students and teachers can create their own musical works, which can be developed, stored, manipulated, and played on computer disks providing both motivation and opportunities to compose original pieces. With CD technologies, students and teachers can selectively access high-quality sound from a storage medium.

Second, through MIDI, students can practice performance skills on synthesizer keyboards and explore musical theory on microcomputers by using special composition software.

Third, MIDI users input data on a synthesizer keyboard rather than a traditional computer keyboard.

Fourth, individualized and personalized learning are encouraged.

What are some specific products of computer desktop music used in education?

• *Beethoven Symphony No. 9* is a product developed by a professor at UCLA and manufactured by Voyager Company for use on the *Macintosh* computer. In addition a CD player and *HyperCard* stacks are also required. (See Chapter 13 for a description of *HyperCard*.) The listener not only hears Beethoven's famous symphony but also through a multimedia format can see graphics and read text concerning this composer.

• *The Magic Flute* from Warner New Media is another CD-ROM product which contains three discs of opera and concert music. In this program both German and English librettos are available, a summary of the story line, an analysis of the piece, a glossary of terms and several other features. In *The Magic Flute*, the music is stored in MIDI format and is accessed through MIDI software. So, you will need a Macintosh computer with hypertext capabilities and a CD player.

• *Music in Education* by Yamaha is a technology-assisted music program in which electronic components are integrated into general music classes. The system utilizes student keyboards, an overhead projector, a compact disc player, and a remote control device which are all linked to a microcomputer running a customized software program.

What are some examples of desktop computer music used in education?

A successful independent study music curriculum was developed to provide an alternate method for an external college degree program. Through computer assisted instruction (CAI), students were able to study music history, theory of orchestration, musical composition, and keyboarding skills on a synthesizer.

Another example of individualized instruction for musical theory helps correct errors in the student's input. Using a synthesizer, the student plays a musical piece which is shown in notation form on the computer screen. Incorrect rhythm, note, or tempo input is shown in musical notation next to the original passage. Both pieces are played and viewed for analysis and correction.

A study reported the use of MIDI in a middle school in Canada. A special project called the Technology in Music Programme (TIMP) was established. Students at the seventh and eighth grade levels were provided MIDI technology, MIDI wind instruments, and a sound editing and production location. Students were encouraged to cultivate creative activities in musical composition, performing, and listening in a collaborative fashion.

According to the study results, the students successfully achieved curriculum goals of the core music curriculum.

The Association for Technology in Music Instruction is a national support network for novice desktop computer music teachers. If you need help and have questions regarding MIDI, in particular, this group can be a valuable resource.

Band teachers of all levels find the features of MIDI useful. For example, if you are introducing a new ensemble piece, and one passage is difficult, through MIDI you can access that passage and play it at half speed to listen for details.

Vocal teachers use new MIDI software that enables the input of the human voice. When an individual sings, the computer offers feedback about the accuracy of the singer's pitch, which can be compared to the synthesizer's rendition.

What are some desktop computer music problems and solutions?

There are several recurring problems identified by educators regarding desktop computer music:

First, the high cost of desktop computer music. As more schools purchase newer, faster, and higher RAM microcomputers (especially the multimedia personal computers), the decision to integrate desktop computer music in the classroom becomes less expensive. If you already own a microcomputer, other hardware components become add-ons and thus the cost of music programming, CD technologies, or MIDI becomes more affordable.

Second, the lack of sufficient and readily accessible support. One answer is to network with the Association for Technology in Music Instruction or to join local desktop computer users' groups. Ideally, an on-site technician who can offer hardware advice and provide service with hardware problems should be encouraged.

Third, the lack of sufficient training. If formal courses are not available to learn this new technology, then curious educators acquire the necessary knowledge and skills informally either by teaching themselves through manuals and tutorials or receiving assistance from a colleague who is knowledgeable on this topic.

Fourth, the wide range of quality in hardware and software. "Test drive" the hardware and software prior to purchase. Visit a computer store, another educational site, and interact with the system. During a trial period, work with the system to see if it meets your needs and expectations.

Decision-making Guidelines: Desktop Computer Music

1. Objective: Which type of desktop computer music (CDs, programming, MIDI, or CD + MIDI) will be selected for your educational setting?

2. Integration: How will desktop computer music be integrated within the curriculum? Does your selection best fit in a music class curriculum, in a self-contained class curriculum, or for research as a reference resource?

3. Cost: What are the initial costs for your selection of desktop computer music?

4. Location: Where will the desktop computer music hardware and software be placed? Will the music room, library/media center, or regular classroom be the best location?

5. Security: How will the desktop computer music hardware and software be protected from theft or vandalism? Who will be responsible for the safety of this equipment?

6. Equal Access: Will both educators and students be provided access to the desktop computer music hardware and software? What policy measures for equal access will be established? Who will be responsible for developing an equal access policy?

7. Updating: Who will be designated as the person responsible to research, compare, and recommend new hardware and software?

8. Training: Who will be trained to use these applications? When and where will the training course occur? Will there be a special time and financial or in-kind benefits offered to the trainees?

Summary

Desktop Computer Music is changing music teaching and learning in educational settings. This topic was divided into three categories: (1) CD technologies, (2) microcomputer music programming, and (3) MIDI. Since MIDI is the most complex category, which requires a basic understanding of music fundamentals, emphasis was placed on the MIDI category.

Recommended Periodicals

American Music Journal
BYTE
Computer Music Journal
The Computing Teacher
Current Musicology
Journal of Research in Music Education

Keyboard Magazine
Sight & Sound
Tech Trends
Technology & Learning

Resources

Adobe Systems. 1585 Charleston Rd., Mountain View, CA 94039. (415) 961-4400.

Advanced Software. 18520 Vincennes #31, Northridge, CA 91324. (818) 349-9334.

Alesis. 3630 Holdrege Ave., Los Angeles, CA 90016. (231) 467-8000.

Altech Systems. 831 Kings Highway, Suite 200, Shreveport, LA 71104. (318) 226-1702.

Apple Computer. 20525 Mariani Avenue, Cupertino, CA 95014. (408) 996-1010.

Association for Technology in Music Instruction. 121 Harris Avenue South, Hopkins, MN 55343. (612) 933-5290.

Audiomedia. Digidesign. 1360 Willow Rd., Suite 101, Menlo Park, CA 94025. (415) 688-0600.

Basic Composer. Education Software Consultant. 934 Forest Ave., Oak Park, IL 60302. (708) 848-6677.

Coda Music Software. 1401 East 79th St., Suite 1, Bloomington, MN 55425. (612) 854-1288.

Digital Music Services. 23010 Lake Forest Dr., Suite D334, Laguna Hills, CA 92653. (714) 951-1159.

Diversified Software. 34880 Bunker Hill, Farminton, MI 48331. (313) 553-9460.

Electronic Arts. 1820 Gateway Dr., San Mateo, CA 94404. (800) 245-4525.

Electronic Courseware Systems. 1210 Lancaster Dr., Champaign, IL 61821. (217) 359-7099.

Great Wave Software. 5353 Scotts Valley Dr., Scotts Valley, CA 95066. (408) 438-1990.

Intelligent Music. 116 North Lake Ave., Albany, NY 12206. (518) 434-4110.

Kurzweil Music Systems. 411 Waverly Oaks Rd., Waltham, MA 02154. (617) 893-5900.

MacMIDI Distributing. 18 Haviland St., Boston, MA 02115. (617) 266-2886.

Mark of the Unicorn. 222 Third St., Cambridge, MA 02142. (617) 576-2760.

Mediagenic (formerly *Activision*). 3885 Bohannon Dr., Menlo Park, CA 94025. (415) 329-0500.

Music Composer. Creative Music Labs. 1901 McCarthy Blvd., Milpitas, CA 95035. (408) 428-6600.

Music Systems for Learning. 311 East 38th St., New York, NY 10016. (212) 661-6096.

Oberheim ECC. 2015 Davie Ave., Commerce, CA 90040. (213) 725-7870.

Opcode Systems. 1024 Hamilton Ct., Menlo Park, CA 94025. (415) 321-8977.

Optical Media International. 485 Alberto Way, Suite 115, Los Gatos, CA 95032. (408) 395-4332.

Passport Designs, Inc. 625 Miramontes St., Suite 103, Half Moon Bay, CA 94019. (415) 726-0280.

Resonate. PO Box 996, Menlo Park, CA 94026. (415) 323-5022.

Sound Master II. Covox. 675-D Conger St., Eugene, OR 97402. (503) 342-1271.

Southworth Music Systems. 91 Ann Lee Rd., Harward, MA 01451. (508) 772-9471.

Studio Master Computer Systems. 229 Sunny Isles Blvd., North Miami Beach, FL 33160. (305) 945-9774.

The Voyager Company. 1351 Pacific Coast Highway, Santa Monica, CA 90401. (800) 446-2001.

Yamaha Corporation of America. 3445 E. Paris Ave., SE Grand Rapids, MI 49512. (714) 522-9011.

References

Ashley, R.D. (1989). *Redesigning the content and sequence in music theory.* Final Report to Fund for the Improvement of Post Secondary Education, Washington, DC.

Barron, A.E. & Orwig, G.W. (1993). *New technologies for education.* Englewood, CO: Libraries Unlimited, Inc.

Casbona, H. & Frederick, D. (1987). *Using MIDI.* Cupertino, CA: Alfred.

Clarkson, A.E. & Austin, K. (1991). *An assessment of a technology in a music programme, technical support 91-2, revised version.* York University Center for the Study of Computers in Education, North York, Ontario, Canada.

DeFuria, S. & Scacciaferro, J. (1988). *The MIDI book: Using MIDI and related interfaces.* Pompton Lakes, NJ: Third Earth Productions, Inc.

Jordahl, G. (1988, October). Teaching music in the age of MIDI. *Classroom Computer Learning, 9* (2), 78-85.

Kearsley, G., Hunter, B., & Furlong, M. (1992). *We teach with technology: New visions for education.* Wilsonville, OR: Franklin, Beedle & Associates, Inc.

Pogue, D. (1991). First steps in the sequence: How to get started in Mac MIDI music without really trying. *MacWorld, 8* (6), 146-53.

Rona, J. (1988). *MIDI: The ins, outs & thrus.* Milwaukee, WI: Hal Leonard Books.

Rumsey, F. (1990). *MIDI systems and controls.* Cambridge, England: Butterworth.

Van Horn, R. (1991). *Advanced technology in education.* Pacific Grove, CA: Brooks/Cole.

Vogel, J. & Scrimshaw, N.B. (1983). *The Commodore 64 music book: A guide to programming music and sound.* Boston, MA: Birkhauser Boston, Inc.

Wallenbach, J. (1991, June). Equipping your PC for high-quality sound production. *PC Today, 1* (5) 32-38.

Yelton, G. (1989). *Music and the Macintosh: How to create and play music with your desktop computer.* Atlanta, GA: MIDI America, Inc.

13

Chapter Thirteen:
Multimedia, Hypermedia,
and Beyond

What is multimedia?

Several technologies are included under the umbrella term of multimedia (e.g., CD technologies, videodiscs, desktop computer music). Prior to microcomputers, multimedia meant a collection of traditional audiovisual (AV) equipment such as slide projectors and audiocassette players used together in a single presentation to enhance instruction. You might remember using a "multimedia kit" that included teaching/ learning aids to enhance a particular curriculum topic.

There were three purposes for using multimedia in classrooms: (1) to increase student motivation through visual and auditory enrichment; (2) to meet individual learning styles; and (3) to extend learning beyond textbook reading. Although the purposes of multimedia today are still the same, the addition of computer-based interactivity has added a new dimension to multimedia. Now multimedia, also called computer-based multimedia, is the combination of two or more electronic media devices controlled by a microcomputer. Sometimes referred to as integrated media, multimedia provides a multisensory and interactive approach unimaginable in most educational settings less than five years ago.

As stated in the introduction to Part IV, multimedia provides the experience of sound, text, video, animation, and graphics networked and delivered primarily via the microcomputer monitor. Users can control the data sequence, respond to multiple-choice questions, and edit information. Because of new developments, multimedia that uses a digitized delivery system is referred to as digital multimedia (e.g., CDs).

What electronic devices are included in a multimedia system?

The configuration of equipment varies. Combinations of technologies, described in previous chapters, such as the videodisc, CD-ROM, MIDI, VCR, television, printer, and software, can be incorporated into a variety of electronic computer-based systems.

There are three approaches to multimedia systems: (1) scavenger multimedia systems; (2) multimedia system upgrade kits; and (3) new preconfigured multimedia systems.

In the past, scavenger multimedia systems were designed by physically wiring computer memory to optical data storage capacities with video and audio capabilities. What electronic devices were connected depended on the needs, interests, knowledge, and cost factors identified by the user. This approach took much time and expertise.

Currently, new hardware products are appearing on the educational market to simplify the process of developing multimedia systems. If you have a microcomputer already, you might be able to purchase a multimedia upgrade kit which includes CD players and software, sound cards, headphones, speakers, and cables. If you would like to buy a totally new preconfigured multimedia system, you can find them on the market today. For example, *IBM* has released its *Ultimedia PC* which generates and displays near-broadcast quality video. *Tandy* has developed its *MPC* or *Multimedia Personal Computer. Macintosh* computers now have built-in speakers and a hypertext programming tool called *HyperCard* to create courseware and presentations.

Besides the "Big Three" in educational computing, other companies offer specialized hardware which facilitates the use of multimedia in the school. One such company, the COMWEB Technology Group, has designed a plug-together hardware network called the "Computer-Video WEB." The WEB is different from traditional networks in that it interconnects microcomputers via their monitor, keyboard, and mouse ports. The person controlling the WEB can present the same multimedia display on a number of monitors at the same time. Since the computers in this arrangement are not linked through a CPU or a file server as in a traditional LAN, there is no interference with the independent functioning of the computers. The system is software independent, which means it can interconnect a variety of operating systems including, for example, MS-DOS and MAC. (See Figure 13.1.)

Figure 13.1. Controlling simultaneous multimedia displays on microcomputer monitors in a group setting. *(Courtesy of COMWEB Technology Group)*

How has multimedia influenced teaching/learning styles?

As the original concept of multimedia provided teachers and students with a more multisensoral and multidimensional approach to learning, the new computer-based multimedia is extending and expanding teaching/learning styles. The most dynamic change has been in the opportunity for user interactivity with an emphasis on discovery-oriented, self-paced instruction. The new multimedia is more closely related to real-world learning. Real-world learning is the serendipitous approach by which we follow our curiosity and interest to understand a new concept rather than follow a sequenced step-by-step workbook.

Rather than passively following predetermined step-by-step sequences of visual and audio information (**linear learning**), you or your student can manipulate and control the presentation of sight and sound data according to individual interest and needs (**non-linear learning** or **branching**.) For example, reading a book or viewing a movie from beginning to end is linear learning. In comparison, developing a concept map on a blackboard linking topic ideas and themes, developing word associations, or serendipitously following your curiosity in learning is branching. Simply, linear learning follows predetermined sequential links of information whereas branching follows associative, intuitive links of data. For example, Figure 13.2 illustrates *Compton's MultiMedia Encyclopedia* which provides eight unique paths for the student to enter the encyclopedia depending on interest, curriculum, and learning style.

With multimedia usage, self-directed learning is encouraged, empowering students to self-discover knowledge, thus, in turn, promoting more self-confidence. As Geoffrey R. Amthor states:

Figure 13.2. The Main Menu from *Compton's MultiMedia Encyclopedia. (Courtesy of Compton's MultiMedia Encyclopedia)*

It (multimedia) taps into our basic need for self-determination, making us active participants in life, explorers and not idle passengers (Amthor, p. 2, 1991).

How is branching used in multimedia?

Suppose you or your students were studying about a famous inventor, using a multimedia system. Rather than manually reviewing facts in traditional book format, it is easy to "call up" an encyclopedia on CD-ROM and read about his life. Then you might want to see a map of his country, or a list of other inventors who lived during the same time period, which, again, you can access through your microcomputer. Next you might want to see a demonstration of his invention, so you request a short video of the experiment. If your curiosity is aroused about lifestyles in that time period, you can "branch" or choose to find out more on that topic as well — all without leaving your microcomputer. As you can see, learning can become more serendipitous or more curiosity-driven rather than a directed step-by-step approach in studying a subject area. Also, since you can access information quickly from your microcomputer, your research time is decreased drastically.

Of course, to enable you to personally research your area of interest, you will need a multimedia system that contains the appropriate hardware and software. Any discovery learning approach system, therefore, needs three software components: (1) an informational electronic database related to your topic of interest, (2) on-screen directions to help guide your search, and (3) tools to manipulate your data.

In summary, multimedia systems provide massive databases for personal investigation. Although you may control the selection and sequence of information, you cannot link and annotate sets of information into larger webs or networked collections. To accomplish this task, you can use a **hypermedia system**.

What is hypermedia?

Hypermedia is a document networking system creating pathways which connect **nodes** (related chunks of data) together. Nodes can be in text, graphics, audio, and video formats. Originally the term **hypertext** was used to describe hypermedia when basically text formats of data were networked. Now the term hypermedia has been expanded to include a variety of audiovisual formats. In comparison to multimedia, which combines more than one media type to disseminate information, hypermedia systems enable you and your students to *create* presentations gathering and storing data from linked networks of electronic sources.

What electronic devices are included in a hypermedia system?

Like a multimedia system, a hypermedia system provides a multisensoral approach to learning. Hardware includes a microcomputer with a mouse and keyboard, CD-ROM, videodisc player, video monitor, and speakers. The user, through the microcomputer, is in control of the text, high-quality sound, animation, and still and motion images.

In hypermedia, you and your students can take part in building your own linked webs of information through browsing, comparing, analyzing, and storing data for presentations or self-studies. Special software programs called **authoring tools** assist in this endeavor. Also referred to as program developer's tools, authoring tools allow you to work with bit-mapped displays, windows, icons, and pull-down menus in a mouse-driven environment.

To better understand this concept, the process used in the *HyperCard* program for the MAC LC microcomputer will be described. *HyperCard* is referred to as a **low-end** or fairly easy to use product. Based on the simple metaphor, the index card, this authoring tool allows you to store text, graphics, sounds, and animation sequences on full-screen sized cards which are grouped in topically-related sets called **stacks**. On each card you design **buttons** which are single characters or icons that point out links in your document. Links via buttons can connect one card to another or control external electronic devices such as CD-ROM drives and videodisc players. Clicking on the buttons will activate the links. See Figure 13.3.

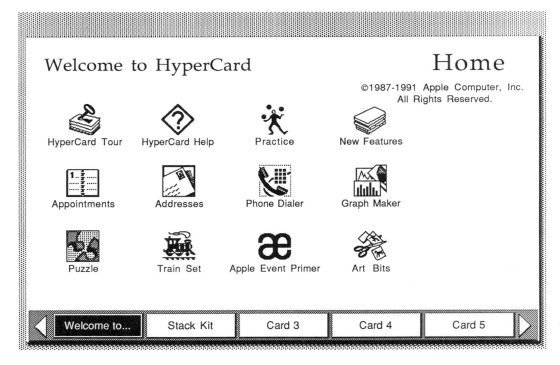

Figure 13.3. A Home Card for HyperCard. *(Courtesy of Claris. HyperCard Software is © 1987 — 1993 Claris Corporation. All rights reserved. HyperCard is a registered trademark of Claris Corporation.)*

You create each button through *HyperTalk*, which is a simple programming language, called **scripting**, that lets you expand and customize buttons, cards, and stacks. For example, if you wanted to develop a computer-based demonstration to explain a topic, you can integrate images, sound, and motion (based on your hypermedia system capabilities) in a program that you personally designed. By using hypermedia or hypertext, you control and organize your own audiovisual presentation by identifying, linking, and storing selections of related information.

What are some other hypertext and hypermedia products?

There are many new products for hypertext and hypermedia. There is an assortment of public domain stacks called **stackware** that you can find available at conferences, in computer and multimedia periodical listings, and through electronic bulletin board systems. Commercial products include the following examples:

• *AmigaVision 1.2* is similar to *HyperCard* but is more an icon or symbol-based programming language. Created for the Amiga PC, AmigaVision uses script flow chart-like programs. Relatively simple to use, this software applications tool is sophisticated yet relatively inexpensive.

• *Audiomedia* is an authoring tool to record, edit, and playback CD-quality sound system which can be connected to multimedia presentation packages for sound enhancement.

• *Authorware Professional* assists in the creation of integrated graphics, sound, text, animation, and video using icons and objects in place of scripting.

• *Course Builder* is a visual authoring tool to create both teaching and testing applications. Besides including graphics, editing, text, animation, and digital sound output, a special extension module for this product can add the enhancement of interactive video to presentations or courseware.

• *The Fourmat Learning Process* is a tool designed specifically for the creation of instructional materials. Tutorials enhanced with sound, video, graphics, text, and animation can be developed without scripting or programming.

• *LinkWay Live!* is an updated version of LinkWay, relatively sophisticated, yet reasonably priced software designed for MS-DOS standalone or networked computers. LinkWay Live! is a point-and-click control system for all multimedia devices.

• *MPG* is multimedia authoring software that is compatible with any IBM PC or clone. Instead of scripting, you simply use a mouse in a point-and-click environment.

• *VideoShow HQ* is a product that provides the possibilities of incorporating full-motion video, live video, stereo sound, photographic images, animation, and graphics into presentations.

What are some of the newest technologies that will influence changes in future education settings?

Besides, for example, videodiscs and CD technologies providing a merger of high-quality sight, sound, and vast information storage capabilities, there are some very new technologies being introduced to wider circles of educators. One of the newest educational technologies is **Desktop Video**. In addition a very new technology called **Virtual Reality** is only on the edge of the educational horizon. Since it has unique potential impact for the teaching and learning environments, a brief introduction will be provided.

What is desktop video?

Desktop video is simply the use of microcomputers to create video productions. Previously, the costs of a traditional video production could be hundreds of thousands of dollars. Now with the advent of the powerful microcomputer video, production costs have decreased. This very new technology has much educational potential. Some advocates project that desktop video will become as important as desktop publishing, but with a video end product, rather than a hard copy from a laser printer.

What is virtual reality?

This fascinating concept that is just in its infancy stage barely touching the educational setting, but an impending force in the restructuring for future educational settings. Virtual reality is the technology that combines the human world and the computer world using a computer-based system displaying synthetic three-dimensional scenes in which you vicariously interact. This **virtual world** mimics reality. According to Sandra Helsel, virtual reality will have an impact on education in two ways: (1) traditional learning styles through text and graphics book format will change to simulations through computer-controlled environments, and (2) a new emphasis on imagery and symbol-based materials will emerge.

An example of virtual reality exists in the world of modern artists. There is a project design that will allow you to walk, fly, or float through a work of art. To do so you need simply to wear a visor called a **visette**, which projects LCD computer-generated images on its screen for you to view. As you move, you "enter" and "explore" the world of virtual reality. Currently, this technology is limited to sight and sound sensations. Future upgrades of current products are projected to include the sense of touch. Developers have created a **dataglove** or tactile sensory glove that will allow you to actually feel items that you view through your visette which, in reality, do not physically exist.

In virtual reality you can visualize simulated computerized surroundings and interact with **knowbots** (computer-based agents that simulate people) and **avatars** (computer-graphic representations of human agents in distant locations). Imagine the possibility of virtual class trips to teach geography and cultures or the possibility of meeting with historic figures from the past? Currently, though, there are very few mass-market applications available to the general public.

However, it is probable that you have already experienced a very rudimentary, small scale form of virtual reality. You might have visited a science museum which provided a simple virtual reality experience. More likely, if you have used a mouse-driven computer environment or a joystick, you can begin to understand the process of interacting with virtual worlds. By moving the mouse or joystick on a desk surface, you have experienced the basics of virtual reality. By controlling the movement of the mouse or joystick, you can control the microworld within the computer.

What are the advantages of using multimedia and hypermedia in education?

Commonly referred to as "the next wave of materials development for technology in the classroom" (Kurshan, 1991), multimedia and hypermedia have at least six basic advantages over traditional methodology: (1) learning motivation increases through nonlinear interactivity; (2) learning is customized to meet individual needs; (3) resources are multisensory; (4) meta-cognitive abilities (thinking about thinking) plus other higher level thinking skills are encouraged; (5) learning is active; and (6) learning sequences and material selection are more teacher/student-controlled than are traditional modes of instruction.

What are some specific uses for multimedia and hypermedia in education?

There are many new multimedia and hypermedia products that are useful to educators. The following list contains several interesting selections:

• *ClipMedia* is a CD-ROM medium containing a variety of multimedia source materials such as graphics, animation, music, sound effects, and video.

• *Deluxe Video III* is desktop video software for creating video productions.

• *Discovery Interactive Library* is a set of videodiscs from the Discovery Channel's Interactive Library focusing upon topics in social studies, science and technology, and natural science.

• *Rain forest* is a multimedia product for students in grades 6-12. Combining a videodisc and a pair of HyperCard stacks, users can access from the first stack of cards six chapters, each including three to seven topics. Chapters include titles such as Watery World, Nocturnal Life, and Forest Canopy. Segments of original film from the rain forests of Costa Rica can be augmented with scripts discussing film segments. Included are Preview Questions for introducing the topic plus Review questions with multiple-choice answers and feedback. An interesting feature is that the second stack of cards will allow students to create their own multimedia presentation by combining information and databases provided on the laserdisc.

What are some multimedia and hypermedia problems and solutions?

As with any new technologies, educators express the following concerns about multimedia and provide suggestions to address them:

First is the issue of cost. To create your own multimedia system, you need not invest in many technologies at once. Components can be added incrementally rather than purchased at one time. For example, a suitable microcomputer might be presently available in your educational setting, including a CPU, keyboard, operating system, color monitor, a hard disk drive, and a mouse. However, you must be aware that your microcomputer must be a fairly powerful one (e.g., MS-DOS 386 or 486 machine) with a high-quality color monitor, a hard disk drive, and audio input/output components.

The next high-cost items are a videodisc and CD-ROM player. Just recently a new product, called an MPC (Multimedia Personal Computer) became available on the market that offers videodisc and CD-ROM abilities in one machine. Lower priced items include a scanner, printer, television, video camera, video and audio digitizers, VCR, speakers, telephone, and a modem.

Second, there is a lack of universal standardization in hardware and software compatibility of older hardware and software in multimedia. This concern can be addressed in one of three ways: (1) assess your present situation: if you have a powerful enough mouse-driven microcomputer and want to use it as part of your multimedia, fine; (2) if you prefer a specific multimedia authoring tool or other software offerings, then select a microcomputer that meets your interests and needs; or (3) purchase a preconfigured multimedia microcomputer system.

The third concern of educators regarding multimedia technology is the need for training. As with any new technology, the best way to develop the knowledge, skills, and understanding of multimedia is by teaching educators about the system prior to placing it in classrooms. Training can begin through various avenues: participation in conferences, workshops, coursework, or self-study. Educators, in turn, after receiving hands-on experiences and gaining the necessary confidence, can assist other educators in learning the new technology, as well as offer advice as to future multimedia purchasing.

One nationally recognized training program is offered at the *Michigan Teacher Explorer Center* in East Lansing, Michigan. This six-hour immersion multimedia workshop is taught by Fred D'Ignazio. Participants are teams of interested teachers and administrators. Hands-on activities are required plus a finished-product videotaped team "journal" of the day at the center. Through the use of multimedia, the educators learn to create a tape using enhancements such as animated computer graphics, digital sound effects, and music from CDs.

Fourth, educators need a technical support system of individuals who can be quickly and easily contacted in case questions or problems arise. A common solution is the provision of an online expert accessed through an 800 number. The best solution is an on-campus or in-house technician who can troubleshoot problems efficiently.

Decision-making Guidelines: Multimedia and Hypermedia

1. Objective: Why use multimedia and hypermedia technology? How will learning/ teaching be enhanced?

2. Integration: How will multimedia and hypermedia be integrated in the teaching/ learning environment? What presently owned media devices will be integrated into a system?

3. Cost: What is the budget cap for multimedia and hypermedia in the school setting? Is there a policy regarding increasing the system with add-on peripherals or electronic devices?

4. Location: Where will the multimedia system be placed? Will there be multimedia and hypermedia systems in classrooms, in the library/media centers, or both locations?

5. Security: How will the hardware and software of the multimedia system be safeguarded against theft or misuse?

6. Equal Access: What policy measures will be developed to provide the opportunities for students and teachers to utilize multimedia and hypermedia systems, particularly if the systems must be shared?

7. Updating: Who will be assigned the responsibility to recommend, add, or delete outdated hardware and software?

8. Training: Who will be trained to use multimedia and hypermedia systems? Where and when will the training occur? Will there be a special time or financial allotments available to the trainees?

Summary

This chapter discussed multimedia and hypermedia. In addition, new technologies such as desktop video and virtual reality were introduced as technologies that will impact educational settings in the future.

Recommended Periodicals

BYTE
Computer Graphics World
Educational Technology
Electronic Learning
International Journal of Robotics Research
Journal of Educational Multimedia and Hypermedia
MPC World
Multimedia Review
PC World
Technology Trends for Leaders in Education and Training
T.H.E. Journal
Technology & Learning

Resources

ABC News InterActive. 7 West 66th St., New York, NY 10023. (800) 524-2481.

Agency for Instructional Technology (AIT). Box A, Bloomington, IN 47402. (800) 457-4509.

Apple Computer, Inc. 20525 Mariani Ave., Cupertino, CA 95014. (800) 538-9696.

Association for Advancement of Computing in Education. PO Box 2966, Charlottesville, VA 22902. (804) 973-3987.

Audiomedia. Digidesign, Inc., 1360 Willow Rd., Ste. 101, Menlo Park, CA 94025. (415) 595-3101.

Authorware, Inc. 275 Shoreline Dr., Suite 535, Redwood City, CA 94065. (800) 288-9576.

Broderbund Software Inc. 500 Redwood Blvd., Novato, CA 94948. (800) 521-6263.

Center for Interactive Multimedia for Education (CIMET). Western Washington University, MH 204, Bellingham, WA 98225. (206) 676-3516.

Children's Television Workshop Interactive Technologies Group. One Lincoln Plaza, New York, NY 10023. (212) 595-3456.

Course Builder. Telerobotics International, Inc., 8410 Oak Ridge Highway, Knoxville, TN 37931. (615) 690-5600.

Deluxe Video III. Electronic Arts, 1820 Gateway Dr., San Mateo, CA 94404. (800) 245-4525.

Discovery Interactive Library. The Discovery Channel, 7700 Wisconsin Rd., Suite 900, Bethesda, MD 20814. (800) 621-2131.

FOURMAT Learning Processor. Fourmat Corporation, 1093 South Orem Blvd., Orem, UT 84058. (800) FOURMAT.

Hypermedia: The guide to interactive media production. MIX Publications, 6400 Hollis St., #12, Emeryville, CA 94608. (415) 653-3307.

IBM Ultimedia. IBM Multimedia and Education Division, 4111 Northside Pkwy., Atlanta, GA 30327. (800) 426-9402.

Intellimation: Library for the Macintosh. PO Box 1922, Santa Barbara, CA 93116. (800) 3-INTELL.

LinkWay Live! IBM Corp. 4111 Northside Pkwy., Atlanta, GA 30327. (800) 426-9402.

MacroMind Inc. 600 Townsend St., San Francisco, CA 94103. (415) 442-0200.

MAD Intelligent Systems. 55 Wheeler St., Cambridge, MA 02138. (617) 492-1982.

Michigan Teacher Explorer Center. Sharon Goth-Taw at Michigan State University, East Lansing, MI. 48823 (517) 337-1781.

Microsoft Corp. One Microsoft Way, Redmond, WA 98052. (800) 426-9400.

MPG. Modern, 515 Madison Ave., Suite 500, New York, NY 10022. (800) 237-7114.

Owl International, Inc. 14218 Northeast 21st St., Bellevue, WA 98007. (800) 344-9737.

Radio Shack. Education Division, 1600 One Tandy Center, Fort Worth, TX 76102. (800) 243-2015.

Rain Forest. National Geographic Society, 17th and M Sts., Washington, DC 20036. (800) 638-4077.

The Voyager Company. 1351 Pacific Coast Hwy., Santa Monica, CA 90401. (800) 446-2001.

References

Ambron, S. & Hooper, K. (Eds.). (1990). *Learning with interactive multimedia: Developing and using multimedia tools in education.* Redmond, WA: Microsoft Press.

Ambrose, D.W. (1991, December). The effects of hypermedia on learning: A literature review. *Educational Technology, 31* (12), 51-55.

Amthor, G.R. (1991, September). Interactive multimedia in education: Concepts and technology trends and model applications, megamedia and knowledge systems. *Special Issue IBM Multimedia: Supplement to T.H.E. Journal,* 2-5.

Anderson, C.J. & Veljkov, M.D. (1990). *Creating interactive multimedia: A practical guide.* Glenview, IL: Scott, Foresman.

Bass, S. (1992, November). Multimedia for the rank and file. *PC World, 10* (11), 344.

Barker, J. & Tucker, R.H. (1990). *The interactive learning revolution: Multimedia in education and training.* New York: Nichols.

Beekman, G. (1990). *HyperCard in a Hurry.* Belmont, CA: Wadsworth.

Billings, L. (1991, September). As ESL tool for the real world. *Electronic Learning, 11* (1), 40 & 63.

Bruder, I. (1991, September). Guide to multimedia: How it changes the way we teach and learn. *Electronic Learning, 11* (1), 22-23.

Byrom, E. (1990, Summer). Hypermedia (multimedia). *Teaching Exceptional Children, 22* (4) 47-48.

Dede, C.J. (1992, May). The future of multimedia: Bridging to virtual worlds. *Educational Technology, 32* (5), 54-60.

D'Ignazio, F. (1989). *The Scholastic guide to classroom multimedia.* New York: Scholastic Publications, Inc.

D'Ignazio, F. (1990, January). Through the looking glass: The multiple layers of multimedia. *Computing Teacher, 17* (4), 25-31.

Fiderio, J. (1988, October). A grand vision. *Byte, 13* (10), 237-244.

Fox, J. (1991, June). The bandwidth blues: Multimedia on networks. *PC Today, 6* (5), 54-61.

Frisse, M. (1988, October). From text to hypertext. *Byte, 13* (10), 247-253.

Galbreath, J. (1992, June). The coming of digital desktop media. *Educational Technology, 32* (6), 27-32.

Galbreath, J. (1993, May). Multimedia: Beyond the desktop. *Educational Technology, 33* (5), 27-32.

Gayeski, D.M. (1992, May). Making sense of multimedia: Introduction to special issue. *Educational Technology, 32* (5), 9-13.

Hasselbring, T.S. *et al.* (1989, Winter). Making knowledge meaningful: Applications of hypermedia. *Journal of Special Education, 10* (2), 61-72.

Helsel, S. (1992, May). Virtual reality and education. *Educational Technology, 32* (5), 38-42.

Hertzberg, L. (1991, November/December). Multimedia authoring languages. *Electronic Learning, 11* (3), 30-32.

Jonassen, D.H. (1991, January). Hypertext as instructional design. *Educational Technology Research and Development, 39* (1), 83-93.

Jonassen, D.H. & Mandl, H. (Eds.). (1990). *Designing hypermedia for learning.* New York: Springer-Verlag.

Kurshan, B. (1991, April). Creating the global classroom for the 21st century. *Educational Technology, 31* (4), 47-49.

Lamb, A. (1992). *IBM LinkWay: Authoring tool.* Orange, CA: Career Publishing.

Leland, J. (1991, June). Desktop Video: The hidden revolution. *PC Today, 6* (5), 23-31.

Loveria, G. & Kinstler, D. (1990, Fall). Multimedia: DVI arrives. *BYTE IBM Special Edition, 15* (11), 105-108.

Lynch, P.L. (1992, April/May). Teaching with multimedia. *Syllabus, 22,* 2-5.

Martin, J. (1990). *Hyperdocuments and how to create them.* Englewood Cliffs, NJ: Prentice-Hall.

Marvin, D. (1991, June). Media integration: Authoring software makes it happen. *PC Today, 6* (5), 15-21.

Multimedia: Getting started. (1990). Sunnyvale, CA: Publix Information Products.

Murdoch, E.E. (1992). *HyperCard the easy way.* Dubuque, IA: Wm. C. Brown.

Pettersson, R. (1993). *Visual information* (2nd ed.). Englewood Cliffs, NJ: Educational Technology Publications, Inc.

Pimentel, K. & Teixeira, T. (1993). *Virtual reality: Through the new looking glass.* New York: McGraw-Hill, Inc.

Schweir, R. & Misanchuk, E. (1993). *Interactive multimedia instruction.* Englewood Cliffs, NJ: Educational Technology Publications, Inc.

Tischer, M. (1991). *Up & running with ToolBook for Windows.* Alameda, CA: Sybex.

Trotter, A. (1992). Schools gear up for 'hypermedia' — a quantum leap in electronic learning. In J.J. Hirschbuhl & L.F. Wilkinson (Eds.), *Computers in Education.* Guilford, CT: The Dushkin Publishing Group.

Wei, C. (1991, March). Hypertext and printed materials: Some similarities and differences. *Educational Technology, 31* (3), 51-53.

Wilson, S. (1991). *Multimedia design with HyperCard.* Englewood Cliffs, NJ: Prentice-Hall.

Glossary

Alphanumeric: Refers to any letter, number, and symbol included on a keyboard.

AM: Amplitude Modulation; type of broadcast radio audio transmission.

Amateur Radio: An interactive communications device that allows for licensed on-the-air communications in a global network; Ham Radio.

American Radio Relay League: Ham radio organization; ARRL.

Analog: Signals in the form of continuous waves or fluctuating electric voltages that are continuously varying over time, e.g., the signal coming from your telephone receiver; opposite of Digital.

Applications Software: Programs for word processing, database, spreadsheet, graphics, and telecommunications; sometimes referred to as Applications Programs.

Archival Copy: Legal backup or second copy of a program for storage purposes.

ARRL: American Radio Relay League; organization for amateur radio interests.

ASCII: American Standard Code for Information Interchange; translates each character on a computer keyboard into a number, e.g., m = 109.

Assistive Technologies: Special electronic hardware devices, software, or a combination of both, that help individuals with disabilities to see better, to hear more clearly, to speak via a synthesized or digitized voice, and/or to become more physically mobile or independent.

Asynchronous Communication: Term that describes two-way communication that is independent of time and space, e.g., message in e-mail is sent, but recipient is unavailable so message is stored temporarily in the computer; also called time shifting.

Audioconferencing: Type of teleconferencing using audio or sound transmissions via telephones plus amplifiers.

Audiographics: Type of teleconferencing in which two-way static image transmissions enhance non-visual sound communication.

Audiotex: Interactive telephone service that uses 800 or 900 area code to connect with a computerized or automated operator who provides information from a computerized database.

Authoring: Creating software programs with content and presentation of your design using an authoring tool.

Authoring Tool: Computer software used to create original programs.

Avatar: Computer-graphic representation of human agent in a distant location; used in a virtual reality environment.

Backup: Duplicate of a program or data disk; sometimes an archival copy; legal software copy.

Barcode Reader: Hand-held device that reads "zebra-stripe" codes; interprets bar coded commands for a videodisc player.

BASIC: Beginner's All-purpose Symbolic Instruction Code; first large-scale computer program available for use in educational settings.

BBS: Bulletin Board System; telecommunications system that permits individuals to use computers for the purpose of posting or exchanging messages; also called Electronic Bulletin Board System (EBBS).

Binary Digits: Series of rapid on-off, or electronic one and zero combinations, used in computers; bits.

BITNET: International education e-mail network available free of charge to individuals affiliated with member universities or colleges.

Bits: Binary digits.

BPS: Bits Per Second; modem transmission speeds; e.g., 300 BPS, 1200 BPS, 2400 BPS, and 9600 BPS; frequently, but incorrectly, called "baud."

Booting Up the System: Loading an operating system into the microcomputer's memory.

Branching: Non-linear learning which follows the individual's self-selected rather than predetermined sequential steps; sometimes referred to as serendipitous learning; opposite of Linear Learning.

Broadcast Radio: One-way direct AM or FM radio transmission of licensed scheduled programming.

Broadcast Television: Commercial and non-commercial (public) television programming.

Bulletin Board System: See BBS.

Bundled Software: Programs that are included in the price of a microcomputer system purchase.

Button: In *HyperCard*, a single character, graphic, or icon that points out a link in the document and when clicked initiates an action (e.g., starting an application, beginning a sound or visual effect, etc.).

Byte: Most commonly an eight-bit set composed of zeros and ones that represents one character, e.g., m = 01101101.

C: High-level computer programming language often taught in secondary and higher education settings.

Cable Television: Paid subscription programming which includes community access channels; Community Access Television or CCTV.

CAI: Computer Assisted Instruction; student-focused courseware; includes Drill and Practice, Tutorial, Simulation, and Problem-Solving courseware categories; associated with CMI.

Carousel: See Jukebox.

CAV: Constant Angular Velocity; a standard videodisc format most often used in education since user flexibility and interactivity are maximized through still and step frame selection, and access of data through multiple speed control; opposite of CLV.

CD: Compact Disc; a format that records digital data on an optical disc; popularly refers to Compact Disc-Audio.

CD-A: Compact Disc-Audio; optical data storage medium for sound and music on a 4.72-inch metalicized plastic disc; commonly referred to as CD.

CD-I: Compact Disc-Interactive; optical storage data medium for graphics, print, and sound on a small metalicized plastic disc; when inserted into a player with a built-in computer processor and connected to a television screen, CD-I can be interactively controlled through the TV screen.

CD-ROM: Compact Disc, Read-Only Memory; nonerasable, prerecorded medium for storing more than 650Mb of digital data on a disc.

CD-ROM Bundling: Package of software selected by the manufacturer sometimes available to the buyer of a CD-ROM player.

CDTV: Commodore Dynamic Total Vision; multimedia, interactive environment that combines digital audio, video, and graphics on a CD.

CD-WORM: Compact Disc, Write Once Read Many (times); optical data storage medium for text and graphics; information can be written once and read many times.

Chapter: Common division of videodisc data which is a set of frames in consecutive sequence.

Clandestine Activities: Prohibited radio transmissions.

Clicking: Pressing a button on a mouse to make a selection on a computer screen.

Clip Art: Generally in desktop publishing software, a collection of computer designs or graphics that can be selected and placed within a text document.

Clone: Copy of an original hardware product; usually a less well-known, less expensive microcomputer.

Closed Circuit Television: Private, non-licensed audio-video delivery system; used by visually-impaired individuals to enlarge printed materials; CCTV.

CLV: Constant Linear Velocity; one standard videodisc format that allows sequential viewing from beginning-to-end; sometimes referred to as extended-play videodisc; opposite of CAV.

CMC: Computer-mediated Communications.

CMI: Computer Managed Instruction; teacher-focused courseware used for clerical responsibilities; includes CBT or Computer-Based Testing; affiliated with CAI.

COBOL: Common Business-Oriented Language; high-level computer programming language taught in secondary and higher education settings.

Codec: Code/Decode Electronic Device used in telephone trunk line transmissions.

Commercial Software: Marketed software sold by a publishing company.

Compact Disc: Optical technology recognized for its great storage ability and clarity of sound; CD; other Compact Disc categories include CD-A, CD-I, CD-ROM, CD-WORM, and DVI.

Compatible: Able to work with other operating systems or hardware configurations.

Compression: Process to condense the amount of memory space required to store audio and video digitized data.

Computer Conferencing: Use of a computer network to facilitate group work and private individual interaction among participants in geographically diverse locations.

Computer-mediated Communication: Electronic method for sending and receiving textual messages via computer; includes electronic mail and computer conferencing; referred to as CMC.

Computer Virus: A hidden, sometimes undetectable program that hides within another program for the purpose of altering or destroying programs or data.

Contract Course: In ITV, a fee-based series of instructional lessons requested and received at a remote viewing site.

Converter Box: Special device needed to access Cable Television programming.

Courseware: Instructional software including tutorial, drill and practice, problem-solving, and simulation programs.

CPS: Characters Per Second; measurement of printer speed.

CPU: Central Processing Unit; the "brain" of the computer which directs all activities, including processing and controlling data flow between devices connected to the computer.

CTU: Coordinated Universal Time; Greenwich Mean Time or GMT.

Data: Information stored in a computer's memory.

Database Software: An applications software package in which an organized collection of information can be created and easily arranged.

Dataglove: Tactile sensory glove that allows the user to "feel" items viewed through a computer-imaging visette in a virtual reality environment.

DBS: Direct Broadcasting by Satellite; television programming delivery system.

Demo Disk: Free or low-cost sample software program to allow a "test drive" of the product prior to purchase.

Desktop: Size of microcomputer that fits on your desk; most common computer in education.

Desktop Computer Music: Creating and playing digitized music using CD technologies, microcomputer music programming, and MIDI.

Desktop Publishing: Refers to the process of creating professionally typeset documents on the microcomputer, which are printed on a laser printer; typesetting tasks include layout of text columns, pasting clip art; also referred to as DTP.

Digital: Signals in the form of abrupt on and off pulses representing binary digits, e.g., computer signals; opposite of Analog.

Digitization: The conversion of a sound or graphic sequence into digital electronic form.

Diskette: Circular, electromagnetic mylar disk used to save data; two sizes, 5 1/4″ and 3 1/2″; floppy disk.

Disk Drive: Computer component that reads and writes data and programs stored on magnetic disks.

Disk Operating System: Operating System or Platform; e.g., MS-DOS, Apple OS.

Disk Version: In connection with software on floppy disks, refers to the software compatibility with a particular operating system, e.g., MS-DOS, Apple OS.

Distance Learning: Allows for learning to take place from distant locations. Teleconferencing and telecourses are examples.

Documentation: Descriptive manual for computer or multimedia software use; "The Docs"; sometimes educational program documentation contains instructional ideas and reproducible worksheets.

Downlinking: Receiving transmissions from orbiting satellites.

Downloading: Accessing and printing data from a host computer to a microcomputer in an electronic computer network; opposite of Uploading.

Downtime: Non-usable computer time due to computer inoperability or malfunctioning.

Dragging: Holding down a button on a mouse while pulling the arrow or icon across the screen.

Drill and Practice: Skills-development CAI courseware; emphasizes response accuracy, speed, self-pacing, and convergent question-answering abilities; sometimes referred to as electronic review sheets.

DVI: Digital video interactive; format for recording digital data on a compact disc; optical storage data medium with universal standardization for digitized video and audio providing 72 minutes of full motion/full screen video; when connected to a computer and television, the video sequence can be controlled by the user.

Educational Radio: Audio transmissions used in the instructional process.

Educational Software: Programs to assist the learning/teaching process; in MIDI, programs that instruct the user to play and better understand musical concepts.

Electronic Mail: See E-Mail.

Electronic Mailbox: Assigned designated storage area for individual messages in a voice mail system.

E-Mail: Electronic transmission of data via networked computers in LANs or telecommunications; part of Computer-mediated Communication (CMC).

Electronic Searching: Researching information through CD-ROM or Electronic Database Systems.

Electronic Sound Synthesis: Electronic process in desktop computer music in which sounds of instruments are created.

Entertainment Software: In MIDI, programs that display color, computer-generated screen images timed to musical sound emissions or fractals.

Erasable Optical Discs: Compact discs which can be erased and re-encoded.

Expandable: The ability to add more memory power to the computer, e.g., 2Mb to 4Mb.

FM: Frequency Modulation; type of broadcast radio audio transmission.

Facsimile: Electronic method for sending and receiving textual and graphic messages via telephone lines; commonly referred to as fax.

Fax: See Facsimile.

Fiber Optic Cable Systems: Cabling which transmits television, telephone, and computer data transmissions over glass fibers by means of lightwaves; benefits include rapid speed of transmission and high capacity of telephone channels (i.e., one cable carries more than 30,000 telephone channels); also referred to as fiber optics or optical fibers.

File Server: A computer dedicated to storing and controlling programs shared by users on a computer network or LAN.

Fixed Downlink: Single directional satellite setting for program reception; opposite of Steerable Downlink.

Fixed Keyboard: Non-movable alphanumeric input device attached directly to the computer; opposite of Independent Keyboard.

Floppy Disk: See Diskette.

Floppy Disk Drive: Disk drive for floppy disk; see Disk Drive.

Font: In word processing and desktop publishing applications, a collection of characters that combine to make a specific standardized typestyle, e.g., Dutch, Helvetica, Ravinia, Swiss, Times; same as Typeface.

Footprint: (1) Regarding microcomputers, the amount of surface or desk space required for a microcomputer; (2) Regarding satellites, signal transmission coverage area on the earth's surface of an orbiting satellite.

FORTRAN: Formula Translation; high-level computer programming language sometimes taught in math/science secondary or higher education settings.

Fractals: Computer-generated display images which can be timed to sound emissions particularly in MIDI.

Frame: A single videodisc image.

Frequency: A measurement of radio waves.

Freeware: No-cost software.

Full-motion Video Data: Standard NTSC North American television transmission of 30 NTSC frames per second.

Function Key: A key on a computer to facilitate a specific command; e.g., arrow keys, F1 key, F2 key.

Geostationary: See geosynchronous.

Geosynchronous: Space orbit in which a satellite remains in a fixed location above the earth; see Geostationary.

GMT: Greenwich Mean Time; the time in Greenwich, England; see Coordinated Universal Time or CTU.

Graphics-based Environment: In microcomputers, screen displays that are guided by icons usually manipulated with a mouse; also called GUI or Graphical User Interface; opposite text-based environment.

Graphics Tablet: Computer input device which allows the user to write or draw on a flat surface with a plastic tipped pen; data is then transferred to the computer screen for viewing.

Ground Waves: Long wave radio signals that travel along the earth's surface; Surface Waves.

Groupware: Software which can be simultaneously shared by an entire class or small group of students.

GUI: Graphical User Interface; popular mouse-driven computer environments in which users are guided through screen displays by icons; also called graphics-based environment; opposite text-based environment.

Hacker: Individual who spends an inordinate amount of time working on computers. Sometimes refers to a person who maliciously accesses unauthorized computer networks.

Ham Radio: See Amateur Radio.

Handshaking Protocol: In telecommunications, signals that link computers to understand each other.

Hardware: Electronic devices and components for technology systems, e.g., monitor, keyboard, mouse, etc.

Hard Copy: Paper copy of computer's output; opposite of Soft Copy.

Hard Drive: Fixed, non-removable, disk drive built into the computer to store programs and data.

Head End: Cable Television distribution site.

Hypermedia: Document networking system connecting nodes of text, audio, and visual information from various sources together. The user selectively stores and retrieves information among the linked resources such as videodiscs, CD-ROMs, etc.

Hypertext: Document networking system connecting text-based information; predecessor of hypermedia.

Icon: In microcomputers, a screen-displayed graphic image which indicates a function (e.g., trash can to indicate deleting a document) usually controlled by a mouse in a GUI or graphics-based environment.

Independent Keyboard: Movable alphanumeric input device attached to the computer by a flexible cord; opposite Fixed Keyboard.

IBM-compatible: computer brands compatible with IBM operating systems; sometimes referred to as IBM clones.

ILS: Integrated Learning System in which the computer plays a central role in the educational learning process; contains both curriculum-oriented hardware and software primarily for basic skills programs along with management software; also referred to as an Instructional Learning System.

Input: To put data into the computer via the computer keyboard, mouse, or other device.

Instructional Gaming: Electronic computer conferencing for students incorporating simulations with e-mail.

Instructional Television: Audio and video transmissions used to teach lessons; common component of Distance Learning; ITV.

Integrated Software Package: Collection of applications programs in one software package; usual combinations include word processing, database, spreadsheet, graphics, and telecommunications capabilities.

Interactive Radio: Traditionally simulated interactivity between the audience and broadcaster.

Interactive Video: Computer-controlled video playback allowing users to control the sequence of the presentation; analog-based technology.

Internet: Largest worldwide computer e-mail and BBS network.

ITFS: Instructional Television Fixed Service; specially assigned microwave spectrum used for educational purposes.

ITV: See Instructional Television.

Ionisphere: A layer of the upper earth's atmosphere between 60 to 300 miles from the earth's surface.

IMI: Integrated Multimedia Instruction; the use of multimedia in the educational process.

ISDN: Newly developed Integrated Services Digital Network which enables digitized sound, data, and video images to be sent via telephone lines.

Joystick: Small peripheral input device that is generally placed next to the computer on a flat surface; specific joystick movements effect specific image movements on the screen.

Jukebox: CD or CD-ROM player which can simultaneously hold and access selections on a multiple set of discs; Carousel.

Keyboard: Input device comprised of keys, similar to a typewriter, arranged on a flat surface; includes alphanumeric keys plus arrow and function keys.

Keyboard Synthesizer: Special piano-like keyboard used for electronic computer music; used commonly with MIDI.

Keyboarding: Inputting data on a computer via the keyboard; electronic typing.

Knowbot: Computer-based agent that simulates a person; used in a virtual reality environment.

LAN: Local Area Network; hardware and software which permits microcomputers to be interconnected and operated together, and the sharing of resources, such as printers, CD-ROMs, hard disk drives, etc.

Laptop: Small, lightweight portable microcomputer that fits on your lap.

Laserdisc: Analog medium using optical data technology to store sound, written text, still images, motion video, and animation on an 12- or 8-inch disc; also referred to as a videodisc.

LCD Output Device: Liquid Crystal Display mechanism which, when connected to a computer and placed on the flat surface of an overhead projector, permits the image from a computer monitor to be enlarged and projected onto a wall screen.

Lexicon: Electronic dictionary which is usually included in word processing software.

Light Pen: Pen-shaped input device used to touch screen displays for computer response.

Linear Learning: Predetermined step-by-step sequences of visual and audio instructional information; opposite Branching.

Loading: Inputting the operating system from the disk into the microcomputer's memory; sometimes called Booting Up the System.

Logo: A programming language and philosophy of education developed by Seymour Papert at M.I.T.

Low-end: An easy to use, simple technology-related product.

Mainframe Computer: Largest, fastest, most powerful, and most expensive category of computer designed for up to 100 users to share one CPU.

Memory: Data storage within the computer; can be RAM or ROM.

Microcomputer: Personal computer designed for one user, but can be part of a network; sizes include desktop, transportable, laptop, notebook, and palmtop microcomputers.

Microprocessor: CPU.

Microwave Dish: Circular dish or parabolic antenna used to send and receive microwave transmissions.

Microwave Transmission: Television signals that broadcast in the microwave spectrum of sound (more than 2000 megahertz or MHz).

Microworld: Concept, commonly associated with Logo programming, referring to the controllable workspace within a computer.

MIDI: Musical Instrument Digital Interface; computer-based hardware and software that enables the user to compose and play high-quality electronic music.

Minicomputer: Smaller, slower, less powerful, and less expensive category of computer as compared to a mainframe, but larger, faster, more powerful, and more expensive than a microcomputer designed for up to 20 users to share one CPU.

Modem: MOdulator-DEModular; electronic "interpreter" device used to link computers through telephone lines. Modulation changes sending computer data signals to telephone tone signals through telephone wires. Demodulation changes telephone tone signals back to computer data signals for the receiving computer to understand. See Analog Transmission and Digital Transmission.

Modem Networking: Long distance transmission of data via computers, telecommunications software, and modems.

Monitor: Electronic viewing device; screen.

Mouse: Input device; small palm-sized pointer peripheral connected via its "tail" by cable to a keyboard or computer; sometimes described as an "upside-down trackball."

Multimedia: The integration of two or more electronic media sources controlled by a microcomputer. The sequence and content of the instructional program are influenced by user decision-making through such avenues as menu choices, questions, and simulated crises; also referred to as Computer-Based Multimedia or Integrated Multimedia.

Multi-timbral Sound: Several sounds being played simultaneously; used in electronic computer music and MIDI.

Music Generator Software: Type of software used in MIDI to store piano, bass, and drum sounds.

Musical Sound Devices: Computer-based hardware which enables the user to develop and play high-quality electronic music.

Networking: Connecting computers together to share peripherals, software, files, and telecommunications such as computer conferencing and e-mail.

Nodes: In e-mail, distant computer network locations; in hypermedia, related chunks of information.

Non-commercial Software: Freeware or shareware.

Notation Software: type of software used in MIDI to change MIDI data into standard musical notation.

Notebook: Light-weight microcomputer; can be as little as 4.4 pounds.

NTSC: Abbreviation for National Television Standards Committee; provides transmission standardization (525-line screen scan) in North America and most of the Far East including Japan; incompatible with other standards including PAL and SECAM.

OCR: Optical Character Recognition; system used by blind and impaired individuals to "read" printed word. The system consists of scanner connected to microcomputer equipped with speech synthesizer and OCR software. When passed over printed word a voice synthesizer "speaks" the data being scanned.

Online: To be connected to another computer in an electronic computer network.

Online Database: Collection of related information that can be accessed quickly generally through a computer network.

Open System: Hardware peripherals that are compatible with different operating systems; opposite Closed or Proprietary System.

Operating System: Set of programs that controls the overall operation of a computer; common ones include Apple Pro-DOS, Mac-OS, MS-DOS, PC-DOS; also referred to as Disk Operating System or Platform.

Optical Data Storage: Encoded data on a metal disk surface that can be decoded through a beam of laser light (e.g., CD disc).

Output: Data received from the computer; can be viewed on either screen or printed page, or can be heard as sound.

Packet Switching: In Computer-mediated Communications, a data communications system which avoids long distance telephone charges by using local access numbers.

Palmtop: Smallest-sized, most lightweight laptop microcomputer.

Parabolic Antenna: See microwave dish.

Pascal: High-level computer programming language taught in secondary and higher education settings; common for business and scientific applications.

Password: Private access code to enable an individual to legally access a computer network or software program.

Password Protected: Common in computer networks, individual security code that provides privacy in the accessing of computer-based data.

PBS: Public Broadcasting Service; non-commercial licensed television programming in the United States.

PC/Fax: Combination of hardware (a fax modem) and software that permits the sending and receiving of faxes directly from a microcomputer.

Peripheral: Electronic hardware device that is added on to a basic technology system.

Personal Computer: PC; microcomputer.

Pirate: In computers, an individual who illegally copies software; in radio, an individual who illegally broadcasts.

Pixels: Picture Elements which define monitor clarity.

Platform: Operating System.

Point-to-Point Communication: Type of broadcast transmission signal used by AM and FM radio programming.

Pointing: Using a mouse to indicate and select a text or graphic item on the computer screen.

Points: Letter sizing in applications and desktop publishing software, e.g., 72-point sizing equals one inch, 12 point is common type size.

Polyphonic Sound: Several notes being played simultaneously; used in electronic computer music and MIDI.

Pop-Up Dictionary: Software program included in a word processing package to provide dictionary assistance.

Pop-Up Thesaurus: Software program included in a word processing package to provide word alternatives, e.g., synonyms, antonyms.

Ports: Add-on, plug-in areas for peripherals located at the back of the computer.

PPM: Page per minute; measurement of printer speed for printers; most commonly used to measure laser printer output.

Printer: Output electromechanical device for computers includes four types: dot matrix, daisy wheel, ink jet, and laser; computer peripheral.

Problem-Solving: CAI courseware that further develops logical or visual-spatial relationships skills; entails inductive and deductive reasoning strategies.

Process: To manipulate by the computer.

Programming: A specific set of computer language rules for step-by-step problem solving; includes Logo and BASIC computer languages.

Prohibited Transmission: Illegal broadcasting.

Proprietary System: A computer brand with no clone, e.g., Macintosh computer; Closed System; opposite of Open System.

Queue: To share a printer on a first-come-first-serve basis among many microcomputers in a network.

QuickTime: Video compression technique to store information on a compact disc; limited to one-quarter screen video.

QWERTY: Traditional letter arrangement on a computer keyboard based on a typewriter keyboard where the first row of letters on left side of the keyboard contains the sequence QWERTY.

RAM: Random Access Memory; primary memory for the temporary storage of information in the computer; RAM that is changeable, allowing both reading and writing to occur, e.g., 128K, 2MB; computer power must be constant to retain RAM contents; if not saved, RAM contents are lost when computer is turned off; opposite and complement to ROM.

Receivers: Devices to "receive" or access radio transmissions.

Recurring Feeds: Regularly scheduled satellite programming.

Remediation Loops: Programmed digressions from the main sequence of learning steps in tutorial CAI programs.

Remote: Commonly, distance learning ITV program site.

Rewritable Optical Disc: Compact disc which can be written upon, erased, and rewritten upon many times.

Robotics: Currently computer-controlled hardware that can replicate human movement.

ROM: Read-Only Memory; factory-programmed memory of computer instructions which can be read but not changed; constant computer power is not required to retain ROM contents; opposite and complement to RAM.

Satellite Transmission: Use of orbiting devices in space to receive and send signals from earth-based stations.

Satellite Frequency: Satellite transmission signals usually Ku-Band and C-Band.

Scanner: Input device that can "read" text, photos, graphics, and handwriting from paper into your computer by digitizing the information.

Scrambling: Method used to encode Cable Television programming so that only paid subscribers can legally decode and access transmissions clearly.

Screen: Monitor.

Scripting: In *AppleTalk*, a simple program using English-like words and syntax in *HyperCard*.

Sequencer Software: Type of software used in MIDI to combine sound data.

Shareware: Low-cost software.

Shortwave Radio: Device to receive multilingual transmissions from at least 160 nations and 1,000 licensed broadcasting stations worldwide; World Band Radio.

SID: Sound Interface Device; chip added to microcomputers to produce sounds and music.

SIG: Special Interest Group particularly in educational technologies to help share problems and solutions, interests and new ideas; can be accessed through BBSs.

Simulation: CAI courseware containing interactive computer analogies of real-life decision-making situations; sometimes referred to as adventure or scenario software.

Site Licensing Fee: Cost paid to software dealer for permission to legally share software programs among many networked users; fee structure is based on the number of microcomputers connected in a network or LAN.

Skip: A radio signal that is bounced from the earth to the ionisphere.

Soft Copy: Screen display of computer's output; opposite of Hard Copy.

Software: General term applied to programs or instructions written in special computer languages which make computers function; commonly purchased on disks.

Sound Source: Internal sound card used in electronic computer music and MIDI.

Spell Checker: Software program available in many word processing packages that assists in identifying and correcting spelling errors listed in the software lexicon; sometimes referred to as Spelling Checker.

Spreadsheet Software: Applications software that enables the user to create, store, calculate, and predict numerical data; referred to as an electronic bookkeeper since data are organized in a general ledger with a row and column format.

Stack: In *HyperCard*, a topic-related set of cards.

Standard: Universally accepted.

Stand-alone: A microcomputer that is a self-sufficient unit with its own peripherals and individual CPU.

Steerable Downlink: Multi-directional, adjustable dish settings for reception of satellite programming; opposite Fixed Downlink.

Step Frame: Capability of a videodisc player that moves from one frame to the next in forward or reverse order.

Still Frame: Single selected video frame on a videodisc that is presented as a static image.

Store: To save data in the computer's memory.

Subnetwork: A subsidiary network organized as part of a larger network; for instance, one that is part of Internet.

Supercomputer: Largest, fastest, most powerful, and most expensive mainframe computer.

Surface Waves: Ground Waves.

Surrogate Reality: Virtual Reality.

Synthesized Speech: Two different styles of imitated human speech patterns, which are digitized and "spoken" by computer voices.

SysOp: Systems Operator who controls Bulletin Board Systems by setting up and posting messages.

Systems Operator: SysOp.

Telecommunicate: To share information electronically.

Telecommunications Device: Hardware that allows you to send and receive information from other computers and electronic devices.

Telecommunications Software: Required software for e-mail systems using modems.

Telecourse: Class sessions televised live (in real-time) or via videotape format to learners in diverse locations through a variety of delivery systems.

Telephone Tag: A cycle of unsuccessful attempts at contacting individuals via telephones and limited-message answering machines.

Terrestrial Microwave Transmission: Television programming access via parabolic antennas or microwave dishes.

Text-Analysis Program: Computerized feedback from a software program used in word processing to analyze grammatical structure, e.g., sentence length, readability index, sexist language, repetitious word frequencies.

Text-based Environment: In microcomputers, display screens that are controlled by typed text commands and functions. Opposite GUI or graphics-based environments.

Text Commands: Typed lists or requests made on the computer keyboard.

Time Shifting: See Asynchronous Communication.

Touch Screen: Input device which is activated by the user's touching the computer screen.

Track: One rotation of 360 degrees on videodisc upon which information is decoded by a laser videodisc player.

Trackball: Input device which looks like a large marble and is controlled by the thumb, sometimes built into the keyboard; movement controls the cursor on the computer screen; serves the same purpose as the mouse.

Transmission Speeds: In telecommunications, modem speeds measured in BPS.

Transponder: Channel in satellite programming transmission.

Transportable: Size of microcomputer that is not as light in weight as a laptop but more portable than a desktop computer.

Turtlegraphics: Logo graphics computer program in which the user controls the movements of the on-screen "turtle" through Logo program development.

Tutorial: CAI courseware which introduces new concepts and facts to the user.

TVRO: Abbreviation for Television Receive-Only; reception of satellite television programming via satellite dishes.

Two-track Audio: Capability of a videodisc to utilize two separate and distinct audio tracks.

Typeface: In word processing or desktop publishing applications, the specific variety of type style; same as Font.

Typestyle: In word processing or desktop publishing applications, the general outline or shape of a character.

Upgraded Keyboard: Available optional input device from some computer companies; generally better-quality and more expensive than the standard keyboard.

Uplinking: Sending transmissions to orbiting satellites.

Uploading: Sending data from a microcomputer to a host computer in an electronic computer network.

UUCP: Unix to Unix Copy worldwide e-mail network.

Video Technology: Any media format that uses a screen for visual presentation of information; includes televisions, videocassettes, personal computers, videodiscs, interactive video, and video games.

Videoconferencing: Type of teleconferencing in which live (real-time) video and audio transmissions are usually exchanged in education via a satellite, cable or microwave network.

Videodisc: See laserdisc.

Virtual Memory: The use of a computer's hard drive as an extension of the RAM memory; programs and data not in current use are temporarily stored and exchanged for programs and data in current use providing more RAM work space.

Virtual Reality: Interactive technology that simulates the real world within a computerized three-dimensional environment (e.g., the holodeck on *Star Trek* exemplifies a sophisticated virtual world); sometimes referred to as Surrogate Reality.

VIS: Video Information System; Compact disc storage for video images; limited to one-quarter screen viewing; uses credit card-sized cartridge.

Visette: Visor to view LCD computer-generated images on its screen in a virtual reality environment.

Voice Mail: Similar to a telephone answering machine, a device to send and receive mail; system entails a digitally-stored voice, computerized database, and a touch-tone telephone; also referred to an Automated Answering Systems and Voice Messaging Units.

Wavelength: A measurement of radio waves.

Windows: In microcomputing, special software program to convert a text-based environment into a graphics-based or GUI environment; a mouse or trackball is used to manipulate screen-displayed icons.

Word Processing: Microcomputer applications program that enables the individual to use the microcomputer as an electronic typewriter to enter, edit, store, and retrieve data.

World Band Radio: Shortwave Radio.

WYSIWYG: What-you-see-is-what-you-get; in applications programs, what you view on the screen in soft copy is exactly what will print in hard copy.

Index

A

AARL (American Radio Resource League), 110

ABC News Interactive by Optical Data Corporation, 168–169

ACSOFT (academic software), 72

AGE (Apple Global Education Network), 88

ALANET, 78–79

Alphanumeric keys, 12

AM (amplitude modulation), 105

Amateur radio, 109–110

  advantages compared with AM/FM radio, 110

  Amateur Radio License required for, 109–110

  carried by OSCARS (Orbiting Satellites Carrying Amateur Radio), 109

  clandestine activities, 115

  educators lacking knowledge of, 114

  interactivity an advantage of, 112

  learning to use, 110

  pirating illegal, 115

  prohibited transmission rules, 115

  transmission affected by daily and seasonal changes, 115

  valuable in emergencies, 112

Amateur Radio License, 109–110

American Radio Resource League (AARL), 110

AmigaVision 1.2, 193

Amplitude modulation (AM), 105

Apple Global Education Network, 88

Apple OS, 6

AppleTalk, 35

AppleWorks, 61

Applications software, 31

  advantages of use in education, 60

  AmigaVision 1.2, 193

  curriculum integration of, 62

  database software, 58–59

  decision-making guidelines, 63

  documentation for, 62

  examples of educational uses of, 61

  graphics software, 56, 58

  integrated software, 59–60

  pirating illegal, 62

  problems and solutions, 61–62

  recommended periodicals, 63–64

  resources, 64–65

  size of text display, 62

  spreadsheet software, 59

  virus problems, 62

  word processing software, 53–56, 57

Archival copies, 8, 46

ASCII (American Standard Code for Information Exchange), 22

Assessment and Evaluation of Integrated Learning Systems: A Kit for School Districts, 46

Assistive technologies, 24, 25

The Association for Technology in Music Instruction, 182

Asynchronous communication, 73

At-risk students, motivated by computer use, 25

AT&T Learning Network, 73, 76–77

Audiographic teleconferencing, 126

Audiomedia, 193

Audio teleconferencing, 126

Audiotex, 95–96

Authorware Professional, 193

Authoring software, 36

  Audiomedia, 193

  Authorware Professional, 193

  Course Builder, 193

  HyperCard, 171, 192–193

  MPG, 193

  PILOT by Apple Computer, Inc., 41

  for repurposing videodiscs, 171

ABOUT THE AUTHOR

Patricia Ann Brock has been a teacher for 25 years. She began her career teaching pre-school, elementary, and junior high students. In 1986 she earned her doctorate at Rutgers, the State University of New Jersey and for the last six years has taught college undergraduate and graduate education courses. Since that time, she has published several articles and has given more than 20 presentations and workshops on educational technology at regional, national, and international conferences.

In 1988, the author received a fellowship from the University of Texas to study teachers and technology at Jagiellonian University, Krakow, Poland. She is currently an assistant professor at Trenton State College and a consultant in educational technology, space studies, and multicultural education. Dr. Brock has recently been selected as a Fulbright Scholar to lecture for a semester at Kyrgyz State University, Bishkek, Kyrgyzstan.